Trust and Skepticis

MW01252751

Children learn a great deal from other people including history, science, and religion, as well as language itself. Although our informants are usually well-intentioned, they can be wrong, and sometimes people deceive deliberately. As soon as children can learn from what others tell them, they need to be able to evaluate the likely truth of such testimony. This book is the first of its kind to provide an overview of the field of testimony research, summarizing and discussing the latest findings about how children make such evaluations—when do they trust what people tell them, and when are they skeptical?

The nine chapters are organized according to the extent to which testimony is *necessary* for children to learn the matter in question—from cases where children are entirely dependent on the testimony of others, to cases where testimony is merely a convenient way of learning. Chapters also consider situations where reliance on testimony can lead a child astray, and the need for children to learn to be vigilant against deception, to ask questions appropriately, and to evaluate what they are told. With an international range of contributors, and two concluding commentaries which integrate the findings within a broader perspective of research on child development, the book provides a thorough overview of this emerging field.

Trust and Skepticism will be essential reading for researchers, academic teachers, and advanced students working in the areas of cognitive development and language development, and will also be of great interest to educational professionals concerned with nursery and primary education.

Elizabeth J. Robinson is Emeritus Professor of Psychology at the University of Warwick, UK. As well as her main research interests in developmental aspects of the transfer of knowledge between people, she has a related side interest in communication in medical settings.

Shiri Einav is a Lecturer in Psychology at the University of Nottingham, UK. Her research focuses on children's developing knowledge attribution, evaluation of oral and printed sources of information, and selective learning.

Current Issues in Developmental Psychology
Series Editor: Margaret Harris
Head of Psychology, Oxford Brookes University, UK

Current Issues in Developmental Psychology is a series of edited books that reflect the state-of-the-art areas of current and emerging interest in the psychological study of human development. Each volume is tightly focused on a particular topic and consists of seven to ten chapters contributed by international experts. The editors of individual volumes are leading figures in their areas and provide an introductory overview. Example topics include: developmental disorders, implicit knowledge, gender development, word learning and categorisation.

Published titles in the series

Current Issues in Developmental Disorders
Edited by Chloë R. Marshall

Trust and Skepticism
Children's selective learning from testimony
Edited by Elizabeth J. Robinson and Shiri Einav

Trust and Skepticism

Children's selective learning
from testimony

**Edited by Elizabeth J. Robinson
and Shiri Einav**

Psychology Press
Taylor & Francis Group
LONDON AND NEW YORK

First published 2014
by Psychology Press
27 Church Road, Hove, East Sussex BN3 2FA

and by Psychology Press
711 Third Avenue, New York, NY 10017

Psychology Press is an imprint of the Taylor & Francis Group, an informa business

British Library Cataloguing in Publication Data
A catalogue record for this book is available from the British Library

Library of Congress Cataloging in Publication Data
Trust and skepticism: children's selective learning from testimony /
edited by Elizabeth J. Robinson, Shiri Einav.
pages cm. — (Current issues in developmental psychology)
1. Trust in children. 2. Truthfulness and falsehood in children.
3. Social adjustment in children. 4. Social perception in children.
5. Child psychology. I. Robinson, Elizabeth J. II. Einav, Shiri.
BF723.T78T78 2014
155.4′192—dc23
2013039407

ISBN: 978-1-84872-185-2 (hbk)
ISBN: 978-1-84872-186-9 (pbk)
ISBN: 978-1-31584-936-2 (ebk)

Typeset in Times
by Swales & Willis Ltd, Exeter, Devon, UK

MIX
Paper from
responsible sources
FSC   FSC® C013056
www.fsc.org

Printed and bound in Great Britain by
TJ International Ltd, Padstow, Cornwall

Contents

Contributors

Kathleen H. Corriveau, School of Education, Boston University, USA

Shiri Einav, School of Psychology, University of Nottingham, UK

Paul L. Harris, Graduate School of Education, Harvard University, USA

Gail D. Heyman, Department of Psychology, University of California San Diego, USA

Christine Howe, Faculty of Education, University of Cambridge, UK

Vikram K. Jaswal, Department of Psychology, University of Virginia, USA

Frank Keil, Department of Psychology, Yale University, USA

Melissa Koenig, Institute of Child Development, University of Minnesota, USA

Katelyn Kurkul, School of Education, Boston University, USA

Asheley R. Landrum, Department of Psychological and Brain Sciences, University of Louisville, USA

Olivier Mascaro, Cognitive Development Center, Central European University, Hungary

Candice M. Mills, School of Behavioral and Brain Sciences, University of Texas at Dallas, USA

Grace Min, School of Education, Boston University, USA

Olivier Morin, Department of Cognitive Science, Central European University, Hungary

Erika Nurmsoo, Department of Psychology, University of Kent, UK

Koraly Pérez-Edgar, Department of Psychology, Pennsylvania State University, USA

Gabrielle F. Principe, Department of Psychology, College of Charleston, USA

Elizabeth J. Robinson, Department of Psychology, Warwick University, UK

Elizabeth Stephens, Institute of Child Development, University of Minnesota, USA

Acknowledgments

Our greatest thanks are to our authors for producing chapters of the highest quality, and on time. Their perfect adherence to deadlines, which as editors will know is most unusual, has ensured that editing this book has been an enjoyable as well as an interesting experience. We are also grateful to Margaret Harris, the series editor, for her advice and support, to Helen de Cruz who provided a really helpful and encouraging review of our manuscript proposal, and to the team at Psychology Press.

Introduction

Shiri Einav and Elizabeth J. Robinson

There are longstanding, very extensive literatures covering the crucial influence of others, including parents, peers, siblings and educators, on children's learning of language, social convention and information about the physical world. In the last 10 years, a sub-field has burgeoned looking at children's criteria for acceptance or rejection of verbal information from others. The label generally adopted to refer to this work is *children's trust in testimony*, and it is this exciting new research area which is the focus of this volume in the series "Current Issues in Developmental Psychology."

As humans we have the great advantage of being able to learn about the world from what other people tell us. In this way we can benefit from the knowledge and expertise of others rather than having to learn everything from our own direct experience. This learning mechanism is particularly significant for children's knowledge acquisition, especially when it comes to learning about facts or events that the child cannot discover for herself (Harris, 2012). Testimony—defined in this sub-field as intentionally communicated verbal information—can shape the child's learning through many guises. It is most clearly observed in instances of deliberate teaching by parents or teachers to which children are highly receptive (Csibra & Gergely, 2009), or when children themselves demand answers to their frequent questions. But it also takes place incidentally: through parents' implicit guidance in their everyday conversations with their children (Callanan, Rigney, Nolan-Reyes, & Solis, 2012; Rogoff, 2003); through children's overhearing of conversations held by others (Akhtar, Jipson, & Callanan, 2001; chapter 9); through exposure to written forms of testimony that constantly surround them (Robinson, Einav, & Fox, 2013); and more generally through the assimilation of subtle cues present in the language used by people in their community (chapter 2). In all these different ways testimony helps children make sense of their world.

Although, for the most part, the information that people offer is true, testimony is not always reliable. In some cases, people may provide deliberately misleading advice with the aim of deceiving the listener, and in others they may be unintentionally wrong, for example, when they are mistaken in their beliefs. So, to balance effectively the benefits and risks of accepting information from others, children need to evaluate the reliability of informants' testimony, rather than show blind trust. This has been variously referred to by researchers in the field as showing selective trust (e.g. Harris & Corriveau, 2011), or epistemic vigilance (Sperber et al., 2010) but both terms describe the ability to distinguish reliable from unreliable sources, and to examine critically the content of communication in order to filter out misinformation. Moreover, given the huge amount of testimony that children encounter everyday, an efficient learning strategy would be to assess the value of such information not only in terms of its likely accuracy but also in terms of its relevance or utility (see Bergstrom, Moehlmann, & Boyer, 2006; Henderson, Sabbagh & Woodward, 2013; Sperber et al., 2010).

The question of how these critical skills develop in childhood has been the focus of intensive research in recent years. A developmental perspective not only informs us about the ways in which children of different ages respond to the above challenges but can also pinpoint the cognitive and metacognitive skills that must come online to enable appropriate evaluation of testimony to take place. As will be discussed by several of the chapters in this volume, these are thought to include executive function (the conscious control of thought, behavior and emotion), theory of mind (the ability to attribute mental states to oneself and others), and source monitoring (the ability to identify the origins of memories, knowledge, and beliefs).

In addition, researchers have been examining the impact of the environment on children's evaluation of testimony. This can of course occur on many levels but we highlight three strands of research here that have been the focus of recent empirical work:

Cross-cultural studies suggest that differences in socialization practices and the promotion of different cultural values (e.g., impression management, modesty, conformity versus individuality, and obedience) may influence children's skepticism, as well as their reasoning about deception, and the type of information they seek from adults when they ask questions (see chapters 4, 6 and 7).

Differences in language structure may also affect the developmental time course of children's selective trust in testimony. For example, some languages including Turkish, and Japanese, but not English, contain obligatory grammatical markers—evidentials—which offer the listener a potential cue as to the reliability of the information conveyed by a speaker. Specifically, whenever a speaker makes a statement in one of these languages, they are grammatically obliged to identify the source of their knowledge (e.g., distinguishing between knowledge gained perceptually or via inference), thereby highlighting to listeners the evidence on which the statement is based. One possibility that has been explored is that children who are exposed to a language in which sources are highlighted by means of evidentials might be especially sensitive to the reliability of testimony. Indeed, a recent study examining the relationship between children's selective trust in testimony and their exposure to linguistic evidentials suggests that Turkish children have an advantage in selective trust over English and Chinese children, consistent with their being aided by their exposure to these markers (Lucas, Lewis, Pala, Wong, & Berridge, 2013; see also Fitneva & Matsui, 2009).

Even within homogeneous cultural and linguistic populations, the conversational environments that children are exposed to at home are diverse and these may have an impact on the development of their critical thinking skills. For example, parents differ in the way they talk spontaneously about the nature of knowledge to their children. These differences have been linked to variation in children's own thinking about knowledge and understanding about evidence (Luce, Callanan, and Smilovic, 2013). Thus, it is important to highlight that children do not just learn information about the social and physical world from the adults around them; adults also model particular ways of thinking and knowing, and these learnt strategies are likely to have some bearing on children's evaluation of sources (see Callanan et al., 2012; chapter 2).

Since around 2005 the number of journal articles on children's selective trust appearing in the literature has accelerated and numerous posters and symposia are included in the programs of major developmental conferences. Most of the published studies use variations on a task developed by Koenig, Harris and colleagues at Harvard and a very similar task developed independently at around the same time by Birch and Bloom at Yale (e.g., Birch, Vauthier, & Bloom, 2008; Koenig, Clément, & Harris, 2004). In this typical task, two informants—dolls, puppets or people seen on video—offer contradicting views about the name or function of an unfamiliar item, and child participants, usually aged between around 2 and 5 years, choose which informant to believe. Variables examined in different experiments are the epistemic credentials of these two informants, for example, how accurate each one has been in the immediate past, what explicit cues about confidence or expertise they give, what their personal attributes are (e.g., age, familiarity, or similarity to the child participant), and whether or not they had access to relevant information when providing their testimony.

The mounting body of evidence indicates that on the one hand, young children are highly selective in their learning from testimony but on the other, they find it very difficult to mistrust individuals (for review see Harris, 2012; Harris & Corriveau, 2011). This tension is borne out throughout the volume, with some chapters highlighting children's effective epistemic vigilance and others drawing attention to the ways in which children can be led astray.

The recent proliferation of empirical research on children's trust in testimony has led to something of an imbalance between 'findings' on the one hand and theoretical interpretation and contextualization on the other (although for a recent theoretical review see Mills, 2013). This volume was put together to give researchers the opportunity to redress this balance, and to consider their findings within a broader context.

Outline of this volume

Chapters 1 to 9 present the latest empirical research on children's trust in testimony and discuss associated theoretical issues. Each chapter focuses on a different facet of this burgeoning literature but many links will be evident throughout. Below, we introduce each of the chapters but first we offer the reader a bird's-eye view of the landscape. The chapters are organized according to the extent to which testimony is *necessary* for children to learn the matter in question:

At one extreme, there is the learning of content for which children are entirely dependent on testimony from others. This includes what Csibra and Gergely (2006) term 'generalizable knowledge' such as the names and functions of objects, and also scientific theories, and religious beliefs. In these circumstances, children's trust is influenced by the perceived reliability of the specific informants who provide the testimony, the type of information being learned (chapter 1), as well as the ways in which such knowledge is endorsed more widely in their surrounding community (chapter 2). At an intermediate position on the dimension, it is often merely convenient to learn from others. For example a child might be told where her shoes are, or that it is raining outside, when she could perfectly well discover that for herself. In these situations, it is most relevant for the child to assess whether the informant has had the particular experience necessary to gain the knowledge under consideration (chapter 3). Whatever the knowledge domain, children are not only offered information, they also actively elicit it by asking questions (chapter 4). In all these cases, children need to be vigilant to deliberate deception (chapters 5 and 6).

At the other extreme, reliance on the testimony of others can lead the child astray in her quest for knowledge, as when she believes falsehoods that go against the evidence of her own eyes (chapters 7 and 8), or ignores the fact that rumors provide only hearsay evidence (chapter 9).

The book concludes with two commentaries on the literature from the perspectives of research in related and relevant areas (chapters 10 and 11). These not only help the reader to make connections between the research described in the preceding chapters and work in other areas, but also to see how taking a different view-point can lead to the formulation of interesting new research questions about children's learning from what others tell them.

In chapter 1, Melissa Koenig and Elizabeth Stephens begin by reviewing the extant evidence concerning the criteria young children use when deciding whether or not an informant is a trustworthy source. Based on this review, and motivated by ideas in social cognition, psychological science, and analytical philosophy, they raise two important observations about testimonial exchanges that provide a theoretical framework for the empirical findings. First, they suggest that when children (and adults) evaluate others, their receptiveness to various speaker cues and characteristics is driven by an underlying sensitivity to two primary dimensions: competence and benevolence. Second, they argue persuasively that whereas to date testimony has largely been treated as a unitary and broad concept by developmental psychologists, there are in fact theoretical and empirical grounds for distinguishing between children's reasoning about generalizable or 'semantic' knowledge, and knowledge that relates to idiosyncratic information that is tied to specific episodes.

While chapter 1 focuses predominantly on children's learning from, and evaluation of, specific individuals, chapter 2 takes a wider lens approach to consider children's assimilation of the testimony they encounter in their surrounding community. In chapter 2, Paul Harris and Kathleen Corriveau discuss the topic of children's belief in the existence of scientific entities such as germs as well as the existence of special beings such as God. To the extent that both types of phenomena are not directly observable, it is likely that children's belief in the existence of each depends on testimony provided by other people. The authors suggest that from a young age, children are sensitive to variation in the way people in their community talk about one type of invisible entity as compared to another. This variation includes the degree of consensus surrounding these phenomena, in addition to tacit signals of presupposition present in people's discourse about them. With this in mind, the authors ask how far children and adults differentiate between the two types of phenomena by examining their confidence in the existence of these entities and the explanations they offer for their beliefs.

Along with further consideration of children's gaining *generalizable* knowledge from others (such as the names of unfamiliar objects), chapters 3 and 4 introduce studies in which children gain *specific* knowledge about the physical world such as which one of a set of objects is hidden in a box. Children could find out by looking themselves, but in these tasks that option is not available to them. Tasks such as this can be designed to allow detailed examination of the criteria children use when deciding whether or not to trust what others tell them.

In chapter 3, Elizabeth Robinson, Erika Nurmsoo and Shiri Einav examine the extent to which children engage in reasoning about informants' knowledge or beliefs when they trust or mistrust them. For example, when children trust an informant who was previously accurate over one who was previously inaccurate, do they take into account how that accuracy or inaccuracy was achieved? What if an informant's previously correct answers were provided by a helper who is no longer present, or were gained from a book which is no longer available? Does the child expect that informant nevertheless to continue to be reliable? Such questions importantly address whether children's selective trust reflects superficial rules-of-thumb based solely on informants' past accuracy, which may leave the child open to drawing the wrong conclusions about the long-term reliability of informants. This chapter also considers why children take into account an informant's knowledge state more readily when the informant offers them information uninvited, than when the child has actively to elicit it by asking a question.

Indeed, in many situations, children must seek out information from others and in chapter 4, Candice Mills and Asheley Landrum examine children's question-asking much more broadly than in chapter 3. The authors begin by unpacking the complex cognitive process that underlies information gathering from others, for the purpose of problem solving. They identify four key steps in this process: (1) recognizing when solving a problem may require assistance from others, (2) deciding whom to question, (3) determining what to ask, and (4) deciding how much information to ask for in order to solve a given problem. The chapter addresses findings related to each of these steps before reviewing research from their own lab that bridges across all four component skills. The authors then discuss the implications of this body of work, making recommendations for future research to understand developmental and individual differences in children's ability to use questions effectively for problem solving.

Children's perception of an informant's communicative intent is crucially important to their decisions regarding whether or not to trust what someone says. It is not enough that an individual has the relevant knowledge; they must also intend to communicate it truthfully. Chapters 5 and 6 consider in different ways children's handling of informants who are intentionally deceptive, as opposed to ignorant or incompetent.

In chapter 5, Olivier Mascaro and Olivier Morin present a theoretical framework for investigating children's developing expertise in lie detection. Specifically, the authors attempt to account for the striking transformation that occurs around the age of 4 years, when children become less likely to assume that assertions are true and more likely to lie themselves. In reviewing the empirical evidence, the authors argue against the view that the emergence of vigilance toward deception is underpinned by cognitive changes such as the development of executive skills or novel metarepresentation abilities that allow the child to represent others' beliefs as separate from reality and to treat assertions as false. Instead, the authors make the case that these capacities are already in place and that the change in children's trust observed around the age of 4 is due to a revision of children's expectations about the honesty of communicators and communication.

In chapter 6, Gail Heyman broadens the discussion on children's notions of deception to examine their growing understanding of the ulterior motives that may drive individuals to stretch the truth, for the purpose of impression management or politeness. For example, when do children recognize the circumstances under which speakers might be motivated to lie about their own achievements or about a peer's behavior? Children's understanding of such motives clearly has implications for their judgments about the moral acceptability of lying within different social contexts, and this topic is explored in the second half of the chapter. As well as highlighting age-related changes in children's awareness of ulterior motives and their implications, the author presents evidence of cross-cultural differences between American and Chinese samples that point to interesting ways in which cultural norms and values may shape children's reasoning about lying.

The chapters above examine children's eventual use of effective criteria to identify when informants are likely to be reliable. In chapters 7, 8 and 9, in contrast, the emphasis shifts to circumstances under which children can be led to ignore the evidence of their own eyes by their trust in testimony.

Like chapter 6, chapter 7 by Kathleen Corriveau, Grace Min and Katelyn Kurkul looks at cross-cultural differences but this time focusing on children's willingness to conform to a false majority view that conflicts with the child's own perception. In such circumstances, the authors have found, Asian-American preschoolers display much higher rates of conformity than Caucasian-American preschoolers. This is consistent with adult findings as well as the documented difference in value placed on conformity versus asserting one's autonomy in collectivitistic and individualistic cultures. While providing an insightful review of the literature, the authors explore how different socialization practices across cultures, such as parenting values and parental discourse, might lead to variation in children's approach to learning—promoting conformity or more independent learning strategies, respectively.

In chapter 8, Vikram Jaswal and Koraly Pérez-Edgar also consider the dilemma faced by children when their own beliefs, based on personal observation, come into conflict with what others tell them. How do they resolve such conflicts? The authors make the case that young children trust in testimony by default and that under some conditions this can override their own experience of the physical world. Nevertheless, as their findings show, there are considerable individual differences in young children's readiness to trust what they are told. The authors present recent data that implicate inhibitory control as a possible source of these differences, and as an underlying mechanism required for skepticism.

In chapter 9, Gabrielle Principe demonstrates that children's susceptibility to being misled by testimony is not limited to their beliefs about the world; their memories of experience are also prone to misinformation garnered from others. The research presented in this chapter examines preschoolers' readiness to believe false rumors about an experienced event in a naturalistic school environment. Importantly, the research shows that children are inclined not only to believe what another child tells them, but wrongly to believe that they have seen the fabricated event themselves. The research has implications for the literatures on children's source-monitoring errors, on children's false memories, and on their reliability as witnesses in legal settings.

In the final two chapters, Frank Keil and Christine Howe each offer a thought-provoking commentary of the published literature on children's trust in testimony from their own perspectives.

In chapter 10, Frank Keil integrates findings from this sub-field with the broader literature on cognitive and social development, as well as relevant research on adults, to explore what changes may account for our increasing distrust with age. Keil examines six factors that could plausibly contribute to children's credulity, such as a lack of interrogation skills, or an inability to deal with information conflicts. In each case, however, the author marshals evidence against the view that children's skills—and conversely their biases—differ in a qualitative way to adults. Rather, the picture of gradual developmental change that emerges is much more complex and interesting, highlighting continuities between young children's and adults' reasoning (with similar biases surfacing especially when adults are under cognitive load), and their receptiveness to cultural influences about trust. Keil concludes by arguing that any dramatic developmental changes that may arise are likely to be due to *interactions* between the different dimensions discussed, and encourages future research to take a pluralistic approach to capture these interactions.

In chapter 11, Christine Howe, a psychologist with particular expertise in peer learning and science education, offers a critique of the approach currently dominating the literature. The author contends that, to date, researchers have tended to focus too narrowly on children's selective learning of specific pieces of information (e.g. object labels or locations), without sufficiently considering the impact of testimony on knowledge building in a wider sense. Using children's understanding in the physical domain and reference to her own research as an example case, the author discusses the symbiosis between verbal communication and physical evidence in supporting the learning process. She argues that talk helps to determine how physical experiences should be interpreted while physical experiences are used to resolve differences of opinion emerging through talk. Howe believes that by considering learning across a broad domain, these bidirectional influences that drive conceptual change can best come to light.

As well as the many links that can be drawn between the empirical chapters, several points of contrast emerge. We highlight two of these here:

First, it is interesting to note that chapters 1 and 3 arrive at similar conceptual distinctions by different routes. Koenig and Stephens (chapter 1) differentiate distinct types of content that children learn from testimony: 'episodic,' and 'semantic, common or conventional' knowledge and they develop the argument that child learners apply different psychological processes when reasoning about these two types of testimonial knowledge. In particular, they argue children are more likely to attend to sources of information in the case of episodic knowledge conveyed by testimony, whether this be the child's awareness of how she herself learned the new knowledge (by being told), or the child's awareness of the informant's source (e.g., that the informant had seen inside the container whose content he reported to the child). In the case of semantic, scientific or conventional knowledge, the child is likely to have heard the information from several people and will not retain details of individual sources. In addition, unlike episodic information, the informant will not have gained semantic information by immediate perceptual access, making the informant's own source less salient and perhaps less relevant.

In contrast, rather than focusing on the content of the knowledge transferred, Robinson, Nurmsoo, and Einav (chapter 3) differentiate between two distinct bases on which a learner can trust the testimony of an informant: on the basis of the informant's known expertise in the relevant domain, or on the basis of the informant having access to the specific information that the learner lacks. The understanding needed by a child learner is importantly different under these two kinds of circumstance. In the former case the child needs to realize what kinds of enduring characteristics indicate that a person is likely to be well informed in a particular domain of knowledge. In the latter case, in contrast, the child needs to understand about knowledge acquisition, for example that somebody who has seen inside a container not only knows what is inside but can also convey that knowledge to another person.

At the same time, Robinson and colleagues do not argue that trust based on information access is relevant only to episodic information. Importantly, within their framework, trust based on information access can apply both to generalizable and to non-generalizable information. An informant could look inside a box and on that basis be trusted to report on its content (non-generalizable knowledge), but an informant could also read the label on an unfamiliar plant and on that basis be trusted to report its name (generalizable knowledge).

Second, there is some disagreement among the chapters about the role of inhibitory control in explaining why it is that young children find it so hard to be skeptical, even toward individuals who have provided them with false information in the past, or who are clearly presented as having deceptive intent. The authors of chapters 5, 6, and 8 all consider the possibility that ignoring false testimony requires exertion of inhibitory control, and that weak inhibitory control may constrain children's ability to respond skeptically. This *executive function hypothesis* is rejected by both Mascaro and Morin (chapter 5) and Heyman (chapter 6) based in part on a study by Heyman, Sritanyaratana, and Vanderbilt (2013) which repeatedly found a lack of significant correlations between children's ability to ignore deceptive advice and their performance on a number of inhibitory control tasks. In contrast, Jaswal and Pérez-Edgar (chapter 8) present new evidence that does offer strong support for the role of inhibitory control. Their data show that children who were more likely to reject false testimony performed better on an inhibitory control task than their more deferential peers. Further research should lead to a resolution of the conflicting accounts, perhaps by identifying a crucial interaction with other factors (see chapter 10).

Some methodological considerations and directions for future research

To date, studies on children's selective trust have generally stayed close to the original experimental paradigm developed by Koenig et al. (2004), described above: participants choose to believe one of two informants who offer conflicting suggestions and differ on a particular relevant dimension (e.g., adult versus child, familiar versus unfamiliar speaker, etc). This procedure has produced robust findings demonstrating children's early sensitivity to a range of markers of reliability, such as informants' past accuracy, as well as revealing biases that may influence them to make non-optimal learning decisions (e.g., bias to trust same-gender informants, Ma & Wooley, 2013). However, there are a number of methodological issues that should be borne in mind.

First, it is important to emphasize that the findings obtained are dependent on the particular methods used and, as such, care should be taken when drawing general conclusions about children's trust in testimony (see also Koenig & Sabbagh, 2013). One case in point concerns the contrast that is set up between the two informants. In some studies, this contrast emerges from the informants' behavior, which the child witnesses during the protocol (e.g., one speaker labels a series of familiar objects accurately whereas the other is inaccurate); in other studies, the child is explicitly told about the informants' divergent credentials or intentions (e.g., "This person knows all about cats, but that person doesn't know anything about cats"; "This person is nice/mean"). In both cases, however, the contrast is likely to highlight the cue of interest, which may lead researchers to overestimate children's sensitivity to it. For example, we cannot assume that children who prefer to learn from the more confident of two informants would attend to a single informant's confidence level and moderate their trust accordingly. Indeed, research that has compared children's trust in two- and one-informant scenarios has found greater sensitivity to certain reliability cues in the former (e.g., Birch, Akmal, & Frampton, 2010; see also Krogh-Jesperson & Echols, 2012). At the same time, as Koenig and Sabbagh (2013) note, null findings in single-speaker paradigms that may rely on between-subject comparisons with low power, should not be taken as evidence of complete insensitivity. Research in this area would benefit from examining the different findings obtained by various methods to achieve a nuanced picture of the conditions under which children of different ages pay attention to various epistemic cues.

Second, research employing the selective trust paradigm has generally focused on children's acceptance or rejection of testimony at the time it is offered, but usually has not examined their subsequent use of the received information (exceptions include Jaswal, Lima, & Small, 2009; Koenig & Woodward, 2010). For example, do children retain the accepted information two weeks on? Conversely, are rejected claims easily forgotten? To what extent do children generalize the accepted information beyond the specific example to which it pertained? Do they expect other people to share this knowledge? And do they trust it sufficiently to pass it on to those who do not share it? We do not yet have firm answers to these fundamental questions but addressing them is a crucial next step for establishing the degree of trust that children invest in testimony from different sources as well as the impact that it has on their long-term learning.

Finally, we must also ask how applicable these decontextualized experimental findings are to the child's real-life practice of receiving and evaluating testimony. In her chapter on rumors in this volume, Principe presents research that is grounded within the child's everyday experience at school. Most studies, however, have been conducted under controlled conditions in the laboratory where children are required to *reason* about testimony in an artificial manner. Of course these standardized procedures have many advantages but they should be complemented by more naturalistic methods that seek to capture instances of testimony transfer in situ. Studies by Callanan and colleagues have highlighted the benefits of taking an observational approach that examines parent–child conversation at home and in learning contexts such as museum exhibits (for a review see Callanan et al., 2012). Similarly, the use of diary records and analysis of extant data sets of natural language like the child language data exchange system (CHILDES; Mac-Whinney & Snow, 1985, 1990) can inform us about the type of questions children ask, and the type of answers they receive in real life.

Clearly, then, there is much still to find out about children's trust in testimony. Nevertheless, this new sub-field of research has already generated interesting and exciting findings: Alongside philosophers' discussions about what grounds we have for trusting testimony, and psycholinguists' research into how children learn language from others, we can now add developmental psychologists' findings and theorizing about how children evaluate what others say to them. We hope that this introduction has offered readers a tempting foretaste of the chapters to come, and that the chapters themselves will be thought-provoking. It would be better still if they provoke further research into the processes by which children learn from what people tell them.

References

Akhtar, N., Jipson, J. L., & Callanan, M. A. (2001). Learning words through overhearing. *Child Development, 72*, 416–430.

Bergstrom, B., Moehlmann, B., & Boyer, P. (2006). Extending the testimony problem: Evaluating the truth, scope and source of cultural information. *Child Development, 77,* 531–538.

Birch, S. A. J., Akmal, N., & Frampton, K. L. (2010). Two-year-olds are vigilant of others' nonverbal cues to credibility. *Developmental Science, 13,* 363–369.

Birch, S. A. J., Vauthier, S. A., & Bloom, P. (2008). Three- and four-year-olds spontaneously use others' past performance to guide their learning. *Cognition, 107,* 1018–1034.

Callanan, M., Rigney, J., Nolan-Reyes, C., & Solis, G. (2012). Beyond pedagogy: How children's knowledge develops in the context of everyday parent-child conversations. In A. M. Pinkham, T. Kaefer, & S. B. Neuman (Eds.), *Knowledge development in early childhood.* London, UK: Guilford Press.

Csibra, G., & Gergely, G. (2006). Social learning and social cognition: The case for pedagogy. In Y. Munakata & M. H. Johnson (Eds.), *Processes of change in brain and cognitive development.* Attention and Performance XXI (pp. 249–274). Oxford, UK: Oxford University Press.

Csibra, G., & Gergely, G. (2009). Natural pedagogy. *Trends in Cognitive Science, 13,* 148–153.

Fitneva, S. A., & Matsui, T. (Eds.) (2009). Evidentiality: A window into language and cognitive development. *New Directions for Child and Adolescent Development, 125.*

Harris, P. L. (2012). *Trusting what you're told: How children learn from others.* Cambridge, MA: Belknap Press/Harvard University Press.

Harris, P. L., & Corriveau, K. H. (2011). Young children's selective trust in informants. *Philosophical Transactions of the Royal Society B, 366,* 1179–1187.

Henderson, A. M. E., Sabbagh, M. A., & Woodward, A. L. (2013). Preschoolers' word learning is guided by the principle of relevance. *Cognition, 126,* 246–257.

Heyman, G. D., Sritanyaratana, L., & Vanderbilt, K. E. (2013). Young children's trust in overtly misleading advice. *Cognitive Science, 37,* 646–667.

Jaswal, V. K. J., Lima, O. K., & Small, J. E. (2009). Compliance, conversion and category induction. *Journal of Experimental Child Psychology, 102,* 182–195.

Koenig, M. A., Clément, F., & Harris, P. L. (2004). Trust in testimony: Children's use of true and false statements. *Psychological Science, 15,* 694–698.

Koenig, M., & Sabbagh, M. A. (2013). Selective social learning: New perspectives on learning from others. *Developmental Psychology, 49,* 399–403.

Koenig, M. A., & Woodward, A. L. (2010). 24-month-olds' sensitivity to the prior accuracy of the source: Possible mechanisms. *Developmental Psychology, 46,* 815–826.

Krogh-Jespersen, S., & Echols, C. H. (2012). The influence of speaker reliability on first versus second label learning. *Child Development, 83,* 581–590.

Lucas, A. J., Lewis, C., Pala, F. C., Wong, K., & Berridge, D. (2013). Social-cognitive processes in preschoolers' selective trust: Three cultures compared. *Developmental Psychology, 49,* 579–590.

Luce, M. R., Callanan, M. A., & Smilovic, S. (2013). Links between parents' epistemological stance and children's evidence talk. *Developmental Psychology, 49,* 454–461.

Ma, L., & Woolley, J. D. (2013). Children's sensitivity to speaker gender when learning from others. *Journal of Cognition and Development, 14,* 100–119.

MacWhinney, B., & Snow, C. E. (1985). The child language data exchange system (CHILDES). *Journal of Child Language, 12,* 271–294.

MacWhinney, B., & Snow, C. E. (1990). The child language data exchange system: An update. *Journal of Child Language, 17,* 457–472.

Mills, C. M. (2013). Knowing when to doubt: Developing a critical stance when learning from others. *Developmental Psychology, 49,* 404–418.

Robinson, E. J., Einav, S., & Fox, A. (2013). Reading to learn: Pre-readers' and early readers' trust in text as a source of knowledge. *Developmental Psychology,49,* 505–513.

Rogoff, B. (2003). *The cultural nature of human development.* New York, NY: Oxford University Press.

Sperber, D., Clément, F., Heintz, C., Mascaro, O., Mercier, H., Origgi, G., et al. (2010). Epistemic vigilance. *Mind & Language, 25,* 359–393.

1   Characterizing children's responsiveness to cues of speaker trustworthiness

Two proposals

Melissa Koenig and Elizabeth Stephens

Introduction

Testimonial exchanges are joint endeavors involving speakers and hearers. These testimonial exchanges have been the recent focus of a broad and productive research program and our review of this large literature will be guided by two main questions: (1) Given the evidence that children selectively respond to many *speaker* characteristics when deciding whom to trust or learn from, do they use all available cues to guide their selectivity or are they especially attuned to specific core or primary dimensions?, and (2) Given that children demonstrate selectivity in response to different testimonial *content*, namely, common or semantic information as well as idiosyncratic or episodic information, do they treat these two types of testimony differently? Using these questions as our guide, we make two proposals about testimonial exchanges. First, in line with recent proposals in adult social cognition, we suggest that children and adults evaluate speakers along two primary dimensions: competence and benevolence (or "moral warmth", see Fiske, Cuddy, & Glick, 2007). Second, consistent with recent proposals in epistemology, we caution against an overly broad treatment of testimony. We will argue for the importance of a 'semantic' versus 'episodic' distinction on two grounds: (1) these two types of messages elicit different intuitions about what is involved in knowing by testimony, and (2) there are empirical reasons to think that the psychological processes that underlie reasoning about 'semantic' versus 'episodic' testimony may be qualitatively different.

1 Two primary dimensions of speaker trustworthiness: benevolence/warmth and competence

In research on person perception, social psychologists have been long aware of a core set of 'central traits' that anchor our impressions of others (Cacioppo, Gardner, & Berntson, 1997; Fiske et al., 2007; Peeters, 2002). Using lists of trait adjectives, Asch (1946) may have been the first to demonstrate the power of 'warm' versus 'cold' traits in changing a person's evaluation of someone else. Building on this research, Rosenberg, Nelson, & Vivekananthan (1968) asked adult subjects to sort 64 traits ('dominating', 'sentimental', 'frivolous', 'unhappy', etc.) into groupings likely to cluster in a single person and found that traits clustered along two primary dimensions: the 'social good-bad' and the 'intellectual good-bad'. More recent work by Wojciszke has shown that 'competence' and 'morality' account for 82% of the variance in adult perceptions of others' everyday behaviors (Wojciszke, 1994; Wojciszke, Bazinska, & Jaworski, 1998). The use of various labels for these dimensions has likely concealed the pervasive use that adults give to these two dimensions. However, as brought to light in a recent review by Fiske et al. (2007), warmth and competence are the leading dimensions that "account almost entirely for how people characterize others" (p. 77).

With this as backdrop, it is interesting that the last 10 years of research on children's selective trust demonstrates children's use of these same dimensions when evaluating speakers. In the standard task for assessing children's selective trust in testimony (e.g., Koenig & Harris, 2005), two speakers, one consistently accurate and one consistently inaccurate, first provide labels for a series of familiar objects. Next, the speakers present conflicting labels or functions for novel objects. Children's tendencies to ask the previously accurate speaker for help with a novel label and to selectively endorse the label provided by the previously accurate speaker over that offered by the inaccurate speaker constitute the outcome measures of interest. Applications of the selective trust paradigm have revealed that children as young as 2 years of age are capable of tracking speaker performance and taking it into account when deciding whom to trust in subsequent learning situations (e.g., Birch, Vauthier, & Bloom, 2008; Clément, Koenig, & Harris, 2004; Ganea, Koenig, & Millet, 2011; Koenig, Clément, & Harris, 2004; Koenig & Harris, 2005; Koenig & Woodward, 2010). By age 7, children and adults treat even a single instance of speaker inaccuracy as reason to prefer another source (Fitneva & Dunfield, 2010). In fact, information about speaker competence may trump other relevant cues to speaker quality including age (Jaswal & Neely, 2006), accent (Corriveau, Kinzler, & Harris, 2013), familiarity (Corriveau & Harris, 2009), and adherence to convention (Scofield, Gilpin, Pierucci, & Morgan, 2013). Even infants appear sensitive to indications that a source or model is incompetent (Zmyj, Buttelman, Carpenter, & Daum, 2010). Early in the second year of life, infants prefer to follow the gaze of an individual who consistently looks in boxes containing objects as opposed to one who consistently looks in empty boxes (Chow, Poulin-Dubois, & Lewis, 2008). Infants also look longer when speakers' pointing gestures fail to coincide with the actual locations of previously labeled hidden objects (Gliga & Csibra, 2009) and when speakers provide inaccurate labels for familiar objects (Koenig & Echols, 2003). Young children attend to several indicators of a speaker's state of uncertainty in addition to prior inaccuracy, including expressions of ignorance (Sabbagh & Baldwin, 2001), provision of insufficiently informative messages (Gillis & Nilsen, 2013; Gweon, Pelton, & Schulz, 2011), lack of perceptual access to relevant information (Nurmsoo & Robinson, 2009a), non-verbal cues of bystander dissent (e.g., head-shaking; Fusaro & Harris, 2008, 2013), and disagreement with the consensus of a majority (Corriveau,Fusaro, and Harris, 2009). When presented with two characters who were described with trait adjectives (e.g., "smart"/"not smart", "truthful/liar") and were seen to behave in accord with those adjectives, children by age 3 preferred to learn from the smarter and more honest character (Lane,

Wellman, & Gelman, 2013). Young children also monitor speakers for specific competencies, or expertise. For example, preschoolers expect a mechanic to have greater knowledge than a doctor regarding the functions of machines, but attribute greater knowledge to a doctor regarding the functions of living things (Lutz & Keil, 2002). Preschoolers also differentiate between informants with causal knowledge and those with lexical knowledge and appropriately direct their questions accordingly (Kushnir, Vredenburgh, & Schneider, 2013). In sum, such findings converge in demonstrating that children, from a very early age, successfully track and attend to verbal and non-verbal cues that signal a person's level of *competence*.

Fewer in number but equally important are studies demonstrating children's sensitivity to information that signals the benevolence/warmth or good motives of a speaker. Such sensitivity is evident very early in development. Infants as young as 3 months of age differentiate helpful and hindering actions and look longer when an actor approaches a previously hindering agent than when an actor approaches a previously helping agent (Hamlin, Wynn, & Bloom, 2010). Six- to 10-month-old infants model this attitude in their independent actions, choosing to reach for a helping actor over a neutral or hindering actor (Hamlin, Wynn, & Bloom, 2007). By preschool, children apply their sensitivity to moral information to guide their evaluations of speakers in novel learning situations. Three- to 5-year-old children selectively endorse novel information offered by previously benevolent speakers as opposed to both malevolent (Mascaro & Sperber, 2009) and neutral (Doebel & Koenig, 2013) speakers. Moreover, older preschoolers systematically reject advice provided by speakers described as liars (Mascaro & Sperber, 2009) and those who consistently tricked others in the past (Vanderbilt, Liu, & Heyman, 2011). Young children appear to evaluate speakers' intentions independently from the outcomes of their advice and demonstrate a preference to accept advice from a helpful speaker over a deceptive speaker, even when the helpful speaker has proved to be consistently incorrect (Liu, Vanderbilt, & Heyman, 2013). Preschoolers' familiarity with a speaker also influences their selective learning. When offered conflicting novel information from a familiar teacher and an unknown source, 3- to 5-year-olds prefer the testimony of their teacher, a preference maintained by the youngest children even when their teacher commits blatant errors (Corriveau & Harris, 2009). Taken together, these findings illustrate that children also successfully track and attend to cues that signal a person's *benevolence*.

These findings are consistent with the proposal that children, like adults, evaluate speakers along two primary dimensions: benevolence/warmth and competence. This proposal does not rule out the utility of other speaker characteristics; it only anticipates the dominance of these two. Of course, it remains to be seen how salient or useful any non-competence or non-benevolence dimension might prove to be in children's learning given that benevolence and competence have largely dominated the characteristics that researchers have chosen to manipulate in their studies. One exception is a recent study by Fusaro, Corriveau, and Harris (2011), who found that when children were presented with two puppet informants who differed in physical strength, children predicted that the stronger puppet would likely be smarter, nicer, and more likely to know facts and new words. In contrast, children judged a more accurate puppet to be 'smarter' and likely to know more words but not stronger or nicer (see also Brosseau-Liard & Birch, 2011). Thus, while physical strength was a dimension that led to broad inferences for children, their inferences based on demonstrations of epistemic competence (i.e., correct naming) were more fine-tuned and accurate. Further research of this type will serve to clarify the conditions under which children appeal to less-epistemic, less-moral characteristics of speakers. In addition, it is important to bear in mind that when children (or adults) appear selective in the face of non-core dimensions like strength or attractiveness, it may be that their selectivity is in response to moral or epistemic cues (e.g., confidence, easy manner) that tend to correlate with these non-epistemic traits (Chaiken, 1979; Chaiken & Eagley, 1983).

According to Fiske et al. (2007), adults evaluate positive versus negative information differently depending on whether the positive-negative information pertains to a person's warmth or competence, and certain parallels exist in the developmental literature. For warmth, for example, adults promptly heed information that disconfirms, rather than confirms, a person's warmth. Unfriendly behavior at a colleague's party is likely to be seen as diagnostic of that person's disposition; whereas friendly behavior is seen as socially prescribed. In a similar spirit, children are better at discriminating negatively behaving agents from neutral ones than they are at discriminating positively behaving agents from neutral ones (Doebel & Koenig, 2013; Vaish, Carpenter, & Tomasello, 2009; Vaish, Grossman, & Woodward, 2008). In contrast, adults tend to be forgiving of occasional but reasonable instances of incompetence as illustrated by absent-minded professors (Fiske, 1980; Skowronski & Carlston, 1987). As we discuss below, while children do sensitively heed errors marking incompetence (Corriveau, Meints, & Harris, 2009 Koenig & Doebel, in press; Koenig & Jaswal, 2011), children also prove capable of forgiving errors when excusable (Kondrad & Jaswal, 2012, Nurmsoo & Robinson, 2009a).

Given this convergence with the adult literature, children's use of cues to speaker morality and competence will strike many as an adaptive practice, especially when learning from testimony. After all, signs of a person's competence or benevolence are good things to track if monitoring for signs of trustworthiness. As many have noted, the unreliability of testimony lies in the fact that informants can make mistakes (competence) and have interests that are not always in line with telling the truth (morality). However, questions concerning how well children monitor speakers for cues to benevolence and competence and how well this practice actually protects them from misinformation remain open, empirical questions. For us, the importance of these skills is that they illustrate that very young children, starting in infancy, are indeed rationally responsive (in the right directions) to considerations of speaker trustworthiness.

2 Against a unitary treatment of testimony

Although most agree that testimony generally serves as a means to verbally communicate true information, this characterization risks being overly broad, overlooks the fact that testimonial exchanges vary considerably across situations, and neglects the possibility that this variation could have important implications for testimonial learning. For example, within the realm of assertions, many have articulated the importance of a shared communication, linguistic, and conceptual system. For Davidson (1984), "we can no more agree than disagree with someone without much mutuality" or "what is shared does not in general call for comment; it is too dull, trite or familiar to stand notice" (p. 199). Wittgenstein did not favor views that argued for the centrality of any single speech act (from which all others are derived) but he made explicit that "if language is to be a means of communication there must be agreement" in definitions and judgments and distinguished these from our more singular "opinions" (para 242, 1954). Coady (1992) draws a distinction between cases where "witness and audience are active explorers of a common world," as in language, and cases of "natural testimony," where examples include "giving someone directions to the post office, reporting what happened in an accident, . . . and telling someone the result of the last race or cricket score." (p. 38). In concert with these distinctions and other considerations, more modern theorists like Lackey (2008), Lipton (1998) and McMyler (2011) agree that it is unlikely that testimony picks out an epistemically unified kind. As we continue to argue here, we too wish to avoid a unitary conception of testimony, and of testimonial knowledge, that puts in the same box knowledge that was arrived at by different routes and considerations.

Here we focus on one basic way in which testimony varies with respect to *content*, namely, what we call 'transient-episodic' versus 'semantic-conceptual' content. To avoid confusion with the use of such terms in other literatures, by 'episodic' testimony we mean assertions of facts tied to a specific time and place, and by 'semantic' testimony we mean assertions about generalizable, conventional, scientific, or conceptual knowledge. On an intuitive basis alone, assertions about episodic facts can be differentiated from those regarding conventional, scientific, and conceptual information (McMyler, 2011; see also Mills, 2013). Assertions of episodic facts are often constrained to specific events, and their truth is based on the authority of individual speakers with informative access to relevant aspects of an episode. In contrast, conventional, scientific, and conceptual information is broadly shared, generalizable knowledge based on the authority of a cultural, scholarly, or other (potentially unknown) collective source. Second, direct observation is often impossible in the cases of common testimony, leaving others' testimony as the sole route to knowledge acquisition. Third, a speaker's perceptual access to the local details of the episode will serve as a source of warrant or support for episodic claims but not as easily for conventional, semantic, or generic ones (see also chapter 3). The very presence of such inherent differences across content domains casts doubt on a unitary theoretical treatment of testimonial learning as well as the idea that children approach testimonial learning situations in a uniform manner. Rather, the processes underlying children's testimonial learning likely differ according to the content of the message. The aim of the remainder of the section will be to substantiate this robust intuitive distinction and reveal important differences in children's selective learning from testimony in semantic and episodic information domains.

In what follows, we turn to the selective trust literature to spell out the psychological differences in children's learning from semantic and episodic testimony. We group these differences into three categories: (1) informant tracking/source memory; (2) significance of errors; and (3) epistemic credentials.

Informant tracking.   In unmarked cases (i.e., where a speaker's benevolence or competence is not in question), when children are presented with a single speaker who offers up a piece of testimony—be it semantic or episodic in its content, children tend to accept that information. In countless experimental studies of word learning, for example, children willingly accept information from an unmarked, unfamiliar speaker (Carey & Bartlett, 1978; ; Jaswal & Hansen, 2006; Woodward, Markman, & Fitzsimmons, 1994). Indeed, work by Jaswal and colleagues shows that 2- to 3-year-old children are willing to re-categorize a perceptually deviant dog-like animal based on the simple, conventional report of an informant (e.g., "That's a cat.") (Jaswal, 2004; Jaswal & Malone, 2007; Jaswal & Markman, 2007; see also chapter 8). Such results are not confined to the preschool years: Chan and Tardif (2013) examined the categorization decisions of American and Chinese kindergartners and second graders. Their task was to classify prototypical objects, for which they had high levels of prior knowledge, and ambiguous objects (that could be appropriately classified multiple ways), for which they had lower levels of prior knowledge. They first performed the task with a teacher, who mislabeled the objects to be categorized, and then performed the task a second time in the teacher's absence. All children were more likely to endorse labels that conflicted with their own perceptual judgments when they had weak prior knowledge of the objects, and the older children exhibited this effect most robustly.

Similarly, for cases of episodic reports from a single speaker who appears benevolent or competent, children accept what they are told. In research by Ganea and colleagues (Ganea et al., 2011), 2-year-old children witnessed an object's location (on the table) or physical state (dry) and were then told by an informant about a change ("moved to the cupboard" or " is now wet"). By 30 months, when children were asked to retrieve the object, they updated their knowledge and retrieved the appropriate object (i.e., the wet one or the one from the cupboard) based solely on someone's episodic testimony. Also, in work by Jaswal (2010), 30-month-old children readily changed their initial judgment about the whereabouts of an object that had been sent down a tubular device into one of three cups based on the episodic testimony of a nearby informant. Thus, for cases of both semantic and episodic testimony from a seemingly benevolent or competent speaker, we see that children (and adults) typically accept what they have been told.

Given children's willingness to accept testimony of both semantic and episodic types, we are not arguing for differences in credulity in the unmarked cases. However, we suggest that beliefs gained from episodic testimony are more likely to carry with them knowledge of the source than are common cultural or semantic beliefs (e.g., about the names of things). Because semantic beliefs are so widespread and the testimonial practice that supports them so pervasive, we are unlikely to track and remember source information for commonly held information. In contrast, we are more likely to remember the source of many episodic claims such as where my lost keys have been hiding, who won the weekend's football game, and what is the best restaurant in town. These episodic claims and the beliefs they engender are not commonly held, making their sources more memorable and easier to track.

In unmarked cases that do not involve error or speaker uncertainty, we are unaware of research that has directly examined children's source tracking or memory when offered semantic and episodic information in a single experiment. However, there are indirect suggestions in the literature that children and adults may monitor the source of a claim more successfully when presented with unmarked episodic information as opposed to semantic information. Preschoolers tend to exhibit strikingly poor source monitoring during semantic learning. For example, 4- and 5-year-olds reported always having known recently learned (non-obvious) animal facts, scientific demonstrations, and color words (4-year-olds only), and expected their peers to know this information as well (Taylor, Esbensen, & Bennett, 1994). In an additional study, preschoolers committed the same error after learning Japanese counting words, but their monitoring performance improved substantially when the linguistic component of the learning task was deemphasized (e.g., "learning how to *count* in Japanese" as opposed to "learning the *meaning* of Japanese counting words;" Esbensen, Taylor, & Stoess, 1997). Preschoolers demonstrated similarly high monitoring performance when learning about the contents of drawers, with 4- and 5-year-olds accurately recalling sources of knowledge at near ceiling levels (Gopnik & Graf, 1988; although obvious procedural differences prevent direct comparison between this and the studies by Esbensen and colleagues).

Research on the relationship between adult language comprehension and belief formation provides additional support for the possibility that differential monitoring processes are engaged for unmarked semantic versus episodic claims. Gilbert, Krull, and Malone (1990) presented adults with a series of assertions containing semantic information such as the meaning of "Hopi" vocabulary words (Study 1) or novel animal facts (Study 3) that were subsequently tagged as true or false. During some of the presentations, participants were distracted by auditory tones and requisite key presses. Results indicated that when distracted, adults were more likely to mistakenly judge assertions previously tagged as false to be true than they were to mistakenly judge assertions previously tagged as true to be false, suggesting that distraction led to decreased monitoring of the falsity of claims. However, the effect was eliminated in subsequent research employing the same task, and monitoring was spared, when assertions contained episodic messages that were informative when false (Hasson, Simmons, & Todorov, 2005). On the basis of these findings, it seems at least plausible that success in monitoring sources associated with statements may depend on the content of information, and, specifically, that monitoring may be engaged more effectively in response to episodic assertions. Future research should address this possibility with both children and adults.

Significance of errors. Recent evidence suggests that young children's responses to speaker errors vary according to whether episodic or semantic information has been asserted. Specifically, younger preschoolers, and at times older preschoolers and school-aged children, exhibit lower responsiveness to speaker errors in cases of episodic assertions compared to cases of object labeling, and they seem to weight semantic errors more heavily when deciding whom to trust in future interactions. When searching for treats, for instance, 3-year-olds continuously endorsed the locations indicated by a speaker in spite of him being explicitly described as a "big liar who always tells lies" (Mascaro & Sperber, 2009). Similarly, preschoolers playing a finding game repeatedly searched for stickers in the locations reported by a speaker who had tricked multiple 'finders' in the past (Vanderbilt, Liu, & Heyman, 2011). In research by Jaswal, after witnessing an object roll down a transparent tube and correctly predicting its location, 30-month-old children repeatedly changed their view and chose to believe an adult's incorrect report of where the object landed (Jaswal, 2010). In fact, children did not become increasingly skeptical over the course of six trials. Finally, Jaswal, Croft, Setia, and Cole (2010) showed that 3-year-olds consistently followed the advice of an inaccurate and deceptive informant (over eight trials) when incorrect sticker locations were communicated through testimony (see chapter 8). To sum, children's sensitivity to the competence or accuracy of informants may decrease when the content is episodic, or event-related. It may be that such errors are less unusual (or more readily explained) because events are often transient, fleeting, or non-recurrent. Another possibility (that warrants empirical exploration) is that differences in the tasks used to assess selective learning in semantic and episodic domains may influence children's performance. Note also that we are not suggesting that children are entirely insensitive to error in the episodic cases (see evidence from Ganea et al., 2011), but that sensitivity to episodic error may be less robust and evident later in development.

In sharp contrast, children appear vigilant and selective in the face of even a small number of semantic errors. Thirteen- and 16-month-old infants indicate their surprise in reaction to labeling errors of an adult (Gliga & Csibra, 2009; Koenig & Echols, 2003). Toddlers by 24 months modulate their willingness to learn from a speaker who recently committed three semantic errors (Koenig & Woodward, 2010). Evidence suggests that 3-year-olds mistrust inaccurate sources paired with neutral ones, and generalize that mistrust across types of information (Corriveau, Meints, & Harris, 2009; Koenig & Jaswal, 2011). In research by Pasquini, Corriveau, Koenig, & Harris (2007), 3-year-olds' selective learning was less affected by the number of semantic errors committed and more by whether the informant had erred or not. Finally, research in our laboratory has demonstrated that preschoolers exhibit a greater selective preference for a previously accurate informant in novel learning situations after being exposed to object labeling errors as opposed to errors in reporting object locations (Stephens & Koenig, submitted). In light of these findings, we speculate that repeated object misnamings call into question an informant's competence because they represent violations of information held *in common*, leading to selective mistrust. Moreover, instances of preschoolers' unchecked credulity in tasks applying episodic inaccuracy may be attributable in part to the fact that episodic errors are often event-specific, transient, and idiosyncratic in nature.

Interestingly, young children are willing to excuse errors made for both semantic and episodic information. For example, when learning episodic information such as the color or texture of hidden objects, preschoolers excused a previously inaccurate speaker who erred only while lacking visual access and chose to accept the speaker's word against their own when she had a positional advantage (Nurmsoo & Robinson, 2009a; Robinson & Whitcombe, 2003). Similarly, when learning semantic information, research by Kondrad and Jaswal (2012) shows that children forgive understandable semantic mistakes. In one condition, 4- and 5-year-old children were presented with two informants who had only a partial view of an object they were to name (e.g., the handle of a comb that also looked like that of a brush). Crucially, both informants provided inaccurate labels but one informant's errors were closer to the mark (e.g., "a brush") than the other informant's errors (e.g., "a thunderstorm"). Children consistently agreed with the "close" informant, even though the inaccuracy of these "close" errors was revealed after each trial. Children also preferred the labels provided by the "close" informant for novel unambiguous objects. This work on error forgiveness is important in that clarifies that, in the eyes of a young child, it is the *inexplicable* semantic errors that really hurt the authority and call into doubt the competence of an informant.

Epistemic credentials.   For semantic information, one wants to learn and use labels accepted by one's own community or group. In contrast, for episodic information, one wants to learn from those who happen to be in a better position to know. For episodic reports, this often amounts to having first-hand access to information or having a positional advantage. Interestingly, in work by Brosseau-Liard & Birch (2011) that directly compared episodic learning (e.g., learning which of two objects was in a box) to semantic learning trials (e.g., learning the name of the object in a box), preschoolers appeared more likely to take into account a speaker's history of accuracy when learning novel semantic information than when learning novel episodic information. Children perceived prior accuracy as less predictive of knowledge in the episodic learning situations (where factors such as a speaker's perceptual access were of greater importance; Brosseau-Liard & Birch, 2011). In contrast, children favor sources with proven linguistic and conceptual knowledge when learning semantic information. For example, when learning novel labels, preschoolers preferred to learn from a speaker who accurately reported conceptual information such as non-obvious internal properties of objects (e.g., whether they were made of "red stuff" or "green stuff") over one who accurately reported objects' non-obvious, but potentially visible, external properties (e.g., whether they had red or green stickers on the back; Sobel & Corriveau, 2010). Preschoolers also selectively accepted novel labels from the speaker who previously labeled objects correctly over one who successfully activated or fixed objects, privileging evidence of conceptual competence (Kushnir et al., 2013). When learning novel conceptual information, children's inferences regarding the internal properties of objects were influenced more by linguistic information (i.e., whether it shared a label with another object with the property in question) than by an object's visual appearance (i.e., whether it looked like another object with the property in question); interestingly, this effect was seen only when the labels were provided by a previously accurate or competent source (Kim, Kalish, & Harris, 2012).

In sharp contrast, in episodic learning situations, children privilege information such as perceptual access, and sometimes do so over semantic accuracy. For example, when figuring out which block would activate a novel machine, preschoolers endorsed the block indicated by an informant who was not blindfolded and thus in a position to apply her knowledge (Kushnir, Wellman, & Gelman, 2008). Young children also recognize when a source has more informative perceptual access than they themselves do and selectively accept suggestions conflicting with their own judgments accordingly (Robinson & Whitcombe, 2003), even when a source has been inaccurate in the past (Nurmsoo & Robinson, 2009a). Similarly, as mentioned above, young children ignore prior accuracy information and exclusively rely on an informant's relevant perceptual access when learning episodic facts such as which of two objects is hidden in a given location (Brosseau-Liard & Birch, 2011). Young children also appreciate the specific relevance of perceptual access to episodic learning situations. When learning about external, visible characteristics of unfamiliar animals and individuals, 6-year-olds chose to rely on visual inspection to acquire information; but, when learning about internal, invisible qualities, they chose to direct questions to individuals with relevant established expertise (Fitneva, Lam, & Dunfield, 2013). Preschoolers have higher confidence in the location or properties of an object after seeing it for themselves over being told from a speaker, especially if the speaker lacks informative access to the object (Clement et al., 2004; Robinson, Haigh, & Nurmsoo, 2008). Finally, even infants preferred to follow the gaze (indicating the potential presence of an object) of an individual who looked with interest in boxes containing objects as opposed to one who looked in empty boxes (Poulin-Dubois & Chow, 2009). In summary, when learning episodic information, children often favor evidence concerning a speaker's positional advantage or relevant perceptual access.

There is plenty of evidence that children as young as 3 (if not younger) attribute knowledge to people who perceive information, but not to those who don't (Meltzoff & Brooks, 2008; O'Neill, 1996; Pratt & Bryant, 1990), and the finding that children appreciate a causal link between perceiving something and knowing about it has been long established. The research reviewed above goes beyond this by indicating that when evaluating a certain kind of *testimony*, namely, episodic assertions, children privilege evidence of a speaker's positional advantage (and do so over prior accuracy). However, in a recent study, Lane et al. (2013) found that children did not privilege access over a trait description ("Sam is smart") until 5 to 6 years of age. Children were asked to attribute knowledge to a "smart" character who lacked access to the contents of a box and a "not smart" character who indeed had access to the box's contents. Three-year-olds used the trait information, rather than perceptual access, to infer informants' knowledge. Only the oldest children (and adults) distinguished between the information conveyed by a positive trait and the more specific indicators of knowledge regarding the box's contents. The understanding that perceptual access should be privileged over other types of information (e.g., trait descriptions) in some learning situations takes time to develop.

Summary

In light of this review, we argue that (1) children monitor speakers according to the primary dimensions of competence and benevolence/warmth and (2) that testimony's extensive variation with respect to testimonial *content* resists a unitary treatment. The current literature on children's selective trust suggests that preschoolers are sensitive to the distinction between semantic and episodic testimony in terms of their *informant monitoring, sensitivity to error*, and evaluations of speakers' *epistemic credentials* in accordance with the type of testimony presented.

The distinction between semantic and episodic testimony has been raised previously in the literature. For example, Fitneva and Dunfield (2010) write, "one of the potentially important differences is that knowledge regarding common objects is widely distributed. In contrast, knowledge about what a person has done in some specific, spatio-temporal context is narrowly distributed." (p. 1383) As discussed by Nurmsoo and Robinson (2009b), who found no evidence for selectivity when semantic errors derived from a blindfolded speaker: "Perhaps children are [. . .] less cautious when they are offered [episodic] knowledge such as which object happens to be in a container at a particular moment in time." (p. 46) And, according to Brosseau-Liard and Birch (2011), who directly compared children's learning of episodic messages with semantic messages, "situation-specific cues are only informative about someone's knowledge in a particular situation: The fact that Sally looks inside a box [. . .] tells us nothing about how knowledgeable she will be on other occasions, even a very similar one." (p. 1789) In support of these ideas, it was our aim to give the distinction between episodic tellings and semantic messages a fuller, more complete treatment here and to more extensively characterize the ways in which children's testimonial learning may indeed depend upon different types of information and associated cognitive processes.

We have focused here on a single distinction—episodic tellings versus shared or semantic practices—because we believe there to be suggestive evidence from children and adults to support the idea that children may treat these two types of claims differently. There are undoubtedly other types of claims that deserve careful consideration. In a recent article, Woolley and Ghossainy (2013), argue that claims regarding the reality status of new entities may initially be resisted by young children, in part because their own first-hand experience does not support such claims. Also, McMyler (2007) argues on intuitive and analytic grounds for an epistemic distinction—knowing at first vs. second hand—and distinguishes testimonial knowledge by appealing to the extent to which the listener has independent evidence that bears on the claim. The more independent evidence that is available to a listener, the more 'first-hand' the knowledge becomes and less trust in the speaker becomes required. Given that epistemic analyses of testimony resist a unitary treatment, we anticipate that our trust in testimony is likely to take different forms as well.

References

Asch, S. E. (1946). Forming impressions of personality. *Journal of Abnormal and Social Psychology, 41,* 258–290.

Birch, S. A., Vauthier, S. A., & Bloom, P. (2008). Three- and four-year-olds spontaneously use others' past performance to guide their learning. *Cognition, 107,* 1018–1034.

Brosseau-Liard, P. E., & Birch, S. A. (2011). Epistemic states and traits: Preschoolers appreciate the differential informativeness of situation-specific and person-specific cues to knowledge. *Child Development, 82,* 1788–1796.

Cacioppo, J. T., Gardner, W. L., & Berntson, G. G. (1997). Beyond bipolar conceptualizations and measures: The case of attitudes and evaluative space. *Personality and Social Psychology Review, 1,* 3–25.

Carey, S., & Bartlett, E. (1978). Acquiring a single new word. *Papers and Reports on Child Language Development, 15,* 17–29.

Chaiken, S. (1979). Communicator physical attractiveness and persuasion. *Journal of Personality and Social Psychology, 37(8),* 1387–1397.

Chaiken, S., & Eagly, A. (1983). Communication modality as a determinant of persuasion: The role of communicator salience. *Journal of Personality and Social Psychology, 45(2),* 241–256.

Chan, C. C. Y., & Tardif, T. (2013). Knowing better: The role of prior knowledge and culture in trust in testimony. *Developmental Psychology, 49,* 591–601.

Chow, V., Poulin-Dubois, D., & Lewis, J. (2008). To see or not to see: Infants prefer to follow the gaze of a reliable looker. *Developmental Science, 11,* 761–770.

Clement, F., Koenig, M. A., & Harris, P. L. (2004). The ontogenesis of trust. *Mind & Language, 19,* 360–379.

Coady, C. A. J. (1992). *Testimony: A philosophical study.* New York, NY: Oxford University Press.

Corriveau, K. H., Fusaro, M., & Harris, P. L. (2009). Going with the flow: Preschoolers prefer nondissenters as informants. *Psychological Science, 20,* 372–377.

Corriveau, K. H., & Harris, P. L. (2009). Choosing your informant: Weighing familiarity and recent accuracy. *Developmental Science, 12,* 426–437.

Corriveau, K. H., Kinzler, K. D., & Harris, P. L. (2013). Accuracy trumps accent in children's endorsement of object labels. *Developmental Psychology, 49,* 470–479.

Corriveau, K. H., Meints, K., & Harris, P. L. (2009). Early tracking of informant accuracy and inaccuracy. *Developmental Psychology, 27,* 331–342.

Davidson, D. (1984). *Truth and interpretation.* New York, NY: Clarendon.

Doebel, S., & Koenig, M. A. (2013). Children's use of moral behavior in selective trust: Discrimination versus learning. *Developmental Psychology, 49,* 462–469.

Esbensen, B. M., Taylor, M., & Stoess, C. (1997). Children's behavioral understanding of knowledge acquisition. *Cognitive Development, 12,* 53–84.

Fiske, S. T. (1980). Attention and weight in person perception: The impact of negative and extreme behavior. *Journal of Personality and Social Psychology, 38,* 889–906.

Fiske, S. T., Cuddy, A. J. C., & Glick, P. (2007). Universal dimensions of social cognition: Warmth and competence. *Trends in Cognitive Sciences, 11,* 77–83.

Fitneva, S. A., & Dunfield, K. A. (2010). Selective information seeking after a single encounter. *Developmental Psychology, 46,* 1380–1384.

Fitneva, S. A., Lam, N. H. L., & Dunfield, K. A. (2013). The development of children's information gathering: To look or to ask? *Developmental Psychology, 49,* 533–542.

Fusaro, M., Corriveau, K. H., & Harris, P. L. (2011). The good, the strong, and the accurate. Preschoolers' evaluations of accurate and strong informants. *Journal of Experimental Child Psychology, 110,* 561–574.

Fusaro, M., & Harris, P. L. (2008). Children assess informant reliability using bystanders' non-verbal cues. *Developmental Science, 11,* 771–777.

Fusaro, M., & Harris, P. L. (2013). Dax gets the nod: Toddlers detect and use social cues to evaluate testimony. *Developmental Psychology, 49,* 514–522.

Ganea, P. A., Koenig, M. A., & Millett, K. G. (2011). Changing your mind about things unseen: Toddlers' sensitivity to prior reliability. *Journal of Experimental Child Psychology, 109,* 445–453.

Gilbert, D. T., Krull, D. S., & Malone, P. S. (1990). Unbelieving the unbelievable: Some problems in the rejection of false information. *Journal of Personality and Social Psychology, 59,* 601–613.

Gillis, R. L., & Nilsen, E. S. (2013). Children's use of information quality to establish speaker preferences. *Developmental Psychology, 49,* 480–490.

Gliga, T., & Csibra, G. (2009). One-year-old infants appreciate the referential nature of deictic gestures and words. *Psychological Science, 20,* 347–353.

Gopnik, A., & Graf, P. (1988). Knowing how you know: Young children's ability to identify and remember the source of their beliefs. *Child Development, 59,* 1366–1371.

Gweon, H., Pelton, H., & Schulz, L. E. (2011). Adults and school-aged children accurately evaluate sins of omission in pedagogical contexts. In *Proceedings of the 33rd Annual Conference of the Cognitive Science Society.*

Hamlin, J. K., Wynn, K., & Bloom, P. (2007). Social evaluation by preverbal infants. *Nature, 450,* 557–559.

Hamlin, J. K., Wynn, K., & Bloom, P. (2010). Three-month-olds show a negativity bias in their social evaluations. *Developmental Science, 13,* 923–929.

Hasson, U., Simmons, J. P., & Todorov, A. (2005). Believe it or not: On the possibility of suspending belief. *Psychological Science, 16,* 566–571.

Jaswal, V. K. (2004). Preschoolers' sensitivity to speaker intent in category induction. *Child Development, 75,* 1871–1885.

Jaswal, V. K. (2010). Believing what you're told: Young children's trust in unexpected testimony about the physical world. *Cognitive Psychology, 61,* 248–272.

Jaswal, V. K., Croft, A. C., Setia, A. R., & Cole, C. A. (2010). Young children have a specific, highly robust bias to trust testimony. *Psychological Science, 21,* 1541–1547.

Jaswal, V. K., & Hansen, M. B. (2006). Learning words: Children disregard some pragmatic information that conflicts with mutual exclusivity. *Developmental Science, 9,* 158–165.

Jaswal, V. K., & Malone, L. S. (2007). Turning believers into skeptics: 3-year-olds' sensitivity to cues to speaker credibility. *Journal of Cognition and Development, 8,* 263–283.

Jaswal, V. K., & Markman, E. M. (2007). Looks aren't everything: 24-month-olds' willingness to accept unexpected labels. *Journal of Cognition and Development, 8,* 93–111.

Jaswal, V. K., & Neely, L. A. (2006). Adults don't always know best: Preschoolers use past reliability over age when learning new words. *Psychological Science, 17,* 757–758.

Kim, S., Kalish, C. W., & Harris, P. L. (2012). Speaker reliability guides children's inductive inferences about novel properties. *Cognitive Development, 27,* 114–125.

Koenig, M. A., Clement, F., & Harris, P. L. (2004). Trust in testimony: Children's use of true and false statements. *Psychological Science, 15,* 694–698.

Koenig, M. A., & Doebel, S. (in press). Children's understanding of unreliability: Evidence for a negativity bias. In S. Gelman & M. Banaji (Eds.), *Navigating the social world: What infants, children and other species can teach us.* Oxford, UK: Oxford University Press.

Koenig, M. A., & Echols, C. H. (2003). Infants' understanding of false labeling events: The referential roles of words and the speakers who use them. *Cognition, 87,* 179–208.

Koenig, M. A., & Harris, P. L. (2005). Preschoolers mistrust ignorant and inaccurate speakers. *Child Development, 76,* 1261–1277.

Koenig, M. A., & Jaswal, V. K. (2011). Characterizing children's expectations about expertise and incompetence: Halo or pitchfork effects? *Child Development, 82,* 1634–1647.

Koenig, M. A., & Woodward, A. L. (2010). Sensitivity of 24-month-olds to the prior accuracy of the source: Possible mechanisms. *Developmental Psychology, 46,* 815–826.

Kondrad, R. L., & Jaswal, V. K. (2012). Explaining the errors away: Young children forgive understandable semantic mistakes. *Cognitive Development, 27,* 126–135.

Kushnir, T., Vredenburgh, C., & Schneider, L. A. (2013). "Who can help me fix this toy?" The distinction between causal knowledge and word knowledge guides preschoolers' selective requests for information. *Developmental Psychology, 49,* 446–453.

Kushnir, T., Wellman, H. M., & Gelman, S. A. (2008). The role of preschoolers' social understanding in evaluating the informativeness of causal interventions. *Cognition, 107,* 1084–1092.

Lackey, J., (2008). *Learning from words: Testimony as a source of knowledge.* Oxford, UK: Oxford University Press.

Lane, J. D., Wellman, H. M., & Gelman, S. A. (2013). Informants' traits weigh heavily in young children's trust in testimony and in their epistemic inferences. *Child Development.* doi: 10.1111/cdev.12029.

Lipton, P. (1998). The epistemology of testimony. *Studies in History and Philosophy of Science, 29,* 1–32.

Liu, D., Vanderbilt, K. E., & Heyman, G. D. (2013). Selective trust: Children's use of intention and outcome of past testimony. *Developmental Psychology, 49,* 439–445.

Lutz, D. J., & Keil, F. C. (2002). Early understanding of the division of cognitive labor. *Child Development, 73,* 1073–1084.

Mascaro, O., & Sperber, D. (2009). The moral, epistemic, and mindreading components of children's vigilance towards deception. *Cognition, 112,* 367–280.

McMyler, B. (2007). Knowing at second hand. *Inquiry, 50,* 511–540.

McMyler, B. (2011). *Testimony, Trust, and Authority.* New York, NY: Oxford University Press.

Meltzoff, A. N., & Brooks, R. (2008). Self experience as a mechanism for learning about others: A training study in social cognition. *Developmental Psychology, 44,* 1257–1265.

Mills, C. M. (2013). Knowing when to doubt: Developing a critical stance when learning from others. *Developmental Psychology, 49,* 404–418.

Nurmsoo, E., & Robinson, E. J. (2009a). Children's trust in previously inaccurate informants who were well or poorly informed: When past errors can be excused. *Child Development, 80,* 23–27.

Nurmsoo, E., & Robinson, E. J. (2009b). Identifying unreliable informants: Do children excuse past inaccuracy? *Developmental Science, 12,* 41–47.

O'Neill, D. K. (1996). Two-year-old children's sensitivity to a parent's knowledge state when making requests. *Child Development, 67,* 659–677.

Pasquini, E. S., Corriveau, K. H., Koenig, M. A., & Harris, P. L. (2007). Preschoolers monitor the relative accuracy of informants. *Developmental Psychology, 43,* 1216–1226.

Peeters, G. (2002). From good and bad to can and must: subjective necessity of acts associated with positively and negatively valued stimuli. *European Journal of Social Psychology, 32,* 125–136.

Poulin–Dubois, D., & Chow, V. (2009). The effect of a looker's past reliability on infants' reasoning about beliefs. *Developmental Psychology, 45,* 1576–1582.

Pratt, C., & Bryant, P. (1990). Children understand that looking leads to knowing (so long as they are looking into a single barrel). *Child Development, 61,* 973–982.

Robinson, E. J., Haigh, S. N., & Nurmsoo, E. (2008). Children's working understanding of knowledge sources: Confidence in knowledge gained from testimony. *Cognitive Development, 23,* 105–118.

Robinson, E. J., & Whitcombe, E. L. (2003). Children's suggestibility in relation to their understanding about sources of knowledge. *Child Development, 74,* 48–62.

Rosenberg, S., Nelson, C., & Vivekananthan, P. S. (1968). A multidimensional approach to the structure of personality impressions. *Journal of Personality and Social Psychology, 9,* 283–294.

Sabbagh, M. A., & Baldwin, D. A. (2001). Learning words from knowledgeable versus ignorant speakers: Links between preschoolers' theory of mind and semantic development. *Child Development, 72,* 1054–1070.

Scofield, J., Gilpin, A. T., Pierucci, J., & Morgan, R. (2013). Matters of accuracy and conventionality: Prior accuracy guides children's evaluations of others' actions. *Developmental Psychology, 49,* 432–438.

Skowronski, J. J., & Carlston, D. E. (1987). Social judgment and social memory: The role of cue diagnosticity in negativity, positivity, and extremity biases. *Journal of Personality and Social Psychology, 52,* 689–699.

Sobel, D. M., & Corriveau, K. H. (2010). Children monitor individuals' expertise for word learning. *Child Development, 81,* 669–679.

Stephens, E. C., & Koenig, M. A. (submitted). The error is key: Preschoolers' selective learning in semantic and episodic domains.

Taylor, M., Esbensen, B. M., & Bennett, R. T. (1994). Children's understanding of knowledge acquisition: The tendency for children to report that they have always known what they have just learned. *Child Development, 65,* 1581–1604.

Vaish, A., Carpenter, M., & Tomasello, M. (2009). Sympathy through affective perspective taking and its relation to prosocial behavior in toddlers. *Developmental Psychology, 45,* 534–543.

Vaish, A., Grossman, T., & Woodward, A. (2008). Not all emotions are created equal: The negativity bias in social-emotional development. *Psychological Bulletin, 134,* 383–403.

Vanderbilt, K. E., Liu, D., & Heyman, G. D. (2011). The development of distrust. *Child Development, 82,* 1372–1380.

Wojciszke, B. (1994). Multiple meanings of behavior: Construing actions in terms of competence and morality. *Journal of Personality and Social Psychology, 67,* 222–232.

Wojciszke, B., Bazinska, R., & Jaworski, M. (1998). On the dominance of moral categories in impression formation. *Personality and Social Psychology Bulletin, 24,* 1251–1263.

Woodward, A. L., Markman, E. M., & Fitzsimmons, C. M. (1994). Rapid word learning in 13- and 18-month-olds. *Developmental Psychology, 30,* 553–566.

Woolley, J. D., & Ghossainy, M. E. (2013). Revisiting the fantasy-reality distinction: Children as naïve skeptics. *Child Development, 84,* 1496–1510.

Zmyj, N., Buttelmann, D., Carpenter, M. J., & Daum, M. M. (2010). The reliability of a model influences 14-month-olds' imitation. *Journal of Experimental Child Psychology, 106,* 208–220.

2 Learning from testimony about religion and science

Paul L. Harris and Kathleen H. Corriveau

Introduction

One of the strongest pieces of evidence for children's trust in testimony is their belief in the existence of ordinarily unobservable special beings such as the Tooth Fairy or God as well as invisible, scientific entities such as germs and oxygen. In earlier work, we established that 5- and 6-year-olds are quite confident of the existence of all of these invisible entities (Harris, Pasquini, Duke, Asscher, & Pons, 2006).

Those initial findings also pointed to a subtle but significant differentiation between scientific entities on the one hand and special beings on the other. Children expressed more confidence in germs and oxygen than in the Tooth Fairy or God. Follow-up studies in Spain (Guerrero, Enesco, & Harris, 2010) and Mexico (Harris, Abarbanell, Pasquini, & Duke, 2007) led to similar results—children expressed more confidence in the existence of unobservable scientific entities such as germs than in unobservable religious entities such as the soul or ancestral spirits.

One possible interpretation of this differentiation is that children have a budding sensitivity to the difference between factual claims, including those that pertain to microscopic entities, as compared to religious claims about special beings and spiritual entities. Indeed, recent findings with children lend some support to this possibility. Children conceptualize religious claims differently from straightforward, factual claims (Heiphetz, Spelke, Harris, & Banaji, 2013).

However, there are two reasons for doubting that children make any principled distinction between religious and scientific claims. First, scrutiny of the original findings by Harris et al. (2006) reveals striking parallels—rather than differences—between the way that children explained their confidence in the existence of religious and scientific entities. In each case, they justified their claims about existence by reference to the properties of the entity—often referring to its causal powers. Second, in the same way that children expressed more confidence in the existence of scientific entities as compared to special beings, so they also asserted that there was a greater consensus around the existence of scientific as compared to religious entities. Recent findings underline the sensitivity of young children to consensus (Corriveau, Min, & Kurkul, chapter 7 this volume; Corriveau & Harris,

2010; Harris, 2012; Harris & Corriveau, 2011, 2013). On reflection, therefore, it is possible that children's greater confidence in the existence of scientific entities such as germs and oxygen is not due to any deep-seated sensitivity to the objective status of such claims—as compared to claims about religious entities—but rather to children's keen antennae for a social consensus.

This latter analysis makes two predictions. First, it predicts that children's confidence in the existence of special beings would be elevated if they were to grow up in a community that displays a complete, or near complete, consensus in a given special being—provided such a community could be found. Second, and conversely, it predicts that children's confidence in the existence of scientific entities—indeed in a wide range of ordinarily unobservable processes—such as evolution or climate change—would be depressed in communities where the relevant consensus is partial or incomplete.

This argument raises the possibility that despite widespread assumptions to the contrary, the process by which trust is established is quite similar for religious and scientific claims. We will discuss recent evidence from children and adults supporting this conclusion. Before doing so, however, it will be helpful to review the above findings in more detail.

Germs and the Tooth Fairy

We asked 5- and 6-year-olds living in the Boston area about the existence of three different types of entity: *scientific* entities (e.g., germs and oxygen), and two types of special being—what we called *endorsed* special beings, i.e., those whose existence is routinely endorsed by adults when speaking to young children (e.g., God and the Tooth Fairy) and finally *equivocal* special beings, i.e., those whose existence is not ordinarily endorsed by adults when speaking to children—except perhaps in the context of stories or pretend-play (e.g., mermaids and ghosts). For each type of entity, children were invited to say whether it really exists (e.g., "Now what about mermaids? Are there really mermaids?") and, following their *yes* or *no* answer, to indicate how sure they were. For example, the interviewer asked: "OK. You say there are (aren't) mermaids. Are you sure about that or not very sure?" Children's existence claims could therefore be measured on a 4-point scale ranging from yes + very sure through to no + very sure. In follow-up questions, children were also asked: to explain their judgment for each item (e.g., "How do you know there are/aren't (any) mermaids?"), to say what other people's judgment would be (e.g., ". . . What about other people—would everyone say there really are/ aren't (any) mermaids?"). And finally, children were asked if they knew about the appearance of the item (e.g., "Do you know what mermaids look like?").

Several notable findings emerged. First, children expressed confidence in the existence of both scientific entities and endorsed beings—considerably more confidence than in the existence of equivocal beings. Thus, in concrete terms children almost invariably said that they were sure that germs exist, they often said that they were sure that God exists but they typically said that mermaids do not exist. Note that children's responses to the scientific entities and the endorsed beings were not identical. They expressed more confidence in the existence of scientific entities. Nevertheless, their justifications for asserting the existence of scientific entities and endorsed beings were quite similar: they referred to the properties, including the causal properties of the entity in question.

We interpreted these findings in light of the testimony that children receive regarding these three different entity types. More specifically, children will generally hear adults endorse the existence of both scientific entities such as germs as well as endorsed beings such as the Tooth Fairy or God. On the other hand, they will not ordinarily hear adults endorse the existence of equivocal beings such as ghosts and mermaids. This focus on the testimonial input that children receive was reinforced by two other findings. First, when children were asked to say what other people believed, their replies displayed a pattern that was similar to the pattern for their own beliefs. Thus, children claimed that other people would believe in scientific entities, would also believe in endorsed beings, albeit less so, and would doubt the existence of equivocal beings. Second, consistent with the idea that children were relying on what they were told and not on any information they had gathered first-hand, children quite often admitted that they did not know what the entity in question looked like—and this was especially true for the scientific entities despite children's strong confidence in their existence. It is worth emphasizing that, in this respect, children are reasoning in a way that is no different from adults. As adults, we might readily admit the existence of cancerous cells or carburetors without having much idea of what they look like or being able to recognize one if we saw it.

Belief in germs, belief in God

In carrying this research forward, we focused on the subtle but intriguing difference between children's responses to scientific entities as compared to endorsed beings. Whether reporting on their own beliefs or other people's, children reported more confidence in the existence of scientific entities. We wondered if this finding reflected the particular sample of children that we had tested—they were drawn from a private school in the Greater Boston area serving predominantly middle-class families. We speculated that such children, growing up in a culturally and religiously diverse urban area such as Boston, might well be exposed to a mix of beliefs about endorsed beings such as God, the Tooth Fairy and Santa Claus, a mix that might undermine their confidence. Also, given their relatively privileged backgrounds and schooling, it was possible that these children had an atypical confidence in the existence of scientific entities such as germs. To explore these possibilities, we conducted two further studies.

We recruited children aged 10 to 12 years from a Catholic school in the city of Cuenca, in central Spain (Guerrero et al., 2010). Our assumption was that the testimony that children received in this school regarding religious phenomena such as God and the soul would be unequivocal. We based this assumption on visible indices of the school's character and philosophy. Most of the teachers in the school were nuns. The classrooms and hallways displayed a variety of religious icons, including pictures of Jesus and the Virgin Mary, devotional inscriptions and crucifixes. Our tentative expectation was that in this setting, children would respond differently from children in Boston—they would be just as confident of the existence of God and the soul as they were of scientific entities such as germs and oxygen. This expectation was not borne out. Like the Boston children, these Spanish children expressed more confidence in the existence of the scientific as compared to the religious entities. Despite the strongly religious environment in which the children were being schooled, the pattern of findings echoed what we had found in Boston.

We also conducted a third study with children of the Tseltal-speaking Mayan community of Tenejapa in Mexico (Harris et al., 2007). This setting provided us with an opportunity to ask children about special beings different from those that are known to children in the United States or Europe. Many villagers in Tenejapa believe in the existence of *ch'ulelal*—the souls or spirits of the dead who have the power to cause an illness in individuals who encounter them. They also believe in the *ijk'al*—small, black creatures that sometimes emerge at night from the caves where they live in order to assault people and even to father children. When questioned about the existence of these endorsed beings as well as scientific entities such as germs and oxygen, the Tenejapa children displayed what had become a familiar pattern. They expressed more confidence in the scientific entities than the endorsed beings.

Given the stability of the findings across three different cultures, we examined two divergent lines of explanation. One possibility is that children reflect in a relatively autonomous fashion on the nature of these various entities and end up with more doubts about the endorsed beings than the scientific entities. A second possibility is that children engage in little autonomous reflection. Instead, they listen with sensitive antennae to the pattern of surrounding testimony and adjudicate in light of what they hear. Below, we weigh these two lines of explanation.

Autonomous reflection or sensitive antennae?

All the various endorsed beings discussed so far—God, the Tooth Fairy, Santa Claus, the *ch'ulelal* and the *ijk'al*—are credited with certain extraordinary characteristic and powers, certainly as compared to human beings. God is credited with omniscience, Santa Claus and the Tooth Fairy with a remarkable, overnight delivery system, the *ch'ulelal* with the power to induce illness at will, and so forth. Arguably, young children are prone to entertain occasional doubts about endorsed beings (as compared to their near certainty concerning scientific entities) because of these alleged extraordinary powers. This account seems plausible at first sight but it actually does a poor job of explaining the detailed pattern of results, especially those obtained in Boston. By any metric, God's extraordinary powers would appear to exceed those of Santa Claus and the Tooth Fairy. Delivering presents to every child or knowing who has just lost a tooth are, we admit, extraordinary feats. But bringing everything into existence would appear to trump either of those achievements in terms of cosmic scope. By implication, if children entertained doubts in proportion to the degree to which any given special being is attributed extraordinary powers, we might reasonably expect God to elicit more doubt than either Santa Claus or the Tooth Fairy. But we saw no sign of that pattern.

In discussing variation among the different endorsed beings that we presented to children, it is important to acknowledge, of course, that God differs from Santa Claus and the Tooth Fairy, not just in the scope of his extraordinary powers but also in at least two other related ways. In the first place, God is more central as an explanatory agent. If children question or dismiss Santa Claus, relatively little is lost in terms of explanatory power whereas if they question or dismiss God, a lot is at stake because he is often presented as the Creator of everything. Second, the costs associated with doubt in Santa Claus might be perceived as modest compared to the costs of doubt in God. However, these special features of God only serve to underline—but not to explain—the pattern of findings that was observed, namely children's more confident endorsement of scientific entities as compared to God. If children were attuned to the central role of God as an explanatory agent—or to the costs of doubting his existence—we might expect them to express great confidence in his existence, certainly as compared to the existence of more localized agents such as germs. But again that is not the pattern that we observe.

Another form of autonomous reflection that children might deploy turns on the notion of microscopic invisibility. By the age of 6 or 7 years, children realize that matter consists of tiny, invisible particles (Au, Sidle, & Rollins, 1993). Armed with this concept, children might conceptualize germs as very tiny creatures—too small to be seen by the naked eye—and thereby retain confidence in their existence, correctly assuming that it can be confirmed with the help of a microscope. Such reasoning would not help to explain the puzzling invisibility of God—or the Tooth Fairy—or the *ch'ulelal* and so, as a result, children might entertain doubts about the existence of these endorsed beings. Again, however, close scrutiny of this line of explanation reveals weaknesses. First, children are confident of the existence of oxygen even though oxygen molecules remain invisible under a microscope. Second, when we asked children to explain why they thought a given entity existed they did not refer to its minute size or to the possibility of observing it with special instruments. More generally, children did not articulate any supposed contrast between, for example, the possibility of seeing germs and the impossibility of seeing God.

So, is it the case that children attend to the surrounding testimony and adjust their credence in any given entity or being according to the pattern that they detect? Two different but potentially correlated metrics might be useful to them in calibrating that testimony: a 'consensus' metric and a 'presupposition' metric.

Recall that when the children were interviewed in Boston, they not only reported on their own beliefs, they were also asked to report on other people's beliefs. In each case, the findings were similar. Children reported more confidence in scientific entities than in endorsed beings. One plausible interpretation of this similarity is that children use their own confidence as a basis for estimating that of adults. They extrapolate from their own case, arguably in a somewhat egocentric fashion. However, the correlation might come about in precisely the opposite fashion. Children might scan the beliefs of the surrounding community, assessing the degree of consensus and calibrate their own confidence accordingly. Thus, if they conclude that everyone believes in germs, they will entertain no doubts themselves. Conversely, if they detect a less than complete consensus, they might temper any predisposition to confidence.

Recent experimental work lends strong support to the idea that young children can and do use a consensus metric. Fusaro and Harris (2008) presented 3- and 4-year-olds with four adults: two informants and two so-called bystanders. Children watched as the two informants were invited to provide names for novel objects. When one proposed a name, the two bystanders expressed agreement (via smiles and head-nods) but when the other proposed a name, the two bystanders expressed disagreement (via frowns and head-shakes). Asked which name they thought was correct, children overwhelmingly selected the name that had triggered bystander agreement. A follow-up study consolidated this result (Corriveau, Fusaro, & Harris, 2009). Three- and 4-year-olds were again presented with four adults. When the adults were asked to point to a novel object ("Show me the modi"), three of them all pointed to the same object whereas the fourth adult dissented by pointing to a different object. Asked which object they thought was the modi, children opted for the object identified by the consensus of three. Indeed, they did so in a further study, in which the consensus was reduced to two—versus a single dissenter.

Both of these studies were done in Boston where children were presented with European-American adults. To check on the generality of the consensus strategy, children in both Boston and Taiwan were tested in a follow-up study (Chen, Corriveau, & Harris, 2013). In each location, some children were presented with European adults and some children were presented with East-Asian adults. In other respects, the procedure was similar to that used by Corriveau et al. (2009). In both locations, and no matter what the ethnicity of the adults, children favored the information provided by the consensus over that offered by the single dissenter.

Could children use this consensus metric to calibrate their relative confidence in the existence of scientific as compared to religious entities? It seems likely that children will encounter a near universal consensus concerning scientific entities such as germs and oxygen. They will rarely, if ever, meet anyone professing doubts about their existence. Note that from a historical perspective, the consensus around the existence of germs is quite recent. Few doctors in 19th-century North America accepted Pasteur's claims concerning the role of microorganisms in the spread of epidemics such as cholera (Rosenberg, 1962). Such a universal consensus is less likely to prevail for religious or supernatural beings. In the case of God, children in Boston or Spain, even those from Christian families or attending Christian schools, will be able to observe varying degrees of church attendance, prayer and piety across individuals and families. Children growing up in Tenejapa may have contact with, or hear about, nearby Ladino communities that practice Catholicism and frown upon beliefs in the spirit world. Finally, if we consider children's belief in the Tooth Fairy and Santa Claus, it seems likely that skepticism and dissent on the part of peers or older children helps to explain children's loss of faith in these endorsed beings. Investigators have frequently supposed that children's emerging skepticism is based on an increasingly probing and rational analysis of the extraordinary powers attributed to these beings (Woolley & Cornelius, 2013). But in light of children's continuing faith in God's yet more extraordinary powers, it seems likely that the testimony of others is actually the more corrosive influence. In line with this analysis, Clément (2013) reports that around the age of 7 to 8 years, many children start to doubt that Santa Claus exists when disabused by another child (often with some contempt towards the naïve believer). Children frequently check with their parents who, at that age, acknowledge that he does not exist.

The presupposition metric is likely to dovetail nicely with the consensus metric. In the case of germs, oxygen or vitamins, individual speakers unreflectively assume the existence of the entities in question. They do not aver their faith or signal any possibility of doubt. Rather, they simply presuppose the existence and properties of the entity in question. For example, they might say: "Don't touch that—it has germs" but not "I believe in germs" or "There really are germs." By contrast, consider the words of a teacher as she led her pupils in prayer in the immediate aftermath of 9/11 (Schweber, 2006):

> We thank you that we can trust in you in that you have this situation under control, even though it seems to us that things are not under control . . . We trust you to work this situation out—for you are good. We ask that people will come to look at you and realize that nothing in the world is secure except you.

The teacher affirms her faith in God while recognizing ongoing doubts—the possibility that God is not in control and that people will need time to recognize the security that God offers. Importantly, she was teaching in a fundamentalist Christian School. By implication, even in an environment in which the presupposition of God's existence and control might be regarded as routine, the teacher's prayer tacitly signals the possibility of doubt even as she affirms the importance of faith.

Research on children's sensitivity to such discourse cues, both explicit and implicit, is still in its infancy but two recent studies suggest that they do play a role in children's beliefs. Woolley, Ma, and Lopez-Mobilia (2011) had children aged 3 to 9 years watch video clips in which two adults conversed casually about animals that were novel to the children (e.g., a bilby, a takin, a civet, etc.). When children heard an implicit reference to the existence of the novel animal in the video (e.g., one of the adults in the video remarked that she had seen a baby takin) 5-, 7- and 9-year-olds (but not 3-year-olds) were likely to judge that the animal was real rather than not real in a subsequent interview. Canfield and Ganea (in press) recorded parents talking to their children about various types of entity, including ordinarily unobservable scientific entities such germs and the brain as well as endorsed beings such as the Tooth Fairy and God. In comparison with the scientific entities, parents were more likely to deny the existence of endorsed beings, or to indicate a lack of expertise ("Well, we don't actually know . . . ") or a lack of consensus ("Some people think . . . ").

In sum, the analysis presented so far is consistent with the proposal that guided by the testimony that they hear, children differentiate between two types of claims: uncontroversial factual claims about scientific entities such as germs and less secure claims about supernatural or religious beings such as God or the *ch'ulelal*. Recent work with children and adults provides further evidence for this differentiation between uncontroversial factual claims and more debatable religious claims.

Heiphetz, Spelke, Harris, and Banaji (2013) presented children and adults with two proponents who made conflicting claims of three different types: (i) conflicting factual claims about science or history (e.g., Germs are very small versus Germs are very big); (ii) conflicting religious claims (e.g., God can do miracles versus Nobody can do miracles); and (iii) conflicting preference-based claims (e.g., Pink is the prettiest color versus Green is the prettiest color). Participants were asked whether the two proponents of these conflicting claims could both be right or whether only one could be right. Both children and adults were likely to judge that only one proponent could be right with respect to conflicting factual claims but that both proponents could be right with respect to conflicting preference-based claims. Judgments about conflicting religious claims were neither seen as fully objective like factual claims nor as fully subjective like preference-based claims. Thus, children and adults conceptualized religious claims in a mixed fashion. They saw some religious claims as more fact based, claiming that only one proponent could be right and others as more preference-based—claiming that both proponents could be right.

The mixed status of religious beliefs also emerged in two further studies in which participants were asked to say how far a given belief might provide information about the world or alternatively provide information about the person holding the belief. Children and adults typically judged that factual beliefs provide information about the world whereas preference-based beliefs reflect something about the person (Heiphetz et al., in press). Again, as in the earlier studies, religious beliefs were viewed as having a mixed status. Thus, participants claimed that religious beliefs sometimes provide information about the world and sometimes about the person. It seems plausible that religious beliefs have this mixed status because children and adults realize that they attract a less systematic consensus than straightforward, factual claims even if they do not display the kind of idiosyncratic variation from one individual to the next that is characteristic of preference-based claims.

Parallels between religion and science

In the study discussed at the outset concerning children's ideas about scientific entities and endorsed beings (Harris et al., 2006), recall that children not only made existence judgments, they also offered an explanation for their existence judgments. Hitherto, we have focused primarily on children's existence judgments and noted a recurrent differentiation between scientific entities, such as germs and endorsed beings such as God. However, children's explanations displayed a different pattern. They revealed important similarities in children's conceptualization of these two types of entity. Explanations were allocated to three primary categories: *encounter* when children referred to some direct contact with the entity in question (or with a veridical representation such as a photo); *source* when children referred to the person or medium of communication that had provided them with relevant information; and *generalization* when they referred to some property or characteristic of the entity.

The profile of children's explanations for scientific entities and endorsed beings was remarkably similar. They rarely mentioned an *encounter* or *source* for either type of entity. Instead, they mostly offered a *generalization*, often echoing the kind of testimony that they had presumably received concerning the particular entity (e.g., "because germs are little thingies and if you don't wash your hands, they make you sick"). The similarity between the explanation profiles for these two types of entity was further highlighted by their contrast with the profile for equivocal beings, such as ghosts and mermaids. For these latter entities, children were more likely to focus both on an *encounter* (or rather, the fact that they had never had an encounter with an equivocal being) as well as the *source* of their information (e.g., a story book); generalizations about equivocal beings were less common than they were for scientific entities or endorsed beings.

The similarity between children's explanation for their belief in God and germs is disconcerting. From an adult perspective, it is tempting to assume that these domains are quite different and warrant different modes of justification. More specifically, it is plausible to assume that anyone familiar with the history of science and the history of religion will realize that the tradition of experimental investigation that has established the existence of germs is a radically different enterprise from the religious tradition that has sustained a belief in God for two millennia. Accordingly, we might expect adults to justify their beliefs very differently in these two cases—for example, to focus on the scientific evidence in the case of germs and to appeal to the religious canon in the case of God. On this view, any similarity in the way that religious beliefs are justified as compared to scientific beliefs would likely be confined to young children and/or participants with limited education.

However, studies of the development of epistemological understanding do not lend strong support to this expectation. Kuhn, Cheney, and Weinstock (2005) presented school children and adults with proponents of conflicting claims in a variety of different domains. Some of the conflicting claims were effectively scientific claims about the physical world (e.g., views about the composition of atoms or the workings of the brain). Participants were invited to say whether only one claim could be right and, if both could be right, to say whether one claim could be judged to have more merit than the other. To the extent that competing claims about the physical world can often be judged as more or less consistent with the available evidence, it would be reasonable to expect participants, especially adult participants, to conclude that one claim could be assessed as having more merit. Such a conclusion would reflect what Kuhn et al. (2005) characterize as the evaluativist stance, i.e., the recognition that some competing claims should not be regarded as freely chosen opinions but as judgments that can be evaluated via argument and evidence. More generally, this evaluativist stance would be expected to predominate if participants regarded claims about the brain or about atomic structure as akin to scientific hypotheses open to adjudication. However, less than half of the participants—30% of school children and 43% of adults adopted the evaluativist stance. The evaluativist stance was even less frequent among a sample of American adults who were presented with competing historical as opposed to competing physical claims and invited to think about their comparative validity. Only 14% displayed the evaluativist stance (Weinstock & Cronin, 2003). Again, such a result is disconcerting. We might expect many adults to grasp the constructed, partial and contested nature of human knowledge about the past.

These findings suggest that the evaluation of conflicting claims on the basis of argument and evidence—a strategy that is often favored by scientists—is not an ideal that is routinely endorsed by adults. To the extent that adults do not recognize and adopt the distinctive epistemological stance favored by science, they may not justify their belief in scientific entities differently from their belief in religious entities.

Guided in part by the developmental findings of Harris et al. (2006), Shtulman (2013) examined the way in which undergraduates at two selective colleges (Occidental College and Harvard) reason in the scientific and religious domains. Thus, as in the developmental study, the students were questioned about scientific phenomena (e.g., electrons, genes, X-rays) as well as religious phenomena (e.g., souls, God, Heaven). They were asked to say whether they believed in the existence of the entity, to indicate their confidence in that belief, to provide a justification for their belief, to say what might change their belief, and to indicate how far they thought that other Americans shared their belief.

Like the children interviewed by Harris et al. (2006), most of the students believed in the existence of the scientific entities and they were very confident in their beliefs. Belief in the existence of the religious phenomena was also widespread but less prevalent than for the scientific phenomena. Moreover, although students expressed confidence in the religious phenomena, they did so less firmly than for the scientific phenomena. The students also resembled the children in their judgments about other people's views: they expected almost everyone to believe in the scientific entities, and they expected many people—but fewer—to believe in the religious phenomena.

So far, these results underline major continuities between children and adults in their overall pattern of judgment concerning the existence of scientific and religious entities. But was there also a similarity in the way that the students justified their belief in those entities? In particular, did the students resemble the children in framing their justifications in a very similar fashion whether they were justifying their belief in, for example, X-rays or in God? As set out above, one might plausibly expect adults, especially those who have had some college education, to justify their religious beliefs differently from their belief in genes and electrons.

Several notable findings emerged. First, once again echoing the pattern observed for children, the overall justification profile for the domains of religion and science was quite similar (even if the particular justifications given by adults and children were different). Thus in both domains, adults offered *deferential* justifications by referring to an authority such as the Bible or to a science teacher, *subjective* justifications by appealing to intuition, preference or personal experience and, finally, *evidential* justifications by appealing to the properties, including the causal properties of the entity, or to other evidential indices (such as the historical record or the ubiquity of reports). For both scientific and religious entities, the majority of justifications fell into these three categories and for both domains, deferential justifications were the most frequently used of the three categories. This parallel also emerged at the individual level. Individuals who resorted to *deferential* justifications particularly often in the domain of science also did so in the domain of religion; a similar cross-domain connection also emerged for individuals' less frequent recourse to *evidential* justifications.

When asked to say what, if anything, might persuade them to change their belief in a given phenomenon, a similar coding system proved applicable. Again, robust within-subject consistency was observed. Thus, individuals used a given type of justification (*deferential, subjective* or *evidential)* more or less frequently across the domains of both religion and science. Such correlations point to the fact that, even if the scientific and religious domains appear to be quite distinct from an epistemic standpoint, when justifying their beliefs individuals deploy strategies that traverse the two domains.

Individuals were also consistent in the way they justified their belief in a phenomenon and the way that they explained what might lead them to change their belief in that phenomenon. Thus, some individuals tended to focus on *deferential* justifications both in justifying their belief in the existence of a given entity and also in discussing what might cause them to change their belief in that entity. Conversely, some individuals tended to focus on *evidential* justifications in both cases.

As Shtulman (2013) emphasizes, even if the students generally expressed more confidence and expected a greater consensus among their fellow Americans for the scientific items, their pattern of reasoning was surprisingly consistent across the scientific and religious items. In each domain, their responses were predominantly couched in terms of deference to authority or—less often—in terms of evidence. Moreover, it is important to emphasize that in each domain, students often denied that anything could change their minds about the existence of the phenomenon in question. Finally, in each domain, confidence was more closely associated with perceived consensus than with citation of relevant evidence. Summing up, even if the students differentiated between the scientific and religious items with respect to their confidence and consensus judgments, their pattern of justification across the two domains was similar. In these respects, the pattern of judgments and justification produced by the adults displayed important parallels with that produced by the children.

Conclusion and implications

From an early age, children embark on two major channels of human thought: religion with its particular assumptions about invisible causal agents and science with its particular assumptions about invisible causal agents. How should we conceptualize the relationship between their thinking in these two domains? One plausible hypothesis, consistent with contemporary assumptions about the difference between science and religion, as manifested in their separate historical chronology, their distinctive institutional structures, and their different status within many contemporary classrooms, is that children will deploy different modes of thinking in the two domains. For example, they will rely on testimonial authority for their religious beliefs and on experimental evidence and its theoretical implications for their scientific beliefs.

A different, perhaps more plausible view is that initially children approach the two domains with the same set of cognitive tools. Nevertheless, by dint of appropriate case studies, they gradually discover that the patterns of reasoning and justification are quite different in science and religion and they hone their tools accordingly. For example, in the course of development they eventually come to realize that claims about scientific concepts are primarily justified by evidence and that theories seeking to explain that evidence are defeasible. Conversely, they also come to realize that claims about religious concepts are primarily justified by reference to the authority of spiritual practitioners or sacred texts.

A third, intuitively implausible view is that the existence of two distinct channels of thinking is, when viewed from a psychological standpoint, illusory. Neither as children nor indeed as adults do most people construe religion and science differently. Rather, from early in development and henceforward, they approach the two domains in much the same way: they accept the testimony of other people concerning the functioning of invisible agents. Asked to assess their belief in those agents, they gauge the tenor of pertinent discourse as well as the degree of consensus in the surrounding community and they express more or less confidence accordingly. Asked to justify their beliefs, they cite the properties of the agents in question or they provide deferential justifications by citing a relevant authority.

Despite its implausibility, the evidence presented in this chapter is consistent with this third view, and not with the first or the second. This conclusion invites two important questions. Why, granted that the history and institutional framework of religion and science have many distinctive features, is this not also manifest at the psychological level—or, rephrasing the question, how is it that science and religion are distinct in so many ways despite their common substrate at a psychological level? And second, is there anything to be said in defense of the ultimately deferential, testimony-based strategy displayed by so many when faced with both religious and scientific claims? Ought we not to find ways of nurturing a more critical, evidence-oriented stance in both (Kuhn, 2008)?

A short answer to these two questions can be given as follows. Science, especially as practiced by a community of scientists, is a rare and late-appearing phenomenon in human history. By contrast, religious communities, and the supernatural beliefs that they espouse and transmit to succeeding generations, have a much more ancient human pedigree. It is likely then that the intellectual proclivity that has favored the transmission of religious ideas for thousands of years, notably a deferential receptivity to testimony about invisible agents and their causal properties, remains part of the human psyche. That proclivity facilitates the assimilation of religious ideas and increasingly, in recent centuries, the assimilation of scientific ideas. By contrast, the type of experimental and evidence-based evaluation that is characteristic of progress within organized scientific communities does not come naturally to human beings. It calls for prolonged education, specialized forms of reporting and trust (Shapin, 1994), and typically, some form of apprenticeship in research. Those who have benefited from that apprenticeship may regard it as an intellectual ideal, an ideal by which they seek to measure and critique more ancient forms of knowing. But psychology—including developmental psychology—is not ultimately a normative or educational enterprise. As a science, it also needs to concern itself with ancient forms of knowing—because they continue to prevail—and figure out how they work.

Acknowledgments

We thank Ileana Enesco, Susan Engel, Carl Johnson, Deanna Kuhn, and Andrew Shtulman for helpful discussion of this paper. The co-authorship of Paul Harris was supported by an ESRC (Economic and Social Research Council) Large Grant (REF RES-060-25-0085).

References

Au, T. K., Sidle, A. L., & Rollins, K. B. (1993). Developing an intuitive understanding of conservation and contamination: Invisible particles as a plausible mechanism. *Developmental Psychology, 29,* 286–299.

Canfield, C., & Ganea, P. A. (in press). "You could call it magic": What parents and siblings tell preschoolers about unobservable entities. *Journal of Cognition and Development.*

Chen, E. E., Corriveau, K. H., & Harris, P. L. (2013). Children trust a consensus composed of outgroup members—but do not retain that trust. *Child Development, 84,* 269–282.

Clément, F. (2013). *Why do children stop believing in Santa Claus?* Paper in preparation.

Corriveau, K. H., Fusaro, M., & Harris, P. L. (2009). Going with the flow: Preschoolers prefer non-dissenters as informants. *Psychological Science, 20,* 372–377.

Corriveau, K. H., & Harris, P. L. (2010). Preschoolers (sometimes) defer to the majority in making simple perceptual judgments. *Developmental Psychology, 46,* 437–445.

Fusaro, M., & Harris, P. L. (2008). Children assess informant reliability using bystanders' non-verbal cues. *Developmental Science, 11,* 781–787.

Guerrero, S., Enesco, I., & Harris, P. L. (2010). Oxygen and the soul: Children's conception of invisible entities. *Journal of Cognition and Culture, 10,* 123–151.

Harris, P. L. (2012). *Trusting what you're told: How children learn from others.* Cambridge, MA: Belknap Press/Harvard University Press.

Harris, P. L., Abarbanell, L., Pasquini, E. S., & Duke, S. (2007). Imagination and testimony in the child's construction of reality. *Intellectica, 46–47,* 69–84.

Harris, P. L., & Corriveau, K. H. (2011). Young children's selective trust in informants. *Proceedings of the Royal Society B, 366,* 1179–1190.

Harris, P. L., & Corriveau, K. H. (2013). Respectful deference: Conformity revisited. In M. R. Banaji & S. A. Gelman (Eds.), *Navigating the social world: What infants, children, and other species can teach us*. New York, NY: Oxford University Press.

Harris, P. L., Pasquini, E. S., Duke, S., Asscher, J. J., & Pons, F. (2006). Germs and angels: The role of testimony in young children's ontology. *Developmental Science, 9*, 76–96.

Heiphetz, L., Spelke, E. S., Harris, P. L., & Banaji, M. R. (2013). The development of reasoning about beliefs: Fact, preference, and ideology. *Journal of Experimental Social Psychology, 49*, 559–565.

Heiphetz, L., Spelke, E. S., Harris, P. L., & Banaji, M. R. (in press). What do different beliefs tell us about? An examination of factual, opinion-based, and religious beliefs. *Cognitive Development.*

Kuhn, D. (2008). *Education for thinking*. Cambridge, MA: Harvard University Press.

Kuhn, D., Cheney, R., & Weinstock, M. (2005). The development of epistemological understanding. *Cognitive Development, 15*, 309–328.

Rosenberg, C. (1962). *The cholera years: The United States in 1832 and 1866*. Chicago, IL: University of Chicago Press.

Schweber, S. (2006). Fundamentally 9/11: The fashioning of collective memory in a Christian school. *American Journal of Education, 112*, 392–416.

Shapin, S. (1994). *A social history of truth: Civility and science in seventeenth-century England*. Chicago, IL: University of Chicago Press.

Shtulman, A. (2013). Epistemic similarities between students' scientific and supernatural beliefs. *Journal of Educational Psychology, 105*, 199–212.

Weinstock, M., & Cronin, M. A. (2003). The everyday production of knowledge: Individual differences in epistemological understanding and juror-reasoning skill. *Applied Cognitive Psychology, 17*, 161–181.

Woolley, J. D., & Cornelius, C. A. (2013). Beliefs in magical beings and cultural myths. In M. Taylor (Ed.). *Oxford handbook of the development of imagination*. New York, NY: Oxford University Press.

Woolley, J. D., Ma, L., & Lopez-Mobilia, G. (2011). Development of the use of conversational cues to assess reality status. *Journal of Cognition and Development, 12*, 537–555.

3   Does understanding about knowledge and belief influence children's trust in testimony?

Elizabeth J. Robinson, Erika Nurmsoo,
and Shiri Einav

Introduction

Imagine you are in the supermarket and have forgotten your glasses so can't read the prices. You are unlikely to search for an expert on the prices of supermarket items. A much better solution is to rely on your companion, no more expert than you are, but who can read the prices. We often rely on others in ways similar to this, for example by asking a partner if there is enough milk in the fridge instead of looking for ourselves, by believing a colleague who has read the email announcing that a lecture is cancelled, or by avoiding a biscuit when our guest points out that the dog licked it when we briefly left the room. In each of these circumstances, we use another person not as an expert in a particular domain of knowledge, but rather as a proxy for ourselves: They can supply the information we need because they had the relevant experience that we lack.

Young children can evaluate information appropriately in circumstances similar to these. In tasks suitable for their age, children from the age of around 4 years believe somebody who is better informed than they are themselves, and ignore someone who is less well informed or equally poorly informed. For example, children believed what they were told about a hidden toy's hardness only when their informant felt it (Robinson, Champion, & Mitchell, 1999; Robinson, Haigh, & Nurmsoo, 2008; Robinson & Whitcombe, 2003). Importantly, if the informant subsequently had doubts about his access to the target object, saying "I'm not sure I felt it properly", 4- to 5-year-olds appropriately lost confidence in what he had told them (Robinson et al., 2008). This is just as we would expect if they were reasoning "I originally believed what you told me because I thought you were well informed; if after all you were not, then you could have been wrong." Three-year-olds showed reduced confidence in the informant's claim immediately after he expressed doubt about his access, but did not do so after a brief delay, suggesting they had only a tenuous grasp of the source of their knowledge.

Children seemed to assume therefore, as adults would, that their informant had gained the knowledge they themselves would have gained from that same experience. However, children do not trust what they are told as much as they trust their own direct experience (Robinson et al., 2008; Robinson, Mitchell, & Nye, 1995). For example, children updated their own mistaken belief about the content of a box more frequently when they subsequently had the opportunity to see inside, than when the experimenter looked and told them what was inside (Robinson et al., 1995). Indeed whether or not adults *should* have as much confidence in testimony as in direct knowledge has long been a matter of discussion among philosophers (see for example Coady, 1994; Lackey, 2008).

Nevertheless, ignoring the rather lower weight given to testimony than to direct experience, the evidence to date suggests that by the age of around 4 years, children can treat others as proxies for themselves when deciding whether or not to believe what they are told: They assume that someone else can supply the information they need if, and only if, the other person has had the relevant experience they themselves lack.

Circumstances of this kind stand in marked contrast to those discussed in many of the other chapters in this volume, when an informant is judged by virtue of their history or enduring characteristics to be knowledgeable in a particular domain. In a frequently used procedure (Koenig & Harris, 2005), the child watches while one informant names familiar objects accurately and another names them inaccurately for no obvious reason. Then an unfamiliar item is introduced, and each informant offers the child a different label. Children from the age of 3 or 4 years typically accept the label offered by the informant with the history of accuracy. The child learner in this case knows nothing about how the informant found out the name of the unfamiliar object, and need give no thought at all to that question. The informant is treated as generally knowledgeable in the relevant domain, rather than having gained the particular knowledge the child lacks.

We cannot assume that children who appropriately identify individuals who are likely to be knowledgeable in a certain domain also make appropriate judgments about who, by virtue of specific experience, has the particular knowledge they lack. Different processes might be involved in these two kinds of judgment. Concerning history of accuracy as an indicator of future accuracy, children could use a cognitively undemanding rule-of-thumb, merely generalizing from the informant's past behavior to their future behaviour (as suggested but dismissed by Birch, Vauthier, & Bloom, 2008). The child need have no understanding of why this can be an appropriate way of evaluating an informant's reliability. In contrast, children need to understand something about knowledge acquisition if they are to trust an informant who has gained the particular knowledge they lack by virtue of a particular experience. For example, they need to know that someone who has seen inside a container can give them an accurate account of what it contains, whereas someone who has not seen (and has no other relevant experience) cannot. Similarly, they need to know that someone who has just read the label on a rare and exotic plant can now report what it is called, unlike someone who has not (and has gained no other relevant experience).

Furthermore, although generalizing in a superficial way from past to future behavior can be a useful and undemanding rule-of-thumb, it is far from foolproof. On a walk across a wild and isolated moor, we might not wish to rely on a leader whose success at finding the route on a previous day was due to heavy use of a map, which she leaves behind today. On the other hand, if another leader took us the wrong way on a previous day due to dense fog, we might be ready to trust her today if the weather is clear. If we relied just on history of accuracy, we would trust the first leader but not the second. To relate this to the published literature on children's trust in testimony, suppose a history of inaccurate labeling of familiar objects was due to the informant being temporarily unable to see the objects. A child might lose out on a helpful learning opportunity if she assumed that the informant would continue to be inaccurate when labeling an unfamiliar object that they can now see.

Interestingly, this is exactly what happened when we made a small modification to the procedure used in Koenig and Harris's (2005) procedure mentioned above (Nurmsoo & Robinson, 2009a). Children watched a video in which two adults were asked to name three familiar objects. One speaker always answered correctly, and the other incorrectly. On subsequent test trials each person offered a different label for an unfamiliar object, and children were asked to identify the correct label. In the *standard condition*, when all speakers could see the objects throughout, children performed as expected: They preferred the label given by the previously accurate person. In our *modified condition*, the inaccurate person had been made to wear a blindfold when she was asked to name the familiar objects, so erred through no fault of her own. On the test trials, the blindfold was removed. In this modified condition there was no good reason to prefer the previously accurate over the previously inaccurate person, and yet children still preferred the label offered by the previously accurate one. Perhaps it was sensible to play safe and rely on the person who had proved their accuracy. Yet in a further condition, in which both adults were inaccurate on the history trials, one wearing a blindfold (whose errors were excusable) and the other not (whose errors were unexplained), children showed no preference for the previously blindfolded person's label. Here it certainly was sensible to avoid the person who made errors for no apparent reason and to give the previously blindfolded one the benefit of any doubt. Yet 4- to 5-year-olds did not do this. This work provided no evidence that young children took into account the reasons for errors on the history trials. Rather, results suggested that children were generalizing on the basis of a superficial rule-of-thumb.

Nevertheless, further experiments provide ample evidence that children do take into account both reasons for an informant's history of inaccuracy and a history of accuracy. In these experiments, summarized in the next two sections below, we departed more seriously from the typical procedure used in the research on children's trust in testimony. Instead, we modified games used in the work mentioned earlier (e.g., Robinson & Whitcombe, 2003).

Taking into account reasons for inaccuracy

In Nurmsoo and Robinson (2009b) children aged 4 and 5 years played a game with a puppet operated by the experimenter. At the start of the game the child examined pairs of toys that were identical except for their color, for example two toy bears, one white and one brown, or identical except for their feel, for example two ducklings, one hard and one soft. On each trial, one toy from a pair was slipped in secret into a tunnel and the aim was to find out which one it was. The tunnel had a curtain on one side that could be raised to allow a view of the hidden toy through a window. It also had a curtain at one end, through which an arm could be placed to feel the hidden toy.

After practicing with the tunnel, children entered one of two conditions, *puppet informed* or *puppet uninformed*. In both conditions, children had three history trials followed by two test trials. On the history trials the child was always allowed informative access (i.e. looked when the identifying feature was color, or felt when the identifying feature was hardness) and so knew the correct answer. The puppet always gave the wrong answer, so in both conditions it built up a history of inaccuracy. For children in the puppet informed condition, the history trials were as follows: The puppet was allowed informative access to the hidden toy, was asked by the experimenter "Which one do you think it is?", and gave the wrong answer. Then the child was also allowed informative access, was asked the same question, and of course gave the correct answer. In this way the child experienced the puppet giving inaccurate answers despite having informative access. For children in the puppet uninformed condition, the sole difference was that the puppet was allowed only uninformative access on each of the three history trials. Hence children in this condition experienced the puppet giving inaccurate answers for justifiable reasons.

Children in both conditions then had two test trials. On these, the child was allowed only uninformative access (e.g., feeling to identify color), was asked by the experimenter "Which one do you think it is?" and made a guess. Then the puppet was allowed informative access, was asked the same question, and contradicted the child's judgment. For example, if the child, having felt a toy identified by color, had said "The brown one," then the puppet, having looked, said "The white one." Finally the experimenter asked the child again which one she thought it was, using a puzzled tone of voice in the light of the conflicting answers given by the child and the puppet.

We examined when children changed their answer to match that of the puppet, indicating that they believed the puppet. Did they do so more frequently in the puppet uninformed condition (when the puppet's history of inaccuracy could be excused) than in the puppet informed condition (when the puppet had been wrong despite being well informed)?

Children did show that pattern. Nearly three-quarters of the 4- and 5-year-olds in the puppet uninformed group changed their answer to match that of the puppet on both test trials. Recall that this puppet was well informed on the test trials despite having been uninformed on history trials. These children appropriately treated the puppet's response as more reliable than their own guess. In contrast, children in the puppet informed group were as likely to change their answers as not, behaving as if they were simply guessing rather than relying on the puppet's suggestion, again appropriately. That is, children did not simply discount an informant based on their history of inaccuracy; both puppets had the same history of inaccuracy. Rather, children took into account the reasons for the inaccuracy. When the puppet's inaccuracy had arisen due to circumstances that no longer applied on test trials, children excused the errors and treated the puppet as a reliable informant.

Children could only show this pattern of responding if they understood the explanation for the puppet's errors in the puppet uninformed condition. Without understanding that the color of the object cannot be identified by touch alone for example, they had no grounds for excusing the puppet's inaccuracy. One important implication of this result is that it suggests that the more children understand about the reasons why people behave as they do, the more possibilities open up for them to excuse past errors rather than dismiss an informant as unreliable. That is, children with more advanced understanding about knowledge and belief and their influences on behavior can become more trusting. Conversely, as we shall see later, they can also become more wary of mere accuracy. They can show appropriate flexibility of trust, rather than just making broad and superficial generalizations.

The relationship between trust and extent of understanding about knowledge acquisition is illustrated by a study in which a puppet made errors not due just to lack of access to the necessary information, but due to a legitimate false belief (Robinson & Nurmsoo, 2009). Four- and 5-year-olds were shown a series of three boxes whose contents they confidently expected to identify based on the picture on the outside, for example a cornflakes packet. For each box in turn they said what they thought was inside, and then saw, to their surprise, a toy cat. This led them to expect that a fourth box would also contain a cat, despite the fact that it showed crayons on the outside. Before the child was asked about the contents of the crayons box, a puppet was introduced, was shown the first three deceptive boxes and asked what they contained. Half the children were in the *puppet ignorant* condition, in which the puppet was not allowed to look inside and gave the expected contents of each box, e.g., 'cornflakes.' This puppet was, therefore, inaccurate because it had a legitimate false belief, and it made the same mistakes that the children themselves made before seeing the true contents. The other half of the children were in the *puppet unreliable* condition, in which the puppet was allowed to see inside each box but nevertheless answered wrongly, e.g., 'cow'. There was no obvious explanation for this puppet's inaccuracy.

Next, children in both conditions were asked what they thought was inside the crayons box, without being allowed to look. Most children expected the box to contain a cat. The puppet then had a look inside the crayons box, and contradicted the child's suggestion, for example by saying 'crayons.' Finally, children were asked again what they thought was inside the crayons box. We were interested in whether or not they changed their answers to match the puppet's. Specifically, did children rely on the puppet more frequently in the puppet ignorant condition, when its previous history of inaccuracy could be excused, than in the puppet unreliable condition, when it could not?

They did: 57% of children in the puppet ignorant condition changed their judgment to match that of the puppet, compared with only 20% in the puppet unreliable condition. Note that children did not need to understand about false belief in order to show this pattern of responding. Children could differentiate in this way simply by understanding that seeing inside the boxes was necessary for the puppet to know what they contained. However the puppet that made errors in the 'puppet uninformed' condition had not just guessed; it had particular and predictable false beliefs based on the pictures on the boxes. If children understood this, over and above understanding about seeing and knowing, they had even stronger grounds for trusting the puppet to be accurate when it did look inside the box on the test trial. In the puppet ignorant condition, we identified children who gave false belief explanations for the puppet's errors on history trials, by saying things like 'Because it's got cornflakes on the front' as opposed to 'Because he's silly.' Three-quarters of the children who gave false belief explanations went on to believe the puppet's suggestion about the content of the crayons box, compared with only 41% of those who did not give such explanations. That is, the more children understood about the reasons why people (or puppets) behave as they do, the more ready they were to excuse legitimate errors and trust the informant when the circumstances leading to the error no longer obtained.

In a vein similar to the studies described in this section, Kondrad & Jaswal (2012) showed that children excused and subsequently trusted a speaker who made a mistake due to having an ambiguous view of the target object, but not a speaker who made the same errors for no good reason.

Going back to the blindfold study mentioned earlier (Nurmsoo & Robinson, 2009a), why did children fail to excuse the previously blindfolded informant when they were prepared to excuse the poorly informed puppets in Nurmsoo and Robinson (2009b) and in Robinson and Nurmsoo (2009)? Perhaps children were more sensitive to the sources of the puppet's knowledge or beliefs in these more interactive games than when they were passively watching a video. Perhaps they were thrown by the strangely unresponsive adults in the video in the standard condition who held their neutral expressions when their colleague named familiar objects wrongly for no obvious reason, as happens in all of the published studies using this procedure. Another, more interesting, possibility is that children are more cautious about excusing inaccuracy when they are learning the names of unfamiliar objects than when they are identifying a hidden toy. Unlike the identities of hidden toys, objects names are generalizable; they can be applied at other times and in other places (although in most of the published experiments children are given nonsense names, so hopefully they will not in fact generalize them). It might therefore be particularly important not to risk learning wrong names. Nurmsoo, Dickerson, and Griggs (2013) compared children's preference for the suggestion of a previously accurate over a previously inaccurate speaker when the information conveyed on history and test trials was either about the names of objects (generalizable in this context), or about their color (non-generalizable in this context), and found no significant difference between these trial types.

More evidence is needed before we can be confident whether or not children use a stricter criterion for evaluating generalizable, as opposed to non-generalizable, knowledge. This remains an important question for future research. However, in the experiments to be described below, children learned the names of unfamiliar creatures (generalizable knowledge) and yet did take into account how their informants achieved past accuracy (as opposed to inaccuracy in the experiments described above). This means that we can at least reject the possibility that children use superficial rules-of-thumb based on history alone for assessing the likely reliability of informants who supply generalizable knowledge, while using more nuanced criteria for non-generalizable knowledge about hidden targets.

Taking into account reasons for accuracy

Just as a history of inaccuracy does not necessarily predict future inaccuracy, a history of accuracy does not necessarily mean that an informant will be accurate in the future. In the next two studies we examined whether or not children would rely on an informant whose accuracy had arisen from specific circumstances that no longer held.

In a series of experiments by Einav and Robinson (2011), children aged 3, 4 and 5 years played a game with puppets. On three history trials, two puppets appeared one at a time. For each puppet, the child held up a picture of a familiar animal for the puppet to name. The puppet looked at the picture and paused as if thinking and did not give an answer. At that point, a third character, Ted (operated by the experimenter), asked "Would you like some help?" One of the puppets always answered "No thank you" and gave the correct answer. The other puppet said "Yes please," whereupon Ted audibly whispered the right answer to the puppet, who repeated it. In this way, one puppet built up a history of giving correct names without help, while the other puppet built up a history of giving correct names with the help of Ted. The procedures then differed in detail across experiments, but Ted always left the scene and the child had to decide which puppet to trust regarding the names of novel animals. The 4- and the 5-year-olds tended to rely on the puppet who had not needed help on the history trials. In contrast, 3-year-olds were equally likely to rely on either puppet despite having remembered which puppet had received help. These younger children apparently judged on the basis of accuracy alone and ignored how it was achieved. These results add to those summarized above concerning inaccurate informants, showing that around the age of 4 years, children are likely to take into account the reasons for an informant's history of accuracy as well as the reasons for inaccuracy.

In all the work discussed so far, children were told new information from people or puppets with whom they interacted face to face, or watched on video. However in literate societies we are not dependent on such face-to-face encounters when gaining knowledge from others. We can read the work of authors who are physically remote or long dead. Children's trust in the printed word is a topic of considerable interest for various reasons (see Eyden, Robinson, & Einav, 2013; Eyden, Robinson, Einav, & Jaswal, 2013; Robinson, Einav, & Fox, 2013), but the work we summarize in this chapter also provides another way of examining children's sensitivity to the reasons for an informant's history of accuracy, as opposed to attending just to accuracy per se.

In Einav, Robinson, and Fox (2013), 4- and 5- year-olds played a game designed to find out if children realized that an informant who gave accurate answers by reading from a print source could not be relied on to supply new information when the print source was no longer available. On each of three *word trials*, children saw a sheet with a mix of pictured familiar and unfamiliar items (e.g., fruit). Each sheet was accompanied by two picture strips, each strip bearing small versions of all of the pictures on the large sheet. One of the strips had printed labels beneath each picture; the other did not. Two dolls were given one of the strips each, and the dolls sat beside their strips which were placed on each side of the large sheet. Hence the child had a clear view of the large sheet and the two strips, one with names and one without, and the dolls sitting by their strips. On each trial the dolls' task was to help the child identify an unfamiliar item, for example a fig. The doll with the strip with names said "This word says 'fig'" and placed a pointer on its strip, by the correct word and its picture. The other doll said "This is a fig" and placed its pointer by an incorrect unfamiliar picture on its strip. The child was asked which doll was right, and to identify the fig on the large sheet. This procedure continued for a further two trials, with the same doll having the names strip each time. In this way, one doll consistently justified its choice by using the correct printed word, while the other doll, who had no words, consistently selected a different picture.

We were interested in whether children trusted the words as the more reliable source. Since the words were read aloud, children might do this even if they could not yet read for themselves. If they did trust the words as the more reliable source, then the doll with the names strip built up a history of accuracy. The further question of interest, and of most relevance to this chapter, was whether children realized that the doll's accuracy was based on having access to particular printed names rather than on any general knowledge about the names of fruit and vegetables. We examined this in the following way:

After the word trials was a *no-word trial*, on which children were shown two pictures of unfamiliar animals (a ferret and a weasel), with no printed labels. The doll that had previously had the names strip and a new doll, with no history, each put their pointers on a different picture, each saying "This one's a ferret." Children were asked which doll was right. We introduced a new doll with no history because we wanted to be sure that children who preferred the suggestion of the doll who had previously had the names strip were positively choosing that doll rather than avoiding the doll who had had no names.

Finally we checked children's ability to read the target word on each of the names strips. Using new strips without pictures and with the words re-ordered, we asked children to point to each target word. We classified children as early readers if they pointed correctly to two or three of the target words. This constituted a very easy test of reading skill, enabling us to identify children on the very cusp of being able to read.

Looking first at children's performance on the three word trials, we identified children who consistently preferred the suggestion from the doll with the names strip and judged that doll to be correct. These children treated the printed labels as reliable. They were likely to be early readers as assessed by their ability to identify the target words. Seventy-two percent of early readers relied on the suggestion of the doll with the names strip on at least two of the three word trials, compared with only 31% of pre-readers. Printed text read aloud seemed to hold no special authority for the pre-readers, who were mainly aged 3 to 4 years. The walls of their nursery classrooms were covered with labeled objects, and they had probably observed adults using print sources such as books, web pages and text messages to provide information. These experiences were apparently insufficient for them to treat the printed labels as authoritative.

On the no-word trial we were interested in the early readers, who had consistently judged the doll with the names strip to be reliable on the preceding word trials. On the no-word trial they were significantly less likely to rely on the suggestion of that doll than they had on the word trials. That is, children who treated the printed labels as authoritative, and so treated the doll with the names strip as having a history of accuracy, no longer treated that doll as particularly reliable when it had no names. That is, the early readers took into account the reasons for the doll's prior accuracy. They apparently understood that print supplies only the particular knowledge of the names on the strips, and the doll's accuracy did not indicate wider knowledge about animal names.

We see parallels with children's understanding that Ted's whispering provided only knowledge of the names of the particular pictured animals (Einav & Robinson, 2011), and with their understanding that prior inaccuracy due to a legitimate false belief does not predict future inaccuracy (Robinson & Nurmsoo, 2009). The more children understood about how informants can achieve past accuracy or inaccuracy, the more nuanced their evaluations could be about the likely future reliability of those informants.

Deciding when to ask

In the work discussed so far, children have been offered information by others, and their task was to decide whether or not it was likely to be reliable. Yet in their everyday lives they do not wait to be offered information. They actively seek it by asking questions. Children might direct questions at whoever happens to be available and rely on them to admit ignorance if they cannot supply the right answer. Alternatively, children might direct their questions to people who are likely to have the knowledge they lack. To reiterate the distinction we made earlier, their informant might be knowledgeable in a certain domain, or their informant might act as the child's proxy, gaining by virtue of a particular experience the specific knowledge the child lacks. As before, it is this latter case on which we focus; this allows us to assess the child's understanding of the processes of gaining and transmitting knowledge.

At first sight there are good grounds for expecting 4- and 5-year-olds to realize that their informant can supply the correct answer only if they have the relevant information. Children much younger than 4 to 5 years often ask questions and gain new knowledge as a consequence (Chouinard, 2007). In the frequently used task already described (e.g., Koenig & Harris, 2005), children experience informants with different histories of accuracy, then choose which informant to ask for the name of an unfamiliar item. Children aged 4 years ask the previously accurate informant. In tasks in which children are offered information, 4-year-olds take into account whether or not their informant has the relevant experience they lack (e.g., Nurmsoo & Robinson, 2009b). By around the age of 4 years, then, children appear to have the understanding necessary to be efficient question-askers.

On the other hand, the work by Mills and colleagues (e.g., Mills, Legare, Grant, & Landrum, 2011; chapter 4 of this volume) identifies weaknesses in 4-year-olds' ability to identify which of two informants is more knowledgeable, as well as in their skill at formulating appropriate questions and using the information supplied to identify a hidden picture. Those tasks were quite complex however, because Mills and colleagues were interested in the development of inquiring skills in general. Children's poor performance on their tasks might be due to factors we are not concerned with here. Our research question was much narrower than theirs: Do children proactively seek information from someone who they know has just gained the information they lack? We found out in the studies summarized below (Robinson, Butterfill, & Nurmsoo, 2011).

Children aged 4 to 5 years played an *ask* game with the experimenter involving three identical containers, each of which contained a different toy. On each trial one of the containers was chosen at random and the aim was to find out which toy it contained. On every trial children first made a guess which they indicated by putting a marker on one of a set of pictures of the possible contents. Then the experimenter either did or did not look inside the container. Next, children had the opportunity to find out what the experimenter guessed or knew was in the container: They could raise a toy mobile phone to their ear (without having to say anything) to indicate that they wanted the experimenter to say what she thought. Finally, children made another judgment about the hidden toy, this time on behalf of a puppet. Were children more likely to ask the experimenter (and rely on her answer when they responded for the puppet) when she had looked inside the container than when she had not looked?

Surprisingly, 4- and 5-year-old children were no more likely to 'ask' for the experimenter's view when she had seen inside the container than when she had not. Yet in comparison tasks children this age performed well. First, in a *seek* condition, the experimenter looked into the container or did not look, and placed a marker on one of three pictures of the contents of the containers. The experimenter's pictures were behind a barrier, so the child had to stand up and look over it to find out what the experimenter thought. Children more frequently looked over the barrier at the experimenter's response when she had looked inside the container than when she had not. The results were the same in an *ask to see* condition. This was like the seek condition except that instead of standing up to look over the barrier, children had to raise the toy mobile phone to their ear to indicate that they wanted the experimenter to lift the barrier to reveal which picture she had put her marker on. Children used the phone more frequently when the experimenter had looked inside the container. Hence 4- to 5-year-olds were adept at relying on the well-informed experimenter when they had to be proactive by looking over the barrier or using the phone to ask for the barrier to be lifted. Yet they were not so adept when they had to use the phone in exactly the same way to ask the experimenter to announce her answer.

We do not know why children failed to take into account the experimenter's knowledge when they had to elicit her response. Whatever the explanation, children's understanding of the processes of knowledge acquisition and knowledge transfer appears not to be as secure as it seemed on the basis of the results presented in previous sections of this chapter, in which children evaluated information they were offered rather than information they elicited. Perhaps there is something about the way children represent the experimenter's state of knowledge or ignorance that makes it hard for them to realize that they can *elicit* an accurate response from her only if she has seen inside the container, even though it is easy for them to *evaluate* a response she has already made, despite it being hidden. Perhaps the difficulty arises from the interruption of the causal sequence from the experimenter's seeing or not seeing inside the container, to giving her answer. In the ask to see and seek conditions, the experimenter looks or does not look; this determines which of her pictures she then puts her marker on, and then the child chooses to consult it or not. In the ask condition, the experimenter looks or does not look, but then does nothing unless the child asks for her answer. The immediate cause of her answering is the child's asking. Perhaps this makes it harder for the child to hold in mind the relevance of the experimenter's having seen or not seen (despite remembering what happened).

Whatever the explanation turns out to be, the results suggest that although young children very frequently ask questions about, for example, where their favorite toy is or where to find their shoes, they may fail fully to understand the circumstances under which they can expect to receive an accurate answer. Interestingly, by the age of 4 to 5 years, 15% of questions are about the location of objects, as frequent as questions about the names of objects (13%). These figures come from Chouinard (2007), who analyzed a large data-base of real life talk between children and their caregivers. Although Chouinard made detailed analyses of the caregivers' responses, it remains unclear how frequently questions about location were misdirected, nor what feedback caregivers provided when this happened. As with all the work on children's evaluations of other people's suitability as sources of knowledge, we have much yet to understand about the underlying developmental processes and what role children's social experiences might play.

Conclusions

When children aged 4 to 5 years believe what they are told by a previously accurate informant, or disbelieve what they are told by a previously inaccurate one, they could be applying a cognitively undemanding criterion that ignores reasons for accuracy or inaccuracy. The evidence summarized here suggests that under some circumstances at least, this is not what children do. Rather, they excuse a history of inaccuracy that arose due to temporary lack of relevant experience. Similarly, they ignore a history of accuracy that arose due to external help that is no longer available. This flexibility of trust and mistrust means that children need not miss out on helpful learning opportunities, nor rely on an informant who is not really knowledgeable. However, in order to show this flexibility, children need a certain level of understanding about how people gain and transmit knowledge.

This suggests that as children's understanding about the processes of knowledge acquisition and transmission develops, they become increasingly able to make nuanced rather than crude judgments about the likely reliability of informants.

An important topic for future work concerns the distinction we have drawn between assessing an informant as having gained the particular knowledge we lack versus being generally knowledgeable within a certain domain. In the first case we attend to the person's particular relevant experience, whereas in the second we attend to their history. Yet the knowledgeable informant became so through specific experiences. Repeated instruction from Ted, or prolonged study of the pictures strips with names, could transform the ignorant puppet and doll into experts. Readers draw on print sources not just to find out the answers to specific questions; they devour them in order to learn about entire domains of knowledge. Here, the literature on trust in testimony connects with research on children's understanding of expertise (see for example Aguiar, Stoess, & Taylor, 2012; Danovitch & Keil, 2004; Koenig & Jaswal, 2011). This connection deserves to be strengthened.

References

Aguiar, N. R., Stoess, C. J., & Taylor, M. (2012). The development of children's ability to fill the gaps in their knowledge by consulting experts. *Child Development, 83,* 1368–1381.

Birch, S. A. J., Vauthier, S. A., & Bloom, P. (2008). Three- and four-year-olds spontaneously use others' past performance to guide their learning. *Cognition, 107,* 1018–1034.

Chouinard, M. (2007). Children's questions: A mechanism for cognitive development. *Monographs of the Society for Research in Child Development, 286, 72*(1).

Coady, C. A. J. (1994). *Testimony: A Philosophical Study.* Oxford, UK: Oxford University Press.

Danovitch, J. H., & Keil, F. C. (2004). Should you ask a fisherman or a biologist? Developmental shifts in ways of clustering knowledge. *Child Development, 75,* 918–931.

Einav, S., & Robinson, E. J. (2011). When being right is not enough: Four-year-olds distinguish knowledgeable from merely accurate informants. *Psychological Science, 22,* 1250–1253.

Einav, S., Robinson, E. J., & Fox, A. (2013). Take it as read: Early readers trust print over oral sources of Information. *Journal of Experimental Child Psychology, 114,* 262–274.

Eyden, J., Robinson, E. J., & Einav, S. (2013). Children's trust in unexpected suggestions: The seductive power of print. Poster presented at Meetings of Society for Research in Child Development, Seattle, April.

Eyden, J., Robinson, E. J., Einav, S., & Jaswal, V. K. (2013). The power of print: Children's trust in unexpected printed suggestions. *Journal of Experimental Child Psychology, 116,* 593–603.

Koenig, M., & Harris, P. (2005). Preschoolers mistrust ignorant and inaccurate speakers. *Child Development, 76,* 1261–1277.

Koenig, M., & Jaswal, V. K. (2011). Characterizing children's expectations about expertise and incompetence: Halo or pitchfork effects? *Child Development, 82,* 1634–1647.

Kondrad, R. L., & Jaswal, V. K. (2012). Explaining the errors away: Young children forgive understandable semantic mistakes. *Cognitive Development, 27,* 126–135.

Lackey, J. (2008). *Learning from words: Testimony as a source of knowledge*. Oxford, UK: Oxford University Press.

Mills, C. M., Legare, C. H., Grant, M. G., & Landrum, A. R. (2011). Determining who to question, what to ask, and how much information to ask for. *Journal of Experimental Child Psychology, 110*, 539–560.

Nurmsoo, E., Dickerson, H., & Griggs, T. (2013). Preschoolers' sensitivity to testimony when learning generalizable vs. non-generalizable information. Oral presentation at Meetings of Experimental Psychology Society, Lancaster, UK, April 2013.

Nurmsoo, E., & Robinson, E. J. (2009a). Identifying unreliable informants: Do children excuse past inaccuracy? *Developmental Science, 12*, 41–47.

Nurmsoo, E., & Robinson, E. J. (2009b). Children's trust in previously inaccurate informants who were well or poorly-informed: When past errors can be excused. *Child Development, 80*, 23–27.

Robinson, E. J., Butterfill, S.A., & Nurmsoo, E. (2011). Gaining knowledge via other minds: Children's flexible trust in others as sources of information. *British Journal of Developmental Psychology, 29, 961–980.*

Robinson, E. J., Champion, H., & Mitchell, P. (1999). Children's ability to infer utterance veracity from speaker informedness. *Developmental Psychology, 35*, 535–546.

Robinson, E. J., Einav, S., & Fox, A. (2013). Reading to learn: Pre-readers' and early readers' trust in text as a source of knowledge. *Developmental Psychology, 49*, 505–513.

Robinson, E. J., Haigh, S. N., & Nurmsoo, E. (2008). Children's working understanding of knowledge sources: Confidence in knowledge gained from testimony. *Cognitive Development, 23*, 105–118.

Robinson, E. J., Mitchell, P. M., & Nye, R. (1995). Young children's treating of utterances as unreliable sources of knowledge. *Journal of Child Language, 22*, 663–685.

Robinson, E. J., & Nurmsoo, E. (2009). When do children learn from unreliable speakers? *Cognitive Development, 24*, 16–22.

Robinson, E. J., & Whitcombe, E. (2003). Children's suggestibility in relation to their understanding about sources of knowledge. *Child Development, 74*, 48–62.

4 Inquiring minds

Using questions to gather information from others

Candice M. Mills and Asheley R. Landrum

Introduction

Children are frequently faced with problems that they cannot immediately solve on their own. For some of these problems, children can learn from listening to claims and advice from others. Indeed, sometimes they need not do anything but passively attend to what they are told or what they overhear to learn something new (e.g., Mills, Danovitch, Grant, & Elashi, 2012). However, in many other situations, children must actively seek information from others by asking questions. Although prior work has shown that children begin to ask questions at a very young age (Chouinard, 2007 includes a substantial review), less is known about the extent to which they can use questions as tools to gather information from appropriate sources for problem solving and learning. How adept are children at formulating effective questions and seeking out enough information to resolve their problems? How much do they take into account the trustworthiness or reliability of an informant when deciding whether or not to ask that informant questions? This chapter examines developmental and individual differences in the ability to question the most knowledgeable, accurate sources when problem solving.

Gathering information from others

The ability to successfully gather information from others for the purpose of problem solving is a complex cognitive process involving at least four steps: (1) recognizing when solving a problem may require assistance from others, (2) deciding whom to question, (3) determining what to ask, and (4) deciding how much information to ask for in order to solve a given problem. In this chapter, we will review each of these steps in turn before reviewing the research bridging across these steps. We will then discuss the implications of this body of work, making recommendations for future directions.

Recognizing when solving a problem may require assistance from others

In order to successfully use inquiry to acquire information from others, it is important to first recognize when others may be able to provide helpful information for solving a problem. This initial step can be challenging. For instance, in a set of studies discussed in the previous chapter, 4- to 6-year-old children were given a choice between answering questions themselves or seeking information from others to determine what was inside a box. In many cases, children (particularly 4- and 5-year-olds) did not attempt to seek out information from others, even though the children demonstrated that they recognized which informant should know the answer (Robinson, Butterfill, & Nurmsoo, 2011). Other research examining 4- to 6-year-old children's understanding of expertise found similar results: when children were given the opportunity to answer some questions themselves or assign those questions to one of three experts (either a doctor, firefighter, or farmer), only 6-year-olds were able to recognize when they did not know the answers themselves and assign test questions to experts fairly accurately (Aguiar, Stoess, & Taylor, 2012).

For children, recognizing a lack of knowledge and the need for information from others can be difficult for many reasons. First, children often overestimate their own knowledge, and sometimes just hearing others ask effective questions or listening to expert explanations helps them recognize what they do not know (e.g., Mills & Keil, 2004). Second, even when children recognize that they lack knowledge or information, they need to know how to gather this information from others—and be motivated to do so. Moreover, this drive to seek out information may also be partially dependent on the strength of our desire to obtain this information (e.g., see Jirout & Klahr, 2012, on exploratory curiosity).

Deciding whom to question

Once the decision has been made that it would be helpful to seek out information from others, the next step is to determine who will be able to provide helpful, accurate information. Much of this book focuses on children's ability to distinguish between sources who vary in trustworthiness and accuracy, often by asking them to choose from which of two sources to seek and endorse information. Ultimately, it is clear that preschool-aged children (and to some extent older infants and toddlers) have some sense that different people can know different things (e.g., Lutz & Keil, 2002) and that some sources are more reliable than others (e.g., see chapter 1).

Yet, determining who will be able to answer our questions is not necessarily easy. In everyday life, it is not always clear what people know or do not know, nor is it clear when they might be untrustworthy. It can also be difficult to distinguish between multiple trustworthy sources that all have some type of expert knowledge. Moreover, even when children recognize that one source is more likely to provide an accurate answer to their questions than another, they *still* may fail to keep that in mind when asking questions. For instance, even though 4- and 5-year-olds knew what doctors, firefighters, and farmers are each likely to know, they frequently failed to keep that in mind when determining whether they or one of those experts should answer a given question (Aguiar et al., 2012; see also

Landrum, Mills, & Johnston, 2013, for related examples of children finding it easier to recognize who would know a given fact than to apply that understanding when problem solving). Although children were better at determining which expert to consult when they had the opportunity to review which expert would know the answer to each question beforehand, they were still nowhere near perfect performance. This suggests that identifying whom to ask for information is more difficult than simply recognizing who knows what.

Deciding what to ask

Once the appropriate source for a particular question is determined, the next step is to determine what to ask. It is evident that children ask many questions, and although their questions can serve the purpose of seeking attention or maintaining social interaction, they do not serve an exclusively social-regulatory function. Instead, children's questions frequently serve an epistemic function; children often use questions to seek additional information about topics of interest to them (e.g., Hickling & Wellman, 2001). To the extent that explicit "why" questions can be used as a prototypical index of information-seeking, developmental research indicates that requests for explanation are widespread even in very young children. For instance, toddlers and preschool-aged children frequently ask for causal explanations about a range of biological, psychological, and physical phenomena (Callanan & Oakes, 1992; Hickling & Wellman, 2001; Wellman, Hickling, & Schult, 1997).

Much of the past research looking at children's questions utilizes one of two methods. In one method, children are presented with situations in which they might want to seek out additional information to solve a problem, and the kinds of questions they ask are monitored. In this research, preschool-aged children can sometimes tailor their questions to obtain specific information, such as to identify an unfamiliar object (Kemler Nelson & O'Neil, 2005), to determine which of two objects is hidden inside of a box (Chouinard, 2007), or to acquire important information about a novel animal or artifact (Greif, Kemler Nelson, Keil, & Gutierrez, 2006). Elementary school-aged children can generate specific questions to determine which item of a set varying in physical characteristics is the target item, but there are developmental improvements, with older children asking more efficient, effective questions than younger children (Mosher & Hornsby, 1966).

In the second method, children are presented with questions or options for hypothesis testing, and children are asked to choose the best question or option provided by an experimenter to solve the problem. This research has traditionally been conducted with elementary school-aged children, who sometimes (but not always) can distinguish between effective and ineffective queries for information (e.g., Samuels & McDonald, 2002; Sodian, Zaitchik, & Carey, 1991).

Taken together, this research demonstrates that even preschool-aged children can generate their own questions in some circumstances to obtain information. However, even elementary school-aged children (and adults) sometimes struggle to determine what an effective question would be.

Determining how much information to ask for

Even after determining whom to question and what to ask, successful learning from others is not guaranteed; it is also important to be able to recognize when enough information has been obtained and then be able to effectively make use of that information. In some cases, children and adults may ask questions and gather information but stop before they have gathered *enough* information to successfully solve their problems. Research examining hypothesis testing, for instance, finds that preschool-aged and elementary school-aged children often cease to gather additional information once they have found evidence to support their hypothesis, even if another hypothesis is correct (e.g., Klahr & Chen, 2003; Klahr, Fay, & Dunbar, 1993). In other cases, though, such as when children are presented with problems of interest to them and given the opportunity to ask questions, children can determine when their questions have not been sufficiently answered (e.g., Frazier, Gelman, & Wellman, 2009; Kemler Nelson, Egan, & Holt, 2004). Given the varied findings in past research, understanding the conditions under which children recognize when they have gathered enough information is important.

Bridging the who, the what, and the how much

Most of the past research examining how children seek information from others for learning and problem solving has focused on only one part of this process. For instance, research examining how children distinguish between different kinds of sources has tended to focus on having children indicate which of two sources seems most accurate (deciding whom to ask) instead of asking them to direct questions to the most accurate sources themselves (deciding both whom and what to ask). Research examining children's question asking, on the other hand, has focused on whether or not children can construct their own questions to gather information from one source (deciding what to ask), without regard to the characteristics of that source.

Examining these skills in isolation can be useful, but doing so also has its weaknesses. One major weakness is that doing so neglects the importance of examining the accumulated strains on cognitive resources when seeking information from others. Indeed, although the amount of information children can track in their working memory increases throughout childhood (e.g., Bayliss, Jarrold, Baddeley, Gunn, & Leigh, 2005), young children's cognitive resources are somewhat limited. Imagine a power grid with a limited capacity. A few processes may function at once without any issues, but if any individual process or combination of processes is too energy-intense, the power grid will fail. Similarly, with children, any step in this process (determining whom to question, deciding what needs to be asked and how to ask it, and determining if they have enough information or need more) can stretch their resources. If these steps together are too taxing, kids may run out of cognitive resources and give up on gathering information, preferring to guess or leave their problems unsolved.

Presumably, some steps of this process are easier than others, but there is little evidence to date to address this issue.

Taking these ideas into consideration, several lines of research in our lab focus on all four of these steps, examining how children use questions as tools to seek information from others for problem solving. We discuss these paradigms and findings below before returning to the big picture.

Questioning informants varying in expertise

In one line of research, we aimed to determine if preschool-aged children could apply their abilities to understand that different people know different things (e.g., Lutz & Keil, 2002) in order to question the appropriate experts to solve a problem. In this particular study (Mills, Legare, Bills, & Mejias, 2010), 3- to 5-year-olds were presented with a simple problem-solving task involving determining which of four special "blickets" (cards varying in background color and in the shape in the center of the card) would open a slot in a box. To solve the problems, children were invited to question two puppet "experts": the shape expert knew all about the shape on each blicket that would work in each slot, while the color expert knew all about the color of each blicket that would work in each slot.

Although past research had modelled questions to children (e.g., Chouinard, 2007), we wanted to refrain from doing so in order to measure what kinds of questions children would ask on their own. Thus, we implemented a warm-up phase in which children interacted with a different puppet with a different type of problem from the test phase; children did not witness any specific questions being asked but were encouraged to notice characteristics of that problem that could be used for questioning (i.e., a raven wanted to know which kinds of leaves to use and where they should come from to build a nest for a friend, and children were encouraged to notice that the four options varied in background color and in shape). During the task itself, whenever children asked a question, each expert responded in a scripted manner according to his expertise, with children permitted to guess when they were ready (even if they had not actually asked any questions). Once children were ready to guess, they inserted their card into the appropriate slot in the box, and an observer would surreptitiously press a remote control that made a doorbell ring inside the box. If children did not hear the doorbell, they were able to ask more questions or guess again.

The design of this study allowed us to examine the component skills previously described: *whom* they asked, *what* they asked, and *how much* information they gathered. First, we examined how frequently children directed questions to the appropriate sources (i.e., the *who*; e.g., questions about color directed to the color expert) over the inappropriate ones. Second, we examined the *quality* of the children's questions (i.e., the *what*). Each question was coded globally for being effective (on-task and able to obtain information that would help distinguish between the options for solving the problem), ineffective (off-task, vague, or otherwise unable to help obtain information for solving the problem), or a clarification of the protocol. In addition, each question received a specific category code based on the characteristics of the question (for more in-depth coding information, see Mills et al., 2010). Third, we examined children's success at problem solving in the task: how much information they gathered through asking effective questions and how many attempts it took for children to obtain the right answer (out of a maximum of four), and whether asking effective questions helped children solve the problems more efficiently (i.e., the *how much*).

As anticipated, we found developmental improvements in knowing *whom* to question as well as *what* to ask. Three-year-olds had difficulty directing questions to the correct experts, and they asked more ineffective questions (e.g., questions that did not help children solve the problem due to being somehow off-task, such as "Is your daddy a fireman?", too vague, such as "Which one is it?", or otherwise unable to distinguish between the options, such as "Is it the blue one?" when all options were blue) than effective ones (e.g., questions aimed at gathering specific information about the problem, such as "Is it green?" when only one option was green). Four-year-olds were more successful at directing questions to the appropriate expert than younger children, but they asked similar proportions of ineffective and effective questions. Five-year-olds, in contrast, succeeded at both knowing whom to ask and at asking more effective questions than ineffective ones. These results provide evidence that preschool-aged children sometimes know whom to ask before they know what to ask, and 5-year-olds ask more effective questions than younger children (see Mills et al., 2010 for additional information on the characteristics of the questions produced by children).

In contrast to knowing *whom* to ask and *what* to ask, we found no developmental improvements in knowing *how much* to ask. At least with this particular task, there were no great differences across development in children's ability to ask enough questions to gather enough information to solve the problems without guessing. This may be partially due to the fact that children were nowhere near ceiling performance on this task: they only asked enough questions to narrow down to one option for less than half of the trials. There are many possible explanations for this finding, including the possibility that having to ask different experts kept children from keeping track of how much information they had obtained. But in a study examining 4- to 6-year-olds' use of questions with only one person to question (i.e., no experts, albeit a more complex task involving cards varying in four dimensions), children still struggled. Although children were frequently asking effective questions, they often did not ask *enough* effective questions to narrow down to one option (Legare, Mills, Souza, Plummer, & Yasskin, 2013). We will return to this finding later in this chapter.

Importantly, regardless of age, children who asked enough effective questions to reduce the options for a possible correct answer down to one option performed better on the task than children who did not. Although 5-year-olds tended to be more likely to ask enough questions than younger children, even younger children could be successful if they asked enough questions. Thus, even during the preschool years, asking the right kinds of effective questions in the right combination is helpful for efficient problem solving.

Questioning informants varying in knowledge status

In another line of work, we examined children's ability to question informants varying in knowledge status (Mills, Legare, Grant, & Landrum, 2011). As noted earlier, informants do not always have clearly identifiable areas of expertise. Instead, informants frequently have varied amounts of knowledge, and we must determine which informant will be most helpful based on inferences about each informant's level of competency. In some cases, explicit signs of ignorance such as a shoulder shrug or admittance of ignorance can help us recognize that someone's knowledge is incomplete. In other cases, though, we may need to rely on other evidence, such as someone's prior demonstrations of accuracy.

In this line of work, 3- to 5-year-olds were presented with pairs of informants contrasting in knowledge levels, similar to much of the past research on selective trust. In two experiments, children were presented with two within-participants conditions. In one condition, a knowledgeable informant was contrasted with an informant who verbally indicated his ignorance (the ignorance condition). In the other condition, a knowledgeable informant was contrasted with an informant who was consistently and clearly inaccurate (the inaccurate condition). The demonstrations of inaccuracy and ignorance varied between experiments. In both experiments, after being introduced to the two informants, children were encouraged to ask them questions to help determine which one of two (or four) cards was inside a box.

As with the prior research examining how children question informants clearly contrasting in expertise, this research measured who children questioned, what they asked, and whether how much information they gathered was related to how successful they were at solving the problems. Like prior work, we were interested in whether there were developmental improvements in children's success in any step of the problem-solving task. But additionally, in this research, we were also interested in whether there were differences in performance based on the ease of distinguishing between the informants. Given that prior research has sometimes found that children are more successful at distinguishing between knowledgeable and ignorant informants than between knowledgeable and inaccurate ones (Koenig & Harris, 2005; see also Chapter 1), we anticipated that children should be more successful in the ignorant condition than in the inaccurate condition. Presumably, when the task of deciding whom to question is easier (i.e., the knowledgeable informant is contrasted with a clearly ignorant one), there are more mental resources available for other aspects of the problem-solving process, such as generating effective questions and integrating the answers to the questions to solve the problem. Finally, we also wanted to examine if, regardless of age, children would be most successful at problem solving if they had asked enough questions to obtain the information needed for problem solving.

In Experiment 1, children were presented with a knowledgeable informant contrasted with a clearly ignorant informant for one set of trials and a clearly inaccurate informant for another set of trials. During a warm-up phase, children were told that one of two pictures was hidden inside a box, and that they could ask some puppet friends any questions about "what the special thing looks like, or sounds like, or feels like, or does, or anything you want that will help you figure out what's in the box." In order to demonstrate the knowledge status of the informants, children witnessed a puppet familiarization phase in which the puppets answered two questions unrelated to the test questions (e.g., why people wear coats in the winter). Each puppet responded according to its knowledge status: the knowledgeable puppet responded accurately, the inaccurate puppet responded with something clearly incorrect (e.g., people wear coats when it is hot outside to keep cold), and the ignorant puppet responded by indicating a lack of knowledge (e.g., I don't know why, I just don't know). This familiarization task clearly unrelated to the test task was intended to avoid constraining children's questions during the test phase (an issue we will return to later).

In this experiment, we found developmental improvements regarding the *who* and the *what* skills: 5-year-olds were better at directing questions to the most knowledgeable informant (with the largest age differences in the inaccurate condition) and better at generating effective questions than younger children. We also found that the ease of distinguishing between sources mattered to some extent: children were better able to direct questions to the most knowledgeable informant in the ignorant condition than in the inaccurate condition, and they also obtained more correct answers in the ignorant condition compared to the inaccurate condition. Additionally, consistent with prior research, we found that regardless of children's age or how difficult it was to distinguish between the sources of information, children's ability to ask enough effective questions to properly narrow down to one possible answer related to problem-solving success.

Experiment 2 involved a knowledgeable informant contrasted with another informant in two conditions: the ignorant condition involved an informant who expressed uncertainty and then guessed (i.e., "I'm not sure, I'll guess [inaccurate but plausible response]"), and the inaccurate condition involved an informant who just provided an inaccurate but plausible response. Thus, the only difference between the guesser and the plausibly inaccurate informant was the paralinguistic cues marking uncertainty provided by the guesser, making the conditions more similar than in the previous experiment. The puppet familiarization task was also updated to be similar to the test phase in order to help children understand how to ask task-related questions.

In this experiment, we found that, overall, children were much more successful at asking effective questions, presumably because of the changes to the familiarization task to provide children with a sense of how to ask effective questions. But distinguishing between the informants was even more difficult, as expected. Moreover, only the 5-year-olds directed more questions to the knowledgeable informant than the other informant, and this was only in the ignorant condition in which the informant marked each response with an indication of uncertainty. Not surprisingly, given the difficulty of distinguishing between the informants, accuracy was low in this experiment, emphasizing how struggles in one aspect of the inquiry process can influence overall learning. But replicating findings in our other research, regardless of age, children who asked enough questions to narrow down the options to one were most successful at solving the problems.

Themes in moving forward

These studies begin to provide insight into how young children seek information from others for learning and problem solving. Clearly, there are barriers at each phase. First, recognizing when assistance from others would be helpful is a challenge that requires children to be able to recognize when they do not have enough knowledge themselves, to know how to gather this information from others, and to have the will to actually do so. Second, determining which source to question can also be difficult, given that determining which source will be most helpful or accurate is not always obvious. Third, determining what to ask can be even more demanding, given that developing an appropriate, effective question involves identifying what is not known, determining what information would be helpful to obtain, and articulating a question that will help obtain that information. Finally, deciding when enough information has been gathered can be difficult, as one has to keep track of what information has been gathered so far and what else needs to be determined.

One important task for future research is to better reflect on the role of cognitive load in children's inquiry process. As discussed earlier, for every part of the process, children may implicitly calculate the costs and benefits of asking questions. In some cases, the costs seem to outweigh the benefits, and children either utilize an unsuccessful strategy or give up on their inquiry. In other cases, the benefits outweigh the costs, and they carry the inquiry process out to its end. Presumably, if one could increase the benefits and reduce the costs enough, children would be more likely to successfully ask questions to gather information.

To increase children's perceptions of the benefits of engaging in inquiry, it may be useful to highlight the efficaciousness of finding accurate information. One way to do this experimentally is to offer extrinsic motivation for correct answers such as rewards for accuracy, and there is some evidence that this helps their performance in seeking information from others. For instance, children are more likely to accurately assign questions to appropriate experts when the benefits of accuracy are higher than when they are lower (Aguiar et al., 2012). But there may also be ways to model an intrinsic drive for explanatory completeness that may encourage children to value finding accurate information.

To decrease children's perceptions of the costs (as well as the actual costs) of engaging in inquiry, it may be useful to determine how to decrease cognitive load for each step of the process. Reducing the costs of knowing which source to question, such as clearly labeling and providing experience interacting with each of the sources, should help children understand what each source knows. Reducing the costs of asking questions, such as giving children greater familiarity with how questions could be useful for a specific task, should prove beneficial for helping children generate effective questions. And reducing the costs of determining if they have received enough information, such as helping children more easily keep track of the eliminated options, may be helpful. Even listening to questions asked by others helps children and adults recognize gaps in their knowledge (Chin & Brown, 2002; Choi, Land, & Turgeon, 2005; Mills & Keil, 2004; Rozenblit & Keil, 2002); thus, children may benefit from listening to others narrow down options to one in order to understand how to do so themselves.

Notably, the costs of engaging in inquiry may have been high in studies to date. Although these recent studies explore children's use of questions to seek out information in action so that each component is not studied in isolation, these studies also involve novel problems that children are being told to solve, with unfamiliar informants to consult. The novelty of the problems and the unfamiliarity of the potential informants both likely increase cognitive load, making it even more difficult to seek out information from others in effective ways. Although some experimental control is useful for being able to measure how children use inquiry to solve problems, the novelty of the experimental task may have been burdensome, and the benefits of accuracy may not have been high enough to outweigh the costly cognitive load. It may be useful for future research to present children with interesting problems that they are likely to want to solve instead of telling them to solve the problems provided to them, given the power of self-directed learning (e.g., see Gureckis & Markant, 2012). It is likely that the process of inquiry will still be somewhat demanding for young children, but if they are highly motivated to perform well, they might have a higher desire to push through a cognitively taxing process.

A second important task for future research is to better understand developmental and individual differences in the inquiry process. One general finding across the research to date is that at least with children ages 3 to 6, using questions effectively to gather information is not easy. Developmental improvements exist across all steps of the process: knowing whom to question, what to ask, and asking enough questions to obtain a correct answer. But there are also some strong individual differences. In some studies, we find that even young 4-year-olds can perform better than older children, as long as they have asked enough questions to narrow down the options to one. These developmental and individual differences most likely influence how costly or beneficial each step of the inquiry process is to a given child.

Therefore, future research needs to examine the role of specific developmental and individual differences in children's success at the problem-solving process. Take, for instance, the ability to decide which informant should be able to provide the most accurate answers to one's questions. Some evidence suggests that children with a deeper understanding about how people can differ in their beliefs, desires, and thoughts (i.e., theory of mind (ToM); e.g., Flavell & Miller, 1998) may be better at recognizing that some sources are more knowledgeable than others. This understanding increases over development, but there are individual differences even within an age group. Indeed, although one study using a three-item false belief task found no relationship between theory of mind performance and selective trust (Pasquini, Corriveau, Koenig, & Harris, 2007), other research has found a correlation between other aspects of theory of mind and selective trust. For instance, DiYanni and Kelemen (2008) found that performance on an eight-point, four-item false belief task correlated with children's ability to recognize which informant was most reliable, and Vanderbilt, Liu, & Heyman (2011) found a relationship between performance on a five-item, more comprehensive ToM scale (Wellman & Liu, 2004) and children's ability to recognize which of two informants was truthful.

Preliminary research in our lab has further examined the relationship between ToM (as measured by the five-item ToM scale mentioned above) and finding appropriate sources for inquiry, focusing on the hypothesis that there is a relationship between ToM abilities and identifying the most *knowledgeable* source of information to question in order to solve problems. In this study, 4- and 5-year-olds were tasked to ask questions to different puppets (i.e., knowledgeable versus ignorant, knowledgeable versus inaccurate) to determine which of four pictures was inside a box. After four trials, children were asked which puppet gave them the most right answers and which puppet gave them wrong answers. Responses were compiled across conditions to create a composite metacognition score (out of 4). On a different day, children were tested on a battery of individual differences measures including five ToM tasks (Wellman & Liu, 2004). As expected, we found developmental improvements on both the ToM and metacognition tasks. Importantly, though, we found that after controlling for age, children's ToM scores significantly predicted children's recognition of an informant's knowledge abilities within this task (the composite metacognition score; $p < .001$). Ongoing research is examining how this ability to recognize the most accurate informant within the task itself related to questioning behavior as well as overall accuracy in problem solving (Williams, Landrum, Pflaum, & Mills, 2013).

In addition to theory of mind, other individual differences may relate to children's success at using questions to gather information from others. For example, early work examining the frequency of question asking and the types of information being sought (e.g., explanations versus procedural inquires) has found differences based on socioeconomic status. Research by Tizard and Hughes (1984) found that 4-year-old girls from middle class families were more likely to ask curiosity-based questions and engage in persistent question asking than 4-year-old girls from working class families. In fact, very early research from McCarthy (1930) found socioeconomic differences in the amount of questions asked from children as young as 24 to 30 months old.

Culture has also been shown to affect children's question-asking behaviors. Gauvain, Munroe, and Beebe (in press) examined children's question asking in Belize, Kenya, Nepal, and Samoa. Although children from these areas also engaged in frequent question asking, these children asked far fewer questions aiming to seek explanations (i.e., how and why questions) than children in the US. Also noteworthy, question asking seemed to vary between these four different cultures based upon the availability of education for parents: the Samoan children, whose parents had access to both primary and secondary education, asked the greatest proportion of information-seeking questions, whereas Kenyan children, whose parents had access only to primary education, asked the least.

Although the specific reasons for these socioeconomic and cultural differences are unclear, some have speculated that the way the parents interact with their children may have a large impact. For instance, Gauvain and her colleagues (in press) mentioned the possibility that some types of child-rearing techniques focus on "passive obedience," which may discourage children from asking questions. Yet, there is little research exploring this possibility or how other aspects of parenting, culture, and socioeconomic status may interact to influence children's abilities to use questions to gather information. Thus, a crucial part of future research will be to investigate the role of socioeconomic status and culture in successfully engaging in the four steps described in this chapter.

When speculating about how this process of gathering information from others through asking questions works in everyday situations, we predict that children may frequently acquire only skeletal, incomplete information. At some level, this may seem like failure, but it is crucial to think about the implications of partial inquiry. Although not acquiring enough information to fully solve their problems may sometimes be detrimental, ceasing to gather information when a comfortable level of satisfaction with the solution has been reached may actually be adaptive. Often, a skeletal understanding provides enough insight to answer basic questions while not being overwhelming in terms of cognitive load (Keil, 2012; see also Mills & Keil, 2004; Rozenblit & Keil, 2002). Moreover, given that it is impossible to know full, complete answers to all question and problems, being satisfied with answers that are sufficient may allow children to develop a broad base of knowledge with which they can build upon for further, more in-depth learning. And when a skeletal understanding is not enough, the hope is that children will be motivated to seek a full understanding from more knowledgeable others through the use of inquiry.

References

Aguiar, N. R., Stoess, C. J., & Taylor, M. (2012). The development of children's ability to fill the gaps in their knowledge by consulting experts. *Child Development, 83,* 1368–1381.

Bayliss, D. M., Jarrold, C., Baddeley, A. D., Gunn, D. M., & Leigh, E. (2005). Mapping the developmental constraints on working memory span performance. *Developmental Psychology, 41,* 579–597.

Callanan, M. A., & Oakes, L. M. (1992). Preschoolers' questions and parents' explanations: Causal thinking in everyday activity. *Cognitive Development, 7,* 213–233.

Chin, C., & Brown, D. E. (2002). Student-generated questions: A meaningful aspect of learning in science. *International Journal of Science Education, 24,* 521–549.

Choi, I., Land, S. M., & Turgeon, A. J. (2005). Scaffolding peer-questioning strategies to facilitate metacognition during online small group discussion. *Instructional Science, 33,* 483–511.

Chouinard, M. (2007). Children's questions: A mechanism for cognitive development. *Monographs of the Society for Research in Child Development, 72,* 1–126.

DiYanni, C., & Kelemen, D. (2008). Using a bad tool with good intention: Young children's imitation of adults' questionable choices. *Journal of Experimental Child Psychology, 101,* 241–261.

Flavell, J. H., & Miller, P. H. (1998). Social cognition. In W. Damon (Series Ed.), D. Kuhn & R. S. Siegler (Eds.), *Handbook of child psychology: Vol. 2. Cognition, perception, and language* (5th ed., pp. 851–898). New York, NY: Wiley.

Frazier, B. N., Gelman, S. A., & Wellman, H. M. (2009). Preschoolers' search for explanatory information within adult-child conversation. *Child Development, 80,* 1592–1611.

Gauvain, M., Munroe, R. L., & Beebe, H. (in press). Children's questions in cross-cultural perspective: A four culture study. *Journal of Cross-Cultural Psychology.*

Greif, M. L., Kemler Nelson, D. G., Keil, F. C., & Gutierrez, F. (2006). What do children want to know about animals and artifacts? Domain-specific requests for information. *Psychological Science, 17,* 455–459.

Gureckis, T. M., & Markant, D. B. (2012). Self-directed learning: A cognitive and computational perspective. *Perspectives on Psychological Science, 7,* 464–481.

Hickling, A. K., & Wellman, H. M. (2001). The emergence of children's causal explanations and theories: Evidence from everyday conversation. *Developmental Psychology, 37,* 668–683.

Jirout, J., & Klahr, D. (2012). Children's scientific curiosity: In search of an operational definition of an elusive concept. *Developmental Review, 32,* 125–160.

Keil, F. C. (2012). Running on empty? How folk science gets by with less. *Current Directions in Psychological Science, 21,* 329–334.

Kemler Nelson, D. G., Egan, L. C., & Holt, L. (2004). When children ask, "what is it?" what do they want to know about artifacts? *Psychological Science, 15,* 384–389.

Kemler Nelson, D. G., & O'Neil, K. (2005). How do parents respond to children's questions about the identity of artifacts? *Developmental Science, 8,* 519–524.

Klahr, D., & Chen, Z. (2003). Overcoming the positive-capture strategy in young children: Learning about indeterminacy. *Child Development, 74,* 1275–1296.

Klahr, D., Fay, A. L., & Dunbar, K. (1993). Heuristics for scientific experimentation: A developmental study. *Cognitive Psychology, 25,* 111–146.

Koenig, M. A., & Harris, P. L. (2005). Preschoolers mistrust ignorant and inaccurate speakers. *Child Development, 76,* 1261–1277.

Landrum, A. R., Mills, C. M., & Johnston, A. M. (2013). When do children trust the expert? Benevolence information influences children's trust more than expertise. *Developmental Science, 16,* 622–638.

Legare, C. H., Mills, C. M., Souza, A. L., Plummer, L. E., & Yasskin, R. (2013). The use of questions as problem-solving strategies during early childhood. *Journal of Experimental Child Psychology, 114,* 63–76.

Lutz, D. J., & Keil, F. C. (2002). Early understanding of the division of cognitive labor. *Child Development, 73,* 1073–1084.

McCarthy, D. A. (1930). The language development of the preschool child. *Institute of Child Welfare Monograph Series, No. 4,* Minneapolis: University of Minnesota Press.

Mills, C. M., Danovitch, J. H., Grant, M. G., & Elashi, F. B. (2012). Little pitchers use their big ears: Preschoolers solve problems by listening to others ask questions. *Child Development, 83,* 568–580.

Mills, C. M. & Keil, F. C. (2004). Knowing the limits of one's understanding: The development of an awareness of an illusion of explanatory depth. *Journal of Experimental Child Psychology, 87,* 1–32.

Mills, C. M., Legare, C. H., Bills, M., & Mejias, C. (2010). Preschoolers use questions as a tool to acquire knowledge from different sources. *Journal of Cognition and Development, 11,* 533–560.

Mills, C. M., Legare, C. H., Grant. M. G., & Landrum, A. R. (2011). Determining whom to question, what to ask, and how much information to ask for: The development of inquiry in young children. *Journal of Experimental Child Psychology, 110,* 539–560.

Mosher, F. A., & Hornsby, J. R. (1966). On asking questions. In J. S. Bruner, R. Oliver, L. P. Greenfield et al. *Studies in Cognitive Growth* (pp. 86–102). New York, NY: Wiley.

Pasquini, E. S., Corriveau, K. H., Koenig, M. A., & Harris, P. L. (2007). Preschoolers monitor the relative accuracy of informants. *Developmental Psychology, 43,* 1216–1226.

Robinson, E. J., Butterfill, S. A., & Nurmsoo, E. (2011). Gaining knowledge via other minds: Children's flexible trust in others as sources of information. *British Journal of Developmental Psychology, 29,* 961–980.

Rozenblit, L. R., & Keil, F. C. (2002). The misunderstood limits of folk science: An illusion of explanatory depth. *Cognitive Science, 26,* 521–562.

Samuels, M. C., & McDonald, J. (2002). Elementary school-age children's capacity to choose positive and negative diagnostic tests. *Child Development, 73,* 857–866.

Sodian, B., Zaitchik, D., & Carey, S. (1991). Young children's differentiation of hypothetical beliefs from evidence. *Child Development, 62,* 753–766.

Tizard, B. & Hughes, M. (1984). *Young children learning: Talking and thinking at home and at school.* London: Fontana.

Vanderbilt, K. E., Liu, D., & Heyman, G. D. (2011). The development of distrust. *Child Development, 82,* 1372–1380.

Wellman, H. M., Hickling, A. K., & Schult, C. A. (1997). Young children's psychological, physical, and biological explanations. *New Directions for Child Development, 75,* 7–25.

Wellman, H. M., & Liu, D. (2004). Scaling of Theory of Mind Tasks. *Child Development, 75,* 523–541.

Williams, R. A., Landrum, A. R., Pflaum, A. D., & Mills, C. M. (2013). *Who to Ask? The relationship between social cognition and recognizing accurate sources of information in preschool-aged children.* Poster presented at the April 2013 meeting of the Society for Research in Child Development, Seattle, WA.

5 Gullible's travel

How honest and trustful children become vigilant communicators

Olivier Mascaro and Olivier Morin

Introduction

> This is the Golden Lasso. Besides being made from an indestructible material, it also carries with it the power to compel people to tell the truth. Use it well, and with compassion.
>
> (Queen Hippolyte to Wonderwoman, *The New Original Wonderwoman*, by Marston & Ross, 1975)

The inventor of Wonderwoman and her golden lasso, William Moulton Marston, did not believe that truth devices were only material for fiction. He claimed to have found a lie-detection technique, one that would "end the 6000-years search for a truth test" (Marston, 1938). It all started when William James invited Hugo Münsterberg to join his laboratory in Harvard. The German émigré soon became a popular professor, laying the foundations of applied psychology and attracting many promising students, young Marston among them. Under Münsterberg's mentorship, the undergraduate started a research on systolic blood pressure variations that would inspire what may have been the most widely used "lie detector" in human history: the polygraph deception test. From its first uses outside the laboratory in the 1920s, the technique quickly rose to fame. The polygraph featured in TV shows and advertisements and became part of popular culture (Adler, 2007; Bunn, 1997). In *Look* magazine, the "disinterested truth finder" was used to read hearts and minds, even to settle marital disputes. Once, the polygraph revealed that a "neglected wife and her roving husband" still had love for one another (Bunn, 1997). The technique was also put to less frivolous use, in police or private investigations, or in job interviews. At the height of his fame, Marston claimed that his lie detector test's accuracy approximated 100%, and was a "psychological medicine" that would "cure crime itself if properly administered" (Marston, 1938). The polygraph deception test, however, proved quite unreliable, with high rates of false positives and false negatives (National Research Council, [USA], 2003).

Despite considerable research, despite public and private investment, the quest for a reliable lie detector has proven elusive. The popular interest in lie detection techniques, however, seems unshakable. This popularity goes beyond the usual curiosity for weird technological contraptions. It has to do, we think, with a deep-rooted interest in lies, in deception, and in ways of avoiding them. Part of this fascination could originate from local cultural specificities (Adler, 2007). Still, the cultural success of lie detectors (as well as of stories and games involving deception and dupes) may exploit a more general feature of human psychology. Among other species, humans stand out by their willingness to offer information, and their reliance on information provided by others (Hauser, 1997; Sperber & Wilson, 1989; Tomasello, 2008). This reliance makes us vulnerable to misleading informants. In this context, the possible occurrence of deception raises a particularly thorny issue: unlike mistakes, lies are typically advantageous to those who produce them. This advantage provides leverage for the evolution of strategies based on the production of persuasive lies. The very fact that human communication is, evolutionarily speaking, a stable practice suggests that some mechanisms allow us to filter misinformation away. Only thanks to these filters is communication advantageous to those who practice it (Dawkins & Krebs, 1978). One may call them mechanisms of "epistemic vigilance" (Sperber, Clément, Heintz, Mascaro, Mercier, Origgi, & Wilson, 2010).

In this chapter, we turn to the developmental origins of these capacities for, and interest in, spotting liars. We will show that our fascination for deception and lies emerges relatively late, around the age of 4. We will review evidence that 2- to 3-year-old children show remarkable conceptual competence in mentally representing beliefs, and in representing communicated information as false, two capacities that are crucial for vigilance towards deception. Yet, 3-year-olds are often remarkably blind to the fact that they may be deceived. Their surprising trustfulness goes along with a robust and remarkable tendency to disregard most opportunities to lie, and to assume that most assertions are true (see also chapter 8). Around the age of 4, children become more likely to recognize the falsity of assertions, more likely to lie, and more likely to be vigilant towards deception. Do these changes spring from the emergence of entirely novel abilities? We doubt it. Rather, they may reflect a change in children's expectations about people and about communication—expectations that they revise as they grow in autonomy and need to interact more with their peers.

Epistemic vigilance grows with difficulties

Lies are not easy to spot. They are much less frequent than honest communication. American adults report producing fewer than two lies per day (DePaulo, Kashy, Kirkendol, Wyer, & Epstein, 1996; Serota, Levine, & Boster, 2010), a relatively small number if contrasted with the impressive amount of honest (though not necessarily reliable) communicative actions they engage in. Moreover, deceivers have no interest in revealing that they are lying. Conventional wisdom notwithstanding, no simple behavioral marker (such as shifting eyes or blushing faces) reliably indicates deception. Lay people's and experts' performances are remarkably low when asked to spot liars with the help of behavioral cues alone—even for people they know well (Bond & DePaulo, 2006). Thus, the natural flow of human communication is hard to sift through for lies, deception being both discrete and rare.

How then does epistemic vigilance develop? Cultural training is one possibility, yet the help that children derive from it is surprisingly meager. They are constantly exposed to games involving deception, to jokes and stories of disguise, of tricks, of lies. These could offer a 'scaffolding' for the development of vigilance towards deception. Quite surprisingly, young children do not seem to learn at all in such games, simple though they may be. Most 3-year-olds show a baffling lack of understanding of hide-and-seek games, for instance. For one thing, they are not proficient hiders; but the problem is deeper: they seem to miss the point of the game entirely. When having to hide, they say where they are going to hide, or hide in full view of the seeker. When playing the role of the seeker, they tell others where to hide, or count with their eyes open (Peskin & Ardino, 2003). This is all the more surprising since 3-year-old children are sensitive to knowledge and ignorance (Pillow, 1989; Pratt & Bryant, 1990). Moreover, they possess sufficient perspective-taking abilities to place objects in such a way that others cannot see them (Flavell, Shipstead, & Croft, 1978; McGuigan & Doherty, 2002). They use this knowledge to hide their transgressions: they will perform a transgression less often when they can be seen in the act (Melis, Call, & Tomasello, 2010). In spite of this, the pleasure that 3-year-olds take in playing hide-and-seek owes, it seems, very little to the experience or practice of deception. Rather they seem to interpret the game of hide-and-seek in a completely different manner—possibly as a game of tag, as a peek-a-boo, or as a game whose enjoyment derives mainly from the thrill of being first separated, then together again.

Similarly, 3-year-old children are remarkably unaware of the fact that they may be lied to in simple games. Couillard and Woodward (1999) designed a task that seems, prima facie, an ideal way of training children's vigilance towards deception. In their experiment, 3- and 4-year-olds had to find a sticker that could be hidden underneath one of two bowls. Before children could guess the location of the sticker, a confederate pointed to one of the bowls. The game was framed as competitive: children were told that the confederate would keep the sticker for herself if they lost, thus implying that the confederate had an interest in misleading participants. Moreover, the confederate consistently deceived the child by pointing to the empty bowl, and was said to be "tricky." Despite repeating the game for 10 trials, with feedback about the real location of the stickers, the youngest participants did not learn to select the box that the informant did not point at. In subsequent studies, 3-year-old children were found to maintain their trust in misleading informants in similar hiding games. Importantly, 3-year-olds extend their trust beyond deceptive informants, to mistaken informants (Call & Tomasello, 1999; Figueras-Costa & Harris, 2001). It is only by the age of 4 to 5 that children manage to distrust a misleading informant who uses familiar communicative means (Heyman, Sritanyaratana, & Vanderbilt, 2013; Jaswal, Carrington Croft, Setia, & Cole, 2010; Mascaro & Sperber, 2009; Vanderbilt, Liu, & Heyman, 2011).

These results are all the more remarkable since young children appear to filter out potentially deceptive information in other tasks: they selectively learn from benevolent informants rather than from malevolent ones (Doebel & Koenig, 2013; Hamlin & Wynn, 2012; Lane, Wellman, & Gelman, 2013; Mascaro & Sperber,

2009). Thus the remarkable gullibility of young children is clearest in tasks of a certain kind—tasks where they have to treat what is conveyed by a single informant as false, and infer that the opposite is true. We shall refer to these tasks as "false communication tasks", to highlight their commonalities with false belief tasks—both in the capacities they require and in the developmental pattern they exhibit (Mascaro & Sperber, 2009).

As we have already suggested, the development of vigilance towards deception raises a paradox. Lies are rare and hard to detect in human communication. Moreover, many children under 4 blissfully ignore the possibility of deception, even in simple artificial situations in which the motivations and strategies of liars are unambiguous. How do children become vigilant towards lies in such circumstances? What cognitive changes (if any) trigger the emergence of vigilance towards deception (and towards misinformation more generally)? And what explains the remarkable trust that 3-year-olds manifest in false communication tasks? We consider three plausible answers for these questions. A first hypothesis is that children recognize, from an early age, that they can be misinformed, but lack the proper executive abilities to act on that knowledge. A second hypothesis holds that children's vigilance towards deception increases around the age of 4 thanks to the development of novel ways of representing representations such as beliefs and utterances (i.e., of novel metarepresentational abilities). According to a third hypothesis, children under 4 have most if not all the capacities required to be vigilant towards deception, but do not use them because they are trustful.

Does children's trust reflect an executive deficit?

Children's executive abilities increase around 4. Moreover, false communication tasks share characteristics with some executive functioning tasks: for instance, they may require children to inhibit accepting communicative cues that have been reliable in the past (Couillard & Woodward, 1999; Jaswal et al., 2010). Recent evidence also suggests that executive abilities contribute to the capacity to filter out misinformation (see chapter 8). Thus, it would not be completely surprising if 3-year-olds' heightened trust in communication were underpinned by an inability to resist accepting what one confident informant asserts. Several lines of evidence, however, speak against this hypothesis.

First, evidence for a relation between executive abilities and the capacity to be vigilant towards deception is scarce. In a series of five carefully crafted studies, Heyman et al. (2013) presented young children with tests of vigilance towards deception, and tests of executive functioning. No robust correlation between tasks of the two types (even closely matched pairs of tasks) was found (see also chapter 6).

Second, in many contexts, children are quite capable of resisting assertions coming from one confident speaker: their executive capacities are sufficient for this purpose. Children as young as 3 reject statements coming from a single confident speaker, when that statement contradicts their perception (Jaswal, 2010; Lyon, Quas, & Carrick, in press) or their memory (Clément, Koenig, & Harris, 2004; see also Ma & Ganea, 2010, although in this case 3-year-olds also need exposure to informants' unreliability to disregard their testimony). Likewise, children as young as 3 are more likely to accept information that contradicts their guesses, when it comes from a better-informed speaker, as opposed to an equally informed one (Robinson, Champion, & Mitchell, 1999; Robinson & Whitcombe, 2003). If young children's executive limitations accounted for their lack of vigilance, then they should make them unable to resist a confident informant, or to consider competing evidence; the data speak to the contrary.

Third, an abundant literature shows that 2- to 3-year-old children select which information to accept when two testifiers provide contradictory information. For instance, they preferentially learn from benevolent and competent informants (e.g., Birch, Vauthier & Bloom, 2008; Corriveau & Harris, 2009; Doebel & Koenig, 2013; Hamlin & Wynn, 2012; Jaswal & Neely, 2006; Koenig & Harris, 2005; Scofield & Behrend, 2008). Were young children prevented by executive limitations from resisting inaccurate testimonies, they would merely trust the last informant speaking in all those studies.

In short, executive functioning abilities play a role in filtering out misinformation, and could contribute to explain inter-individual and age differences in gullibility. Yet, children as young as 3 have sufficient executive abilities to refrain from indiscriminately accepting any testimony, and to select, in a pair, which informant they would learn from. This speaks against the executive interpretation of false communication tasks according to which 3-year-old children are unable to reject what is conveyed by a single confident speaker. We now consider another possibility: the gullibility found in 3-year-olds may reflect a flaw in their manner of representing thoughts, utterances, or beliefs—in their *metarepresentational abilities.*

Does children's trust reflect a metarepresentational deficit?

Vigilance towards deception involves representations of representations: it requires knowing that communication can be used to modify beliefs (mindreading component) by communicating false information (epistemic component). As we will review, children's behavior shows important changes in these two domains around age 4. These changes could be explained by the emergence of entirely novel metarepresentational abilities (Leekam, Perner, Healey, & Sewell, 2008; Wellman, Cross, & Watson, 2001; Wimmer & Perner, 1983). However, we suggest that a closer look at young children's competence indicates that they have, long before they turn 4, a basic grasp of two metarepresentational building blocks of epistemic vigilance: a capacity to represent the effect of communication on beliefs, and an understanding of truth and falsity.

Lessons from the mindreading domain: 3-year-olds are honest

Children's tendency to lie shows an increase around age 4. This change occurs in games where young children have to deceive an opponent (e.g., Russell,

Mauthner, Sharpe, & Tidswell, 1991; Sodian, 1991) as well as in more ecological settings, such as the temptation paradigm (Lewis, Stanger, & Sullivan, 1989), in which children are given an opportunity to deny responsibility for a transgression that they committed (e.g., Talwar & Lee, 2002a, 2008). Until recently, researchers thought that this tendency of 3-year-olds to miss blatant opportunities for deception could be accounted for by a simple hypothesis: children of that age did not represent beliefs. This view was supported by the robust increase in performance that is observed on standard false belief tasks at age 4 (e.g., Wellman, Cross, & Watson, 2001; Wimmer & Perner, 1983). This long-held view has been challenged by an impressive number of studies showing that children before age 4 do possess metarepresentational capacities. Those studies used a variety of measures, including looking behavior, helping, replies to requests, or pointing (for reviews, see Baillargeon, Scott, & He, 2010; Perner & Roessler, 2012). Although there is no consensus on the nature of these early competences, these findings make it worth reconsidering the once prevalent explanation of children's lack of awareness for deception opportunities. Is it true that children fail to grasp deception because they fail to understand that communication is used to modify people's beliefs?

Young children seem to possess an incipient knowledge of the way communication affects beliefs. Children as young as 18 months old expect that truthful communication will correct someone's false belief (Song, Onishi, Baillargeon, & Fisher, 2008). Moreover, infants use communication with the intent to act on their audience's mental states. They point to inform ignorant adult experimenters (Liszkowski, Carpenter, & Tomasello, 2007) or to correct false beliefs in mistaken adult experimenters (Knudsen & Liszkowski, 2012). Likewise, 3-year-olds produce statements that they know to be false, to hide a transgression, or simply to be polite—the increase in lying behavior observed around age 4 notwithstanding (Evans & Lee, in press; Lewis et al., 1989; Polak & Harris, 1999; Talwar & Lee, 2002a, 2002b; see also Reddy, 2007; Wilson, Smith, & Ross, 2003 for observational evidence). The literature thus indicates that children younger than 4 can represent beliefs (or analogues of beliefs). They recognize that communication is used to act on others' mental states. In spite of this, their proficiency as liars shows a sharp increase around age 4.

This increase, we think, does not reflect the appearance of enhanced abilities to execute lies, so much as a heightened perception of opportunities for the planning and execution of lies. Three-year-olds have trouble deceiving others in simple games that require them to mislead an opponent about the location of an item by pointing at an empty container rather than at the real location of the item (e.g., Russell et al., 1991). This difficulty does not result from an executive inability to refrain from pointing at the baited box: 3-year-olds easily point at the empty box if asked to (Simpson, Riggs, & Simon, 2004).

In one study, Carlson, Moses, and Hix (1998) showed that 3-year-olds' performances in deception games are improved when participants respond by rotating an arrow (instead of pointing). This result is often interpreted as indicating that children's difficulty with lying comes from an inability to execute lies. These data, however, are open to reinterpretation: perhaps the difficulty lies not in execution but in planning. In a follow-up experiment, Carroll, Riggs, Apperly, Graham, & Geoghegan (2012) trained 3-year-olds for a deception game where subjects responded with an arrow, and replicated the increase in performance observed in Carlson et al.'s original study. Increased performances also obtained, however, when the same children were later tested, on the same task, but asked to respond this time with a pointing gesture. This result is inconsistent with the view that familiar means of communication prevent children from *executing* lies. What may elude them, rather, is devising a deceiving strategy. Once found, the strategy seems easily implemented (see also Carroll, Apperly, & Riggs, 2007).

Three-year-olds thus appear to understand that communication is used to manipulate others' beliefs. What they may lack is a sensitivity to 'deception affordances,' i.e. situations that afford lying (Mascaro & Morin, 2010): far from being cognitively unable to lie, young children may simply be prevented from deceiving others by sheer honesty. For them, communicative situations seem to afford the communication of true and relevant information more strongly than they do for adults. In other words: Three-year-olds are honest.

Lessons from the epistemic domain: three-year-olds are trustful

A similar developmental pattern is observed in the epistemic domain. Children's tendency to assume that what is communicated can be false increases around the age of 4. In "false signs tasks," children have to interpret a sign that becomes out-dated as reality changes (Parkin, 1994, cited in Leekam et al., 2008), or to predict what will result when a character is given a false piece of information (Bowler, Briskman, Gurvidi, & Fornells-Ambrojo, 2005). In these tasks, young preschool-ers tend to misinterpret the sign—to claim that it is still telling the truth when it is in fact outdated. Children's performance on this type of task correlates moderately with their performance on standard false belief tasks, even after controlling for various dimensions such as age (Parkin, 1994, quoted in Leekam et al., 2008), verbal mental age (Bowler Briskman, Gurvidi, & Fornells-Ambrojo, 2005) and performance on a false photograph task (Leekam et al., 2008) (but see Sabbagh, Moses, & Shiverick, 2006).

Yet, there are reasons to believe that young children can assess the match of a message with other sources—with their perception, their memory, their infer-ences, or with other messages. Infants as young as 9 months old are sensitive to mismatches between words and reality (Gliga & Csibra, 2009; Koenig & Echols, 2003; Parise & Csibra, 2012). Toddlers and 3-year-olds are more likely to request information from labelers who proved accurate in the past (Begus & Southgate, 2012; Koenig & Harris, 2005). They preferentially learn from such accurate informants; they remember their testimony better (e.g., Koenig & Woodward, 2010). Such modulations of trust by accuracy would be very hard to understand if children paid no heed to the fit (or lack thereof) between reality and what speak-ers say about it. Additional studies also indicate that, from toddler age, children have a capacity to assess mismatches between what is communicated and what is really the case. Around age 2, children start to produce jokes that consist in misnaming objects (Dunn, 1991). They also show a capacity to assess whether an utterance is right or wrong (Pea, 1982). It is also around that age that toddlers start to use negation to contradict what others say (Hummer, Wimmer, & Antes, 1993). Toddlers also interpret others' comments on the reliability of testimonies. In Fusaro & Harris (2012), 24-month-olds are more likely to trust what has been said by an informant when a third party assents to it (by nodding), than when the third party dissents (by shaking her head). If, following the (disputed, but) dominant theory of truth in philosophy, we admit that falsity is a lack of correspondence between facts and representations (see e.g., David, 2009), we are led to conclude that 2- to 3-years old children have the conceptual wherewithal to treat communicated information as false. Their difficulties with resisting gullibility must lie elsewhere.

These difficulties may reflect a change in baseline expectations about the reliability of assertions. As a direct test of this possibility, one of us (Mascaro), presented 3-year-olds with a hiding game where participants had to discover the location of an item on the basis of a misleading informant's testimony. This testimony was, as children were directly told, 'not true' (in another condition, the informant 'made a mistake'). Even 3-year-olds were able to reject these testimonies, and to infer the true location of the hidden item. Interestingly, when asked to recall what the informant had said, many mistakenly replied that he had pointed them to the right location. Children showed no such bias when asked to recall which box the informant touched, thus suggesting that they had correctly memorized the puppet's actions (for similar memory effects, see Robinson, Mitchell, & Nye, 1995). These data are consistent with the view that 3-year-olds can treat communicated information as false, but also have a strong assumption that assertions are accurate. In other words: Three-year-olds are trustful.

We have reasons to think that 2- to 3-year-old children possess competences that allow them to represent beliefs, and to treat communicated information as false. Yet around the age of 4, they become more likely to lie, and less likely to assume that assertions are true. This change coincides with the increase of children's vigilance towards deception and mistakes in false communication tasks. There are reasons to doubt that this change is underpinned by the emergence of entirely novel metarepresentational abilities. Rather, it seems that 3-year-olds are more honest, and trustful, than older children and adults. The change in children's trust observed around the age of 4 could be due to a revision of children's expectations about the honesty and reliability of communication and communicators. Three-year-olds are competent, selective social learners. Yet, without being completely gullible, they appear as much more trusting than older children and adults. This higher-than-average trust in communication need not take the form of "unlimited" credulity (Reid, 1764/2007, p.120). In fact, baseline trust is always weighted against available counter-evidence, as evidenced by the fact that even 3-year-olds reject communicated information if it contradicts what they perceive (or remember with enough confidence). Similarly, to say that young children are more trustful than older humans is not tantamount to saying that they are indiscriminate learners. Young children may have a higher baseline level of trust in communicated information, while still being able to choose between better and worse informants (Shafto, Eaves, Navarro, & Perfors, 2012).

What is it that young children trust so much? People, intentional communication, or familiar forms of expression?

Three components could contribute to children's higher-than-average trust in communication. They may be more disposed to place their trust in *people*. Their trust may also be elicited by the recognition of communicative intent. Or else it could be that children set great store by familiar forms of communication (such as pointing). In our view, a plausible case can be made for each of those three options.

First, young children may have a stronger-than-average assumption that people are generally benevolent and competent. In Corriveau, Meints, and Harris (2009), children were familiarized with accurate informants (who named objects by their true names), inaccurate informants (who named objects by wrong names), and neutral informants who merely drew attention to objects. In a subsequent test, 3- and 4-year-olds learned preferentially from neutral (rather than inaccurate) informants. Four-year-olds also selectively learned from accurate (rather than neutral) informants. However, 3-year-olds did not learn preferentially from accurate, as opposed to neutral informants—they seemed to take accuracy for granted. This pattern could reflect a higher baseline level of trust in people's accuracy (see also Doebel & Koenig, 2013 for a similar but more tentative pattern of data, with informants varying in benevolence).

Children's trust in communication, however, is not exhausted by their general trust in people. In Palmquist and Jaswal (2012), 3-year-olds were presented with a hiding game in which one actor hid a ball in one of four cups, while the other actor turned away. Later on, each of the two actors grasped a different cup by the top. In that case, 3-year-olds had no difficulty indicating that the actor who hid the cup was the more knowledgeable of the two. On the contrary, when the actors *pointed* at different cups, instead of grasping them, 3-year-olds were at chance. They could not tell which actor was the most knowledgeable, though they did remember which one hid the ball. Thus, communication (at least in certain forms) creates an assumption of knowledgeability that is stronger than that elicited by other behaviors (such as grasping). This leads us to two additional possibilities: children may have higher-than-usual expectations about communication as such, or about certain forms that communication takes.

Part of young children's trust may be elicited by the recognition of an intention to communicate (Heyman, Sritanyaratana, & Vanderbilt, 2013; Mascaro & Sperber, 2009). By offering information willingly, communicators imply that their input is worth processing, and thus present themselves as benevolent and competent. As a consequence, recognizing an intention to communicate could heighten children's trust. For example, in two independent studies, preschoolers who had to interpret an ambiguous request followed pointing 12.5% of the time when its ostensive, or communicative, nature was reduced (Jaswal & Hansen, 2006), but did so 97.9% of the time when pointing was clearly ostensive (Grassmann & Tomasello, 2010). Likewise, in Leekam, Solomon, and Teoh (2010) 3-year-olds' tendency to follow an unfamiliar signal (e.g., an arrow, or a toy replica) was stronger when the unfamiliar signal was accompanied by positive facial emotions. Possibly, these positive facial emotions make it easier for children to recognize the experimenter's communicative intention. This, in turn, could prompt children to look more keenly into what the experimenter is trying to convey with the unfamiliar signals that he is manipulating. Similarly, in Heyman et al. (2013), 3-year-olds have difficulties mistrusting an informant when he used an unfamiliar signal with an easily identifiable communicative intention.

These last two studies suggest that children's trust in communicated information partly depends on the recognition of communicative intent, regardless of the form of communication employed. That said, some particular forms of communication may be more likely to elicit trust in children—starting with those that have proven reliable in the past, first of all pointing or verbal testimony (Couillard & Woodward, 1999; Jaswal et al. 2010). For example, in Palmquist, Burns, & Jaswal (2012), 3-year-olds' capacity to learn from the better informed testifier was disrupted when informants used pointing to communicate, but not when they used unfamiliar cues (pictures placed as markers). Why should pointing be more disruptive of children's selective learning? Perhaps because it has been reliable many times before, unlike unfamiliar cues (for similar views and further relevant data, see also Couillard & Woodward, 1999, and Jaswal et al., 2010; however note that in these two papers training may lead trustful children to reinterpret unfamiliar signals as honest indicators, revealing which box they should not select).

Conclusion: epistemic vigilance grows in a social environment

Detecting deception on the basis of purely behavioral cues is hard, even with high technology equipment. Yet, in a certain sense, detecting lies and deception is intuitive. In this chapter, we reviewed the early development of capacities that are arguably part of humanity's common toolkit for lies-detection: assessing the truth or falsity of what is said (epistemic component) and anticipating the ploys by which people manipulate others' beliefs (mindreading component). Despite possessing early competence in these domains, 3-year-olds are often oblivious to the possibility that they may be misinformed, or that they may misinform others. Around the age of 4, children revise this trustful stance towards others, and towards communication. This revision is what permits their increased vigilance towards misinformation. It could reflect a change in baseline assumptions concerning the reliability of people, of communication, and (possibly) of some familiar forms of communication. This change is also associated with an increased interest for deception in stories, and in games such as hide-and-seek. It has counterparts in children's use of lies. It coincides with a period in most children's social life when they start to interact more and more with their peers, after many years spent under the care of (usually) benevolent adults. Caregiving relations are typically characterized by a high level of overlap between the interests of caregivers and care-receivers—an alignment of interests and desires that, for children, justifies a stance of trustful dependence. In these circumstances, keeping an eye out for deception (or for malign intentions more generally) is not as important as it will later be. In any event, young children have little choice in the matter. Relations with peers are different. They require a higher level of autonomy and vigilance. The increase in epistemic vigilance observed around the age of 4 is a crucial ingredient of a child's social savvy.

References

Adler, K. (2007). *The lie detectors: The history of an American obsession.* New York, NY: Free Press.

Baillargeon, R. M., Scott, R., & He, Z. (2010). False belief understanding in infants. *Trends in Cognitive Sciences, 14,* 110–118.

Begus, K., & Southgate, V. (2012). Infant pointing serves an interrogative function. *Developmental Science, 15,* 611–617.

Birch, S. A., Vauthier, S. A., & Bloom, P. (2008). Three-and four-year-olds spontaneously use others' past performance to guide their learning. *Cognition, 107,* 1018–1034.

Bowler, D. M., Briskman, J., Gurvidi, N., & Fornells-Ambrojo, M. (2005). Understanding the mind or predicting signal-dependent action? Performance of children with and without autism on analogues of the false belief task. *Journal of Cognition and Development, 6,* 259–283.

Bond, C. F., & DePaulo, B. M. (2006). Accuracy of deception judgments. *Personality and Social Psychology Review, 10,* 214–234.

Bunn, G. C. (1997). The lie-detector, Wonderwoman and liberty: The life and work of William Moulton Marston. *History of the human sciences, 10,* 91–119.

Call, J., & Tomasello, M. (1999). A nonverbal false belief task: The performance of children and great apes. *Child Development, 70,* 381–395.

Carlson, S. M., Moses, L. J., & Hix, H. R. (1998). The role of inhibitory processes in young children's difficulties with deception and false belief. *Child Development, 69,* 672–691.

Carroll, D. J., Apperly, I. A., & Riggs, K. J. (2007). The executive demands of strategic reasoning are modified by the way in which children are prompted to think about the task: Evidence from 3-to 4-year-olds. *Cognitive Development, 22,* 142–148.

Carroll, D. J., Riggs, K. J., Apperly, I. A., Graham, K., & Geoghegan, C. (2012). How do alternative ways of responding influence 3- and 4-year-olds' performance on test of executive function and theory of mind? *Journal of Experimental Child Psychology, 112,* 312–325.

Clément, F., Koenig, M., & Harris, P. (2004). The ontogenesis of trust. *Mind and Language, 19,* 360–379.

Corriveau, K., & Harris, P. L. (2009). Choosing your informant: weighing familiarity and recent accuracy. *Developmental Science, 12,* 426–437.

Corriveau, K. H., Meints, K., & Harris, P. L. (2009). Early tracking of informant accuracy and inaccuracy. *British Journal of Developmental Psychology, 27,* 331–342.

Couillard, N. L., & Woodward, A. L. (1999). Children's comprehension of deceptive points. *British Journal of Developmental Psychology, 17,* 515–521.

David, M. (2009). The correspondence theory of truth. *Stanford Encyclopedia of Philosophy*. Retrieved from http://plato.stanford.edu/entries/truth-correspondence/

Dawkins, R., & Krebs, J. R. (1978). Animal signals: Information or manipulation? In J. R. Krebs & N. B. Davies (Eds.), *Behavioural Ecology* (pp. 282–309). Oxford, UK: Basil Blackwell.

DePaulo, B. M., Kashy, D. A., Kirkendol, S. E., Wyer, M. M., & Epstein, J. A. (1996). Lying in everyday life. *Journal of Personality and Social Psychology, 70,* 979–995.

Doebel, S., & Koenig, M. A. (2013). Children's use of moral behavior in selective trust: Discrimination versus learning. *Developmental Psychology, 49,* 462–469.

Dunn, J. (1991). *The beginnings of social understanding.* Oxford, UK: Blackwell.

Evans, A. D., & Lee, K. (in press). Emergence of lying in very young children. *Developmental Psychology.*

Figueras-Costa, B., & Harris, P. (2001). Theory of mind development in deaf children: A nonverbal test of false-belief understanding. *Journal of Deaf Studies and Deaf Education, 6,* 92.

Flavell, J. H., Shipstead, S. G., & Croft, K. (1978). Young children's knowledge about visual perception: Hiding objects from others. *Child Development, 49,* 1208–1211.

Fusaro, M., & Harris, P. L. (2012). Dax gets the nod: Toddlers detect and use social cues to evaluate testimony. *Developmental Psychology, 49,* 514–522.

Gliga T., & Csibra G. (2009). One-year-old infants appreciate the referential nature of deictic gestures and words. *Psychological Science, 20,* 347–353.

Grassmann, S., & Tomasello, M. (2010). Young children follow pointing over words in interpreting acts of reference. *Developmental Science, 13,* 252–263.

Hamlin, J. K., & Wynn, K. (2012). Who knows what's good to eat? Infants fail to match the food preferences of antisocial others. *Cognitive Development, 27,* 227–239.

Hauser, M. C. (1997). *The evolution of communication.* Cambridge, MA: MIT Press.

Heyman, G. D., Sritanyaratana, L., & Vanderbilt, K. E. (2013). Young children trust in overtly misleading advice. *Cognitive Science, 37,* 646–667.

Hummer, P., Wimmer, H., & Antes, G. (1993). On the origins of denial negation. *Journal of Child Language, 20,* 607–618.

Jaswal, V. K. (2010). Believing what you're told: Young children's trust in unexpected testimony about the physical world. *Cognitive Psychology, 61,* 248–272.

Jaswal, V. K., Carrington Croft, A. A., Setia, A. R., & Cole, C. A. (2010). Young children have a specific, highly robust bias to trust testimony. *Psychological Science, 21,* 1541–1547.

Jaswal, V. K., & Hansen, M. B. (2006). Learning words: Children disregard some pragmatic information that conflicts with mutual exclusivity. *Developmental Science, 9,* 158–165.

Jaswal, V. K., & Neely, L. A. (2006). Adults don't always know best: Preschoolers use past reliability over age when learning new words. *Psychological Science, 17,* 757–758.

Koenig, M. A., & Echols, C. H. (2003). Infants' understanding of false labeling events: The referential roles of words and the speakers who use them. *Cognition, 87,* 179–208.

Koenig, M. A., & Harris, P. L. (2005). Preschoolers mistrust ignorant and inaccurate speakers. *Child Development, 76,* 1261–1277.

Koenig, M. A., & Woodward, A. L. (2010). Sensitivity of 24-month-olds to the prior inaccuracy of the source: Possible mechanisms. *Developmental Psychology, 46,* 815–826.

Knudsen, B., & Liszkowski, U. (2012). 18-month-olds predict specific action mistakes through attribution of false belief, not ignorance, and intervene accordingly. *Infancy, 17,* 672–691.

Lane, J. D., Wellman, H. M., & Gelman, S. A. (2013). Informants' traits weigh heavily in young children's trust in testimony and in their epistemic inferences. *Child Development, 84,* 1253–1268.

Leekam, S., Perner, J., Healey, L., & Sewell, C. (2008). False signs and the non-specificity of theory of mind: Evidence that preschoolers have general difficulties in understanding representations. *British Journal of Developmental Psychology, 26,* 485–497.

Leekam, S. R., Solomon, T. L., & Teoh, Y.-S. (2010). Adults' social cues facilitate young children's use of signs and symbols. *Developmental Science, 13,* 108–119.

Lewis, M., Stanger, C., & Sullivan, M. W. (1989). Deception in 3-year-olds. *Developmental Psychology, 25,* 439–443.

Liszkowski, U., Carpenter, M., & Tomasello, M. (2007). Pointing out new news, old news, and absent referents at 12 months of age. *Developmental Science, 10,* F1–F7.

Lyon T. D., Quas, J. A., & Carrick, N. (in press). Right and righteous: Children's incipient understanding and evaluation of true and false statements. *Journal of Cognition and Development.*

Ma, L., & Ganea, P. A. (2010). Dealing with conflicting information: Young children's reliance on what they see versus what they are told. *Developmental Science, 13,* 151–160.

Mascaro. O., & Morin, O. (2010). L'éveil du mensonge. *Terrain, 57,* 20–35.

Mascaro, O., & Sperber, D. (2009). The moral, epistemic, and mindreading components of children's vigilance toward deception. *Cognition, 112,* 367–380.

Marston, W. M. (1938). *The lie detector test.* New York, NY: Richard R. Smith.

Marston, W. M. (as Moulton, C.), & Ross, S. R. (1975). *The new original wonderwoman.* Warner Home Video.

McGuigan, N., & Doherty, M. J. (2002). The relation between hiding skill and judgment of eye direction in preschool children. *Developmental Psychology, 38,* 418–427.

Melis, A. P., Call, J., & Tomasello, M. (2010). 36-month-olds conceal visual and auditory information from others. *Developmental Science, 13,* 479–489.

National Research Council (USA) (2003). *The polygraph and lie detection.* Washington, DC: National Academy Press.

Palmquist C. M., Burns H. E., & Jaswal V. K. (2012). Pointing disrupts preschoolers' ability to discriminate between knowledgeable and ignorant informants. *Cognitive Development, 27,* 54–63.

Palmquist C. M., & Jaswal V. K. (2012). Preschoolers expect pointers (even ignorant ones) to be knowledgeable. *Psychological Science, 22,* 230–231.

Parise, E., & Csibra, G. (2012). Electrophysiological evidence for the understanding of maternal speech by 9-month-old infants. *Psychological Science, 23,* 728–733.

Pea, R. D. (1982). Origins of verbal logic: Spontaneous denials by two-and three-year-olds. *Journal of Child Language, 9,* 597–626.

Perner, J., & Roessler, J. (2012). From infants' to children's appreciation of belief. *Trends in Cognitive Sciences, 16,* 519–525.

Peskin, J., & Ardino, V. (2003). Representing the mental world in children's social behavior: Playing hide-and-seek and keeping a secret. *Social Development, 12,* 496–512.

Pillow, B. H. (1989). Early understanding of perception as a source of knowledge. *Journal of Experimental Child Psychology, 47,* 116–129.

Polak, A., & Harris, P. L. (1999). Deception by young children following noncompliance. *Developmental Psychology, 35,* 561–568.

Pratt, C., & Bryant, P. (1990). Young children understand that looking leads to knowing (so long as they are looking into a single barrel). *Child Development, 61,* 973–982.

Reid, T. (1764/2007). *An Inquiry into the Human Mind.* J. Bennett (Ed.) Retrieved from http://www.earlymoderntexts.com/pdf/reidinqu.pdf.

Reddy, V. (2007). Getting back to the rough ground: Deception and 'social living'. *Philosophical Transactions of the Royal Society B: Biological Sciences, 362*(1480), 621–637.

Robinson, E. J., Champion, H. H., & Mitchell, P. P. (1999). Children's ability to infer utterance veracity from speaker informedness. *Developmental Psychology, 35,* 535–546.

Robinson, E. J., Mitchell, P., & Nye, R. (1995). Young children's treating of utterances as unreliable sources of knowledge. *Journal of Child Language, 22,* 663–685.

Robinson, E. J., & Whitcombe, E. L. (2003). Children's suggestibility in relation to their understanding about sources of knowledge. *Child Development, 74,* 48–62.

Russell, J., Mauthner, N., Sharpe, S., & Tidswell, T. (1991). The 'windows task' as a measure of strategic deception in preschoolers and autistic subjects. *British Journal of Developmental Psychology, 9,* 331–349.

Sabbagh, M. A., Moses, L. J., & Shiverick, S. (2006). Executive functioning and preschoolers' understanding of false beliefs, false photographs and false signs. *Child Development, 77,* 1034–1049.

Scofield, J., & Behrend, D. A. (2008). Learning words from reliable and unreliable speakers. *Cognitive Development, 23,* 278–290.

Serota, K. B., Levine, T. R., & Boster, F. J. (2010). The prevalence of lying in America: Three studies of self-reported lies. *Human Communication Research, 36,* 2–25.

Shafto, P., Eaves, B., Navarro, D. J., & Perfors, A. (2012). Epistemic trust: Modeling children's reasoning about others' knowledge and intent. *Developmental Science, 15,* 436–447.

Simpson, A., Riggs, K. J., & Simon, M. (2004). What makes the windows task difficult for young children: Rule inference or rule use? *Journal of Experimental Child Psychology, 87,* 155–170.

Sodian, B. (1991). The development of deception in young children. *British Journal of Developmental Psychology, 9,* 173–188.

Song, H., Onishi, K. H., Baillargeon, R., & Fisher, C. (2008). Can an agent's false belief be corrected by an appropriate communication? Psychological reasoning in 18-month-old infants. *Cognition, 109*(3), 295–315.

Sperber D., & Wilson D. (1989). La pertinence: Communication et cognition. Paris, France: Éditions de Minuit.

Sperber, D., Clément, F., Heintz, C., Mascaro, O., Mercier, H., Origgi, G., & Wilson, D. (2010). Epistemic vigilance. *Mind & Language, 25,* 359–393.

Talwar, V., & Lee, K. (2002a). Development of lying to conceal a transgression: Children's control of expressive behavior during verbal deception. *International Journal of Behavioral Development, 26,* 436–444.

Talwar, V., & Lee, K. (2002b). Emergence of white-lie telling in children between 3 and 7 years of age. *Merrill Palmer Quarterly, 48,* 160–181.

Talwar, V., & Lee, K. (2008). Social and cognitive correlates of children's lying behavior. *Child Development, 79,* 866–881.

Tomasello, M. (2008). *Origins of human communication.* Cambridge, MA: MIT Press.

Vanderbilt, K. E., Liu, D., & Heyman, G. D. (2011). The development of distrust. *Child Development, 82,* 1372–1380.

Wellman, H. M., Cross, D., & Watson, J. (2001). Meta-analysis of theory-of-mind development: The truth about false belief. *Child development, 72,* 655–684.

Wilson, A. E., Smith, M. D., & Ross, H. S. (2003). The nature and effects of young children's lies. *Social Development, 12,* 21–45.

Wimmer, H., & Perner, J. (1983). Beliefs about beliefs: Representation and constraining function of wrong beliefs in young children's understanding of deception. *Cognition, 13,* 103–128.

6 Children's reasoning about deception

A cross-cultural perspective

Gail D. Heyman

Introduction

Although the testimony of others is invaluable to children as they construct belief systems about themselves, others, and the world around them, it also presents challenges. One fundamental challenge is the risk of being manipulated or misled by deceptive individuals. This chapter investigates how children manage this challenge, with reference to the question of when and how they reason about (1) ulterior motives that are associated with intentionally misleading communication, and (2) individuals who engage in deception. These issues are examined from a cross-cultural perspective as a means to explore the role of social influences on children's reasoning processes.

1 Reasoning about ulterior motives

Although in everyday conversation there is a general assumption that people will say what they believe to be true (Grice, 1980), many social interactions are subject to motives other than a desire to convey accurate information. For example, speakers may seek to present information in an entertaining manner, or in a simplified form for clarity.

Motives are particularly likely to run counter to the goal of communicating accurately when the social context carries strong evaluative implications. For example, during a job interview concerns with impression management may be paramount. Typically, the candidate will downplay information that creates a negative impression and emphasize information that creates a positive impression, such as when a candidate who considers herself to be lazy and easily distracted seeks to portray herself as hard working and focused.

There is a wide body of evidence suggesting that children learn about impression management during an extended period of development. Children begin to show some sensitivity to it by age 4. For example, young children appreciate that disclosing a fondness for dolls carries more negative implications for boys than for girls (Gee & Heyman, 2007) and that apologies are more likely to lead to favorable social evaluations than are excuses (Banerjee, Bennett, & Luke, 2010). By age 6, children give more positive ratings to a drawing if the artist is present rather than absent (Fu & Lee, 2007). However, 6- and 7-year-olds have difficulty identifying self-presentational motives, such as when an individual seeks to conceal his or her fear from others (Banerjee, 2002; Banerjee & Yuill, 1999).

Evaluating statements about the speaker

Heyman and Legare (2005) found an age-related increase in children's skepticism of speakers who may be influenced by goals relating to impression management. Children aged 6 to 7 and 10 to 11 were asked about whether individuals could be expected to accurately assess their own value-laden traits (e.g., honesty). Older participants treated these self-reports with skepticism and considered them to be a less credible means of assessment than behavioral observation. Younger participants showed the reverse pattern: they generally considered these self-reports to be credible and judged them to be more reliable than behavioral observation. Younger and older children also differed in their explanations of their credibility judgments. Older children were more likely to directly reference ulterior motives (e.g., "people don't want to tell you they're not good at something") or to point out that people are not always truthful (e.g., "you cannot always trust people by what they say because sometimes people make up what they talk about"). Younger children were more likely to claim that people would provide accurate reports because that is what they should do (e.g., "if you ask them to tell the truth, then they better tell the truth, otherwise it would be a lie").

Heyman, Fu, and Lee (2007) found that cultural experience can influence the developmental course of children's reasoning about situations in which concerns about impression management are likely to come into play. In an extension of Heyman and Legare (2005), which was conducted in the US, children were tested both in the US and in China. This cultural comparison was intended to serve as a first step toward examining whether children's patterns of reasoning differ as a function of social norms relating to the communication of value-laden information. These norms differ substantially between China and the US, and the differences include the ways in which people are expected to communicate about themselves. One such difference is a greater emphasis on the importance of engaging in impression management in China, which can be seen in some of the lessons that are typically taught to children. For example, *The good book of wisdom expansion*, which has been used to teach social skills and morality to Chinese children for centuries (see Sun, 2004), instructs readers to reveal only 30% of the truth about oneself to others and to avoid exposing one's "true heart."

In conducting the cross-cultural comparison, Heyman, Fu, and Lee (2007) included children in the same age groups (6- and 7-year-olds and 10- and 11-year-olds) used by Heyman and Legare (2005), and used a similar methodology. Results showed a main effect of age: in both countries, children in the older group were substantially more skeptical about people's reports of their own value-laden traits than were children in the younger group. The presence of this age-related difference within each country indicates that it is not an artifact of specific cultural practices used in the US, and builds on previous research suggesting that middle childhood is likely to be an important developmental period for children's reasoning about impression management.

There was also a main effect of country, with children in China showing higher levels of skepticism than children in the US Although there are many potential explanations for the higher level of skepticism seen among Chinese participants, the results suggest that a cultural emphasis on managing impressions may result in greater awareness of these motives and their implications.

Heyman, Barner, Heumann, and Schenck (in press) found further evidence that during the middle childhood years, children become increasingly skeptical of individuals who may be motivated by a desire to make a good impression. In this study, younger (age 6 and 7) and older (age 9 and 10) participants were asked to judge the generosity of children who offered a gift to a needy peer. The key contrast was whether the gift was offered in public (which is consistent with the ulterior motive of impression management) or in private (which is inconsistent with the ulterior motive). In the public condition, the act of giving was intentionally performed in the presence of an audience of classmates. For example, in the public condition of the crayon-giving scenario participants were told,

> Chelsea's friend wants to draw a picture, but she doesn't have any crayons. Chelsea waits until a lot of her other friends are looking and gives her friend a box of her own crayons. So everyone sees Chelsea give away the crayons.

In contrast, in the private condition the act of giving was intentionally performed outside of the view of this audience. In the private condition of the crayon-giving scenario participants were told that the giver waited until everyone except the recipient was gone before giving the crayons, and that, as intended, no classmates observed the act of giving. Based on previous findings, the prediction was that the older children would relate the contrast between public and private giving to impression management, and would conclude that the private givers were nicer because there is less of a reason to assume that their giving was motivated by impression management rather than a desire to help (see Kelley, 1973 and Lin-Healy & Small, 2013). In contrast, the younger children were expected to make no references to impression management and to be indifferent to the contrast between public and private giving.

As predicted, the older children were substantially more likely to judge the private giver as nicer, and 83% of them referred to impression management strategies when explaining their judgments (within this subgroup, 84% had expressed a preference for private givers). For example, one older child justified his preference for private givers by saying that the public giver "wants people to think he's generous," but that the private giver "isn't making a big deal." Similarly, another explained that the private giver "gave it without being a showoff."

Contrary to the predictions, rather than showing indifference to the public/private contrast, the younger children showed the reverse pattern of the older children by systematically rating public givers as nicer than private givers. Another unexpected finding was that a substantial minority (30%) of the younger children mentioned impression management when explaining their evaluations. However, all of these references emerged in the context of explaining a preference for public givers rather than private givers. Many of these children appeared to equate niceness with social reputation. For example, one younger child explained, "it was clever to do it when everyone is around; it made it so everyone can see she's nice," and another said that the public giver "wanted to show his friends he was a good person." This pattern of results suggests that young children do not believe that the goal of creating a good impression warrants skepticism, and instead view it positively. Taken together, these findings suggest that when it comes to reasoning about self-relevant words and actions, cues that elicit skepticism among older children and adults often do not have the same effect among young children. Even when young children are able to recognize such cues they may dismiss them (e.g., by concluding that an individual isn't lying because lying is bad) or come to different conclusions than older individuals do.

Evaluating statements about the listener

The research that has been reviewed to this point concerns ulterior motives relating to how people present themselves. However, ulterior motives can also be salient in other types of situations. One such context involves evaluative feedback that concerns the listener. In these situations speakers may consider the ways in which the feedback could be expected to influence the emotions or future behavior of the listener, and these considerations may motivate speakers to misrepresent their true beliefs.

In examining children's beliefs about the credibility of evaluative feedback, Heyman, Fu, and Lee (2013) found that children are more skeptical of unfavorable evaluations than favorable ones. Participants aged 7 to 10 in the US and in China heard scenarios in which a peer or teacher provided positive or negative performance feedback to a student in the class concerning the quality of an assigned essay. Participants were asked whether the listener should believe the evaluation or treat it with skepticism. Teacher feedback was generally viewed as more credible than peer feedback, but regardless of whether feedback came from teachers or peers the younger and older children in each country showed *selective skepticism*, which was defined as treating negative feedback more skeptically than positive feedback. For children in the US, selective skepticism is consistent with the cultural emphasis on self-esteem (Miller, Wang, Sandel, & Cho, 2002) and self-promotion (Heine, 2001; Markus & Kitayama, 1991) that is prevalent in the West. The presence of selective skepticism in China, where there is not a widespread cultural norm of encouraging people to think highly of themselves, suggests that it may not be a culturally specific phenomenon.

One possible explanation for children's selective skepticism is that they believe it is appropriate to consider the desirability of evaluative statements when assessing their credibility. As is consistent with this possibility, many participants focused on the likely consequences of accepting the evaluative feedback when they explained why they did or did not find it credible, and many focused on different factors when assessing positive feedback versus negative feedback. For example, a child in the US explained that, "when a teacher compliments work you should take pride in it," but that, "if a teacher doesn't compliment your work, it's only one person so it doesn't mean much." A child in China said, "you should believe it if it is good" when assessing a teacher's praise, but suggested "maybe the teacher made a mistake" when assessing criticism. The possibility that children may be less skeptical of information that they want to be true or think should be true is also consistent with other studies involving children (Woolley, Boerger, & Markman, 2004) and adults (Ditto, Pizarro, & Tannenbaum, 2009) that suggest desirable outcomes may be treated with less skepticism than undesirable ones.

Although Heyman, Fu, and Lee (2013) found evidence of selective skepticism in both the US and China, there were some cultural differences. Chinese children were less skeptical about negative feedback from teachers than were children from the US. This difference may result from a cultural belief in China about the value of using negative feedback to better understand one's own weaknesses and to identify what one must do to improve performance in the future (Heyman, Fu, Sweet, & Lee, 2009; see also Li, 2005).

Summary

The results presented so far suggest that between the ages of 6 and 11, children go through substantial changes in their reasoning about ulterior motives. Over time they become better at recognizing situations in which others are likely to have an agenda that conflicts with the goal of being truthful, and they begin to exhibit higher levels of skepticism in such contexts. Part of the reason for this change is that children become increasingly aware of impression management strategies. However, the ability to understand that others engage in impression management is not always sufficient to produce greater skepticism in contexts in which impression management goals are likely to be present. One reason is that young children may follow moral guidelines when making inferences about others by predicting that people will do what they should do. In addition, they may reason associatively, such as by linking a positive reputation to being nice, rather than thinking through the causal implications of a speaker having ulterior motives. Even among older children, factors other than a rational analysis of the evidence may come into play, including a tendency to give more scrutiny to undesirable outcomes than desirable outcomes under some circumstances.

Cross-cultural research on this topic offers some clues about the extent to which patterns of reasoning tend to generalize beyond Western samples. This work suggests that the age-related trend toward an increasing awareness of ulterior motives and their implications extends to children in China. However, the results also point to interesting ways in which cultural values may shape children's developmental trajectory. For example, the cultural emphasis on impression management in China may lead to an earlier sophistication about ulterior motives than in the US, and the cultural emphasis on self-esteem that is seen in the US may be associated with greater skepticism about evaluative information that has negative implications for the self.

2 Reasoning about overtly deceptive individuals

The first part of this chapter focused on children's developing awareness of contexts in which individuals might be motivated to provide inaccurate information about what they believe to be true. This second part addresses how children's judgments and behavioral responses to an informant's testimony are affected by evidence that the informant has previously offered deliberately misleading information.

Recent research suggests that when predicting an individual's future behavior, pre-school-age children often fail to take into account evidence of the individual's prior deceptive behavior (Lee & Cameron, 2000; Mascaro & Sperber, 2009; Vanderbilt, Liu, & Heyman, 2011; see also chapter 8).

Vanderbilt et al. (2011) presented adult informants to children aged 3, 4 and 5. The informants advised individuals on two occasions about which of two boxes contained a sticker. The goal was to determine whether children would differentiate between helpers, who were shown as happily giving correct advice, and trickers, who were shown as happily giving incorrect advice. The ability to differentiate between informants was assessed behaviorally by children's decision to either accept or reject the advice of each informant concerning the location of a hidden sticker. The ability to differentiate between informants was also assessed through verbal report measures in which subjects were asked about the motives and behavior of informants (e.g., whether they were trying to trick or to help).

The 5-year-olds differentiated between helpers and trickers behaviorally and on the verbal report measures. In contrast, the 3-year-olds showed very high levels of trust for both types of informants, and no tendency to differentiate between helpers and trickers on any of the measures. Four-year-olds differentiated between helpers and trickers on verbal report measures (e.g., they predicted that informants who had been helpful previously would be more likely to provide accurate information in the future). They also showed higher overall levels of skepticism toward informants than did the 3-year-olds. However, like the 3-year-olds, they failed to differentiate between helpers and trickers in their behavioral responses. This pattern of results suggests that young children may have difficulty recognizing the implications of deceptive intent even after they learned how to detect it (see Lee and Cameron, 2000, for related findings).

Heyman, Sritanyaratana, and Vanderbilt (2013) followed up on Vanderbilt et al. (2011) to determine whether 3- and 4-year-olds would show distrust of informants who demonstrate deceptive intent in a salient manner. This study again used a sticker task, and the informant took the form of a familiar story character with malevolent intent: the Big Bad Wolf. This character was depicted using a gray wolf puppet, and children were reminded that he had tricked Little Red Riding Hood. The experimenter explicitly told subjects that the Wolf is "bad" and always gives wrong information. Participants observed the experimenter getting tricked by the Wolf on one demonstration trial, and then observed the experimenter achieve success by rejecting the Wolf's advice on the next demonstration trial. Following each trial, children received material feedback on their performance: they earned a sticker when they rejected the Wolf's advice, and they failed to earn a sticker when they accepted the Wolf's advice. Children also received social feedback: after they rejected the deceptive advice the experimenter verbally acknowledged their success, and when they failed to reject the advice, the Wolf gloated by saying "Ha ha ha ha ha, I tricked you!" Even with these strong cues, the 3-year-olds failed to systematically reject the Wolf's advice, and the 4-year-olds did so on only about three-fourths of the trials.

Why do young children have trouble rejecting information that comes from overtly deceptive informants? One possibility, the *executive function hypothesis*, posits that children's inability to reject deceptive information is due to limitations in executive functioning skills that make it difficult for them to respond in a way that is opposite to what has been indicated by a cue. Heyman, Sritanyaratana, and Vanderbilt (2013) found no support for this hypothesis: performance on executive function tasks such as the day-night task (Gerstadt, Hong, & Diamond, 1994) was uncorrelated with children's ability to reject deceptive advice regardless of whether or not age was controlled for. This lack of correlation is particularly notable because both types of measures require children to reject an item that is being indicated by a cue and then select a different item. (But for evidence in support of the executive function hypothesis, see chapter 8.) Based on their findings Heyman, Sritanyaratana, and Vanderbilt (2013) proposed the *communicative intent hypothesis*, which posits that the difficulty occurs when children conceptualize the task as one in which they must reject intentionally communicated advice, rather than as a task in which they are provided with a completely reliable indicator of which choice *not* to make (see Mascaro & Sperber, 2009; for a related argument in support of the role of communicative intent, see chapter 5).

Beyond the question of how children learn to recognize deception and assess its implications for future behavior, there has been research on reasoning about deception from a moral perspective, including research addressing how children assess the acceptability of lying under various circumstances and whether these judgments differ as a function of age or culture. These issues have typically been explored in contexts in which truth telling comes into conflict with other values, such as the desire to prevent harm.

One focus of research on children's judgments of the moral acceptability of lying has been on lies that serve the goal of politeness, which are sometimes called white lies. White lies lack malicious intent (Bok, 1978) and often concern preferences within the context of social relationships (Bussey, 1999). For example, an individual may claim to like the cake a friend baked for him, even though he really disliked it.

By age 7, children judge white lies more favorably than lies motivated by a speaker's desire to avoid getting in trouble (Bussey, 1999; Heyman, Sweet, & Lee, 2009; Peterson, Peterson, & Seeto, 1983; Walper & Valtin, 1992). Moral evaluations of lying in politeness situations tend to be similar for children in East Asia and in the West (Xu, Bao, Fu, Talwar, & Lee, 2010). However, in Western cultures the focus is on the recipient's emotional well-being, whereas in East Asian cultures the focus is on the social implications for the recipient (i.e., his or her "face" or public persona; Bond & Hwang, 1986).

Another focus of research on children's judgments of the moral acceptability of lying has been on lies that serve the goal of modesty, such as when individuals falsely deny responsibility for their prosocial acts. Children evaluate these types of lies more favorably in East Asia than in the West (Lee, Cameron, Xu, Fu, and Board, 1997). It is likely that this cultural difference results from the strong cultural emphasis on modesty in East Asia. For example, in China, school children are encouraged to be "unsung heroes" (see Lee et al., 1997). Children who grow up in East Asian societies tend to value sacrificing the truth to maintain modesty to an even greater extent in public contexts than in private ones (Fu et al., 2010; Heyman, Itakura, & Lee, 2011). Among adolescents and young adults, approval of modesty-related lying in public is associated with the endorsement of collectivist values (Fu, Heyman, & Lee, 2011; see also chapter 7).

Despite the greater emphasis on modesty norms in East Asia as compared to the West, there are contexts in which avoiding the disclosure of positive information about oneself may be considered more appropriate in the West than in East Asia. One such context involves disclosing one's own successful performance to poorly performing peers. Heyman, Fu, and Lee (2008) found that 10- and 11-year-olds in the US were less likely to approve of disclosure in this context than were their counterparts in China. One likely explanation for this difference is that such disclosure tends to be seen as showing off among children in the US, whereas for children in China it tends to be interpreted as an implicit offer of help to poorly performing students.

A third focus of research on children's judgments about the moral acceptability of lying concerns lies that are told to promote the interests of one's group, sometimes called blue lies (Fu, Luo, Heyman, Wang, Cameron, & Lee, 2013). Fu et al. (2013) found that Chinese participants judged blue lies less negatively than did their American counterparts, and that this difference increased with age. There was also an age-related difference in beliefs about the relative acceptability of lies to promote the interests of different groups. The youngest participants (9- and 11-year-olds) were least critical of blue lies told to benefit a speaker's class, slightly older participants (13-year-olds) were least critical of blue lies told to benefit a speaker's school, and the oldest participants (17-year-olds) were least critical of blue lies told to benefit a speaker's country. This suggests that young children may place the greatest emphasis on smaller groups in which all individuals are likely to be personally acquainted, and that they eventually shift their emphasis to more abstract collectives.

Summary

The results presented in this section suggest that preschool-age children often trust advice from informants who have been observed lying, and that being able to verbally differentiate between informants with deceptive versus helpful intent does not appear to be sufficient to allow children to reject such advice. Children's difficulty with rejecting this type of advice is particularly robust before age 4. Three-year-olds show no evidence of systematically distrusting informants even when the deceptive intent is made highly salient. Preliminary evidence suggests that the act of rejecting advice poses challenges that are social-cognitive in nature rather than simply being a function of executive control. Specifically, it appears that for young children to distrust, they must learn to integrate their knowledge of advice giving, which is generally viewed as prosocial, with their understanding of deceptive intent.

Research on the development of the moral evaluation of lying suggests that by age 7, children differentiate between several different types of lies. There is also evidence that children's reasoning about lies is shaped by the broader cultural values, and that the way children conceptualize relevant cultural values such as those relating to group loyalty may change across development.

Future directions

Future research is needed to further identify the limitations in children's ability to reason about ulterior motives and respond to individuals who show signs of being untrustworthy. This research will need to examine how children's notions of what they find desirable and what they think people should do informs their willingness to consider possible ulterior motives and to formulate appropriate responses to deceptive behavior.

Future research is also needed to better understand how young children's cognitive and moral approach to deception is influenced by their social environment. Although there is now evidence that these conceptions differ as a function of the culture children have been exposed to, and that these differences seem closely related to strong cultural values and socialization practices, the causal mechanisms have yet to be identified. One approach will be to continue measuring the relevant cultural values and examining whether within-culture variation predicts the between-culture variation. Another approach will be to prime values that are thought to be important and then examine the potential consequences for children's reasoning and behavior (see Oyserman & Lee, 2008).

There may also be individual differences in family practices that affect children's reasoning about deception. One possibility concerns children's observations of lying by parents (Heyman, Hsu, Fu, & Lee, 2013; Heyman, Luu, & Lee, 2009). When parents frequently lie to their children or otherwise appear unreliable as sources of information, children may come to view such behavior as more normative and less morally wrong. Children may also learn to treat the claims of unreliable people with skepticism (see Kidd, Palmeri, & Aslin, 2013)

Future research is also needed to identify real-world contexts in which children's reasoning about lying has consequences for their well-being, including how children infer deceptive motives when they are communicating with people they meet online. More information is also needed about how children can be taught to think critically about assessing motivation in these contexts. For example, it will be important to determine when and how to best teach children how to recognize the "promotional intent" in advertisements that are designed to influence the mental states and behavior of the audience by emphasizing positive features of products and deemphasizing negative ones (Moses & Baldwin, 2005).

Finally, it will be important to examine how children's notions of deception are integrated with their broader notions of mental life, and how their reasoning about deception compares with other sources of unreliability, such as deficits in knowledge. For example, even young children have some capacity to distinguish between accuracy and underlying mental states that involve knowledge (Einav & Robinson, 2011; Nurmsoo & Robinson, 2009), and it will be important to assess whether they can also make such distinctions with reference to mental states that involve intentions.

Acknowledgments

I thank Brian Compton for his helpful comments.

References

Banerjee, R. (2002). Children's understanding of self-presentational behavior: Links with mental-state reasoning and the attribution of embarrassment. *Merrill-Palmer Quarterly: Journal of Developmental Psychology, 48*, 378–404.

Banerjee, R., Bennett, M., & Luke, N. (2010). Children's reasoning about the self-presentational consequences of apologies and excuses following rule violations. *British Journal of Developmental Psychology, 28,* 799–815.

Banerjee, R., & Yuill, N. (1999). Children's explanations for self-presentational behaviour. *European Journal of Social Psychology, 29,* 105–111.

Bond, M. H., & Hwang, K. K. (1986). The social psychology of Chinese people. In M. H. Bond (Ed.), *The psychology of the Chinese people* (pp. 213–266). Oxford, England: Oxford University Press.

Bok, S. (1978). *Lying: Moral choices in public and private life.* New York, NY: Pantheon.

Bussey, K. (1999). Children's categorization and evaluation of different types of lies and truths. *Child Development, 70,* 1338–1347.

Ditto, P. H., Pizarro, D. A., & Tannenbaum, D. (2009). Motivated moral reasoning. In B. H. Ross (Series Ed.) & D. M. Bartels, C. W. Bauman, L. J. Skitka, & D. L. Medin (Eds.), *Psychology of learning and motivation, vol. 50: Moral judgment and decision making.* San Diego, CA: Academic Press.

Einav, S., & Robinson, E. J. (2011). When being right is not enough: Four-year-olds distinguish knowledgeable from merely accurate informants. *Psychological Science, 22,* 1250–1253.

Fu, G., Brunet, M. K., Lv, Y., Ding, X., Heyman, G. D., Cameron, C. A., & Lee, K. (2010). Chinese children's moral evaluation of lies and truths—Roles of context and parental individualism-collectivism tendencies. *Infant and Child Development, 19,* 498–515.

Fu, G., & Lee, K. (2007). Social grooming in the kindergarten: The emergence of flattery behavior. *Developmental Science, 10,* 255–265.

Fu, G., Heyman, G. D., & Lee, K. (2011). Reasoning about modesty among adolescents and adults in China and the U.S. *Journal of Adolescence, 34,* 599–608.

Fu, G., Luo, Y. C., Heyman, G. D., Wang, B., Cameron, C. A., & Lee, K. (2013). *Moral evaluations of lying for one's own group.* Manuscript under review.

Gee, C. L., & Heyman, G. D. (2007). Children's evaluation of other people's self-descriptions. *Social Development, 16,* 800–810.

Gerstadt, C. L., Hong, Y. J., & Diamond, A. (1994). The relationship between cognition and action: Performance of children 3 ½–7 years old on Stroop-like day–night test. *Cognition, 53,* 129–153.

Grice, H. P. (1980). *Studies in the way of words.* Cambridge, MA: Harvard University Press.

Heine, S. J. (2001). Self as cultural product: An examination of East Asian and North American selves. *Journal of Personality, 69,* 881–906.

Heyman, G. D., Barner, D., Heumann, J., & Schenck, L. (in press). *Children's sensitivity to ulterior motives when evaluating prosocial behavior. Cognitive Science.*

Heyman, G. D., Fu, G., & Lee, K. (2007). Evaluating claims people make about themselves: The development of skepticism. *Child Development, 78,* 367–375.

Heyman, G. D., Fu, G., & Lee, K. (2008). Reasoning about the disclosure of success and failure to friends among children in the U.S. and China. *Developmental Psychology, 44,* 908–918.

Heyman, G. D., Fu, G., & Lee, K. (2013). Selective skepticism: American and Chinese children's reasoning about evaluative academic feedback. *Developmental Psychology, 49,* 543–553.

Heyman, G. D., Fu, G., Sweet, M. A., & Lee, K. (2009). Children's reasoning about evaluative feedback. *British Journal of Developmental Psychology, 27,* 875–890.

Heyman, G. D., Hsu, A., Fu, G., & Lee, K. (2013). Instrumental lying by parents in the U.S. and China. *International Journal of Psychology, 48,* 1176–1184.

Heyman, G. D., Itakura, S., & Lee, K. (2011). Japanese and American children's reasoning about accepting credit for prosocial behavior. *Social Development, 20,* 171–184.

Heyman, G. D., & Legare, C. H. (2005). Children's evaluation of sources of information about traits. *Developmental Psychology, 41,* 636–647.

Heyman, G. D., Luu, D. H., & Lee, K. (2009). Parenting by lying. *Journal of Moral Education, 38,* 353–369.

Heyman, G. D., Sritanyaratana, L., & Vanderbilt, K. E. (2013). Young children's trust in overtly misleading advice. *Cognitive Science, 37,* 646–667.

Kelley, H. (1973). The process of causal attribution. *American Psychologist, 28,* 107–128.

Kidd, C., Palmeri, H., & Aslin, R. N. (2013). Rational snacking: Young children's decision-making on the marshmallow task is moderated by beliefs about environmental reliability. *Cognition, 126,* 109–114.

Lee, K., & Cameron, C. A. (2000). Extracting truthful information from lies: Emergence of the expression-representation distinction. *Merrill-Palmer Quarterly, 46,* 1–20.

Lee, K., Cameron, C. A., Xu, F., Fu, G., & Board, J. (1997). Chinese and Canadian children's evaluations of lying and truth-telling. *Child Development, 64,* 924–934.

Li, J. (2005). Mind or virtue: Western and Chinese beliefs about learning. *Current Directions in Psychological Science, 14,* 190–194.

Lin-Healy, F., & Small, D. (2013). Nice guys finish last and guys in last are nice: The clash between doing well and doing good. *Social Psychological and Personality Science, 4,* 692–698.

Markus, H. R., & Kitayama, S. (1991). Culture and the self: Implications for cognition, emotion, and motivation. *Psychological Review, 98,* 224–253.

Mascaro, O., & Sperber, D. (2009). The moral, epistemic, and mindreading components of children's vigilance towards deception. *Cognition, 112,* 367–380.

Miller, P. J., Wang, S., Sandel, T., & Cho, G. E. (2002). Self-esteem as folk theory: A comparison of European American and Taiwanese mothers' beliefs. *Parenting: Science & Practice, 2,* 209–239.

Moses, L. J., & Baldwin, D. A. (2005). What can the study of cognitive development reveal about children's ability to appreciate and cope with advertising? *Journal of Public Policy and Marketing, 24,* 186–201.

Nurmsoo, E., & Robinson, E. J. (2009). Children's trust in previously inaccurate informants who were well or poorly informed: When past errors can be excused. *Child Development, 80,* 23–27.

Oyserman, D., & Lee, S. W. S (2008). Does culture influence what and how we think? Effects of priming individualism and collectivism. *Psychological Bulletin, 134,* 311–342.

Peterson, C. C., Peterson, J. L., & Seeto, D. (1983). Developmental changes in ideas about lying. *Child Development, 54,* 1529–1535.

Sun, L. J. (2004). *The deep structure of the Chinese culture.* Guilin, China: Guanxi Normal University Press.

Vanderbilt, K. E., Liu, D., & Heyman, G. D. (2011). The development of distrust. *Child Development, 82,* 1372–1380.

Walper, S., & Valtin, R. (1992). Children's understanding of white lies. In W. Winter (Series Ed.), R. J. Watts, S. Ide, & K. Ehlich (Vol. Eds.), *Politeness in language: Studies in history, theory and practice* (pp. 231–251). Trends in Linguistics: Studies and Monographs, 59. Berlin, Germany and New York, NY: Mouton de Gruyter.

Woolley, J. D., Boerger, E. A., & Markman, A. (2004). A visit from the Candy Witch: Children's belief in a novel fantastical entity. *Developmental Science, 7,* 456–468.

Xu, F., Bao, X., Fu, G., Talwar, V., & Lee, K. (2010). Lying and truth-telling in children: From concept to action. *Child Development, 81,* 581–596.

7 Cultural differences in children's learning from others

Kathleen H. Corriveau, Grace Min,
and Katelyn Kurkul

Introduction

To date, most research on children's selective learning from others has systematically focused on the cues young children use to determine whether or not an informant (or a group of informants) is a trustworthy source. Based on this research, it appears that children use two broad heuristics when determining informant credibility: (1) they attend to available epistemic information about informants, preferring to learn from an informant who has been previously correct (Birch, Vauthier & Bloom, 2008; Koenig & Harris, 2005; Pasquini, Corriveau, Koenig, & Harris, 2007; see Harris & Corriveau, 2011 for a review) and (2) they attend to available social information, preferring to learn from an informant who is met with consensus (Chen, Corriveau, & Harris, 2013; Corriveau, Fusaro, & Harris, 2009; Fusaro & Harris, 2008) or one who is a member of their social in-group (e.g., accent, race, gender, familiarity: Chen et al., 2013; Corriveau & Harris, 2009; Corriveau, Kinzler, & Harris, 2013; Kinzler, Corriveau, & Harris, 2011; Mascaro & Sperber, 2009; Shutts, Banaji, & Spelke, 2010). This work has been instrumental in highlighting children's relative weighting of social and epistemic cues, and in charting the developmental time-course of children's selective learning from others.

The majority of these studies have focused on mean differences in selectivity, without considering differences in children's racial, ethnic, or cultural background. Yet a large body of research in children's developing social cognitive abilities has indicated differences in the development of social cognition as a function of the child's cultural environment. For example, although children's ability to complete a false-belief task emerges around age 4, research by Wellman and colleagues (Shahaeian, Peterson, Slaughter, & Wellman, 2011; Wellman, Fang, Liu, Zhu, & Liu, 2006) indicates that the developmental precursors of false-belief understanding vary by culture. The researchers used Wellman & Liu's (2004) developmental scale that assesses understanding of (a) diverse desires (people can have different desires with respect to the same objects), (b) diverse beliefs (people can have different beliefs about the same situation), (c) knowledge-ignorance (something can be true, but someone might not know that), (d) false belief (something can be true, but someone might believe something different), and (e) hidden emotion (someone can feel one way but display a different emotion). Whereas

Chinese and Iranian children find it easier to understand that someone might not know something that they themselves know (because they do not have access to that knowledge, knowledge-ignorance task), they find it more difficult to understand that someone might hold a belief that they themselves do not share (diverse-beliefs task). By contrast, preschoolers in the United States and Australia display the opposite pattern: they find it easier to understand diverse beliefs than a difference of knowledge based on information access (Wellman et al., 2006; Shahaeian et al., 2011).

One way to interpret this cultural variability in children's emerging understanding of mental states is that knowledge might be construed differently across cultures: as a set of unquestionable facts that are agreed upon, or alternatively, as a set of opinions that are decided individually—similar to desires (Harris & Corriveau, 2013). Indeed, older children's decision to accept evaluative feedback from others echoes this difference in how knowledge is perceived. Chinese children are more willing to take on feedback—even if it is negative—whereas American children put less weight on negative feedback (Heyman, Fu, & Lee, 2013; see also chapter 6).

Based on the work highlighting differences in children's social cognition—specifically in how knowledge is acquired and construed—it is plausible to ask whether children's approach to learning from others is also influenced by culture. In the current chapter, we focus on ethnic and cultural differences in children's learning from others. We focus on the difficult learning task children are faced with when encountering a conflict between their own perceptual evidence and the information conveyed by others. Below, we highlight the basic paradigm we use with young children (a variant of the original Asch, 1956 setup) and discuss our findings with young preschoolers. Next, we focus on differences in children's deference to the consensus based on ethnicity and culture. Finally, we ask why there might be cultural differences in children's relative weighting of their own perception and the information provided by others, and discuss new research highlighting the role of socialization in children's learning. Research suggests that children from Western cultures are more likely to rely on individually based learning, whereas individuals from Eastern cultures are more likely to rely on socially based learning. Based on this framing, we suggest that East Asian children's increased reliance on conformity, a socially based learning strategy, should be considered an appropriate and culturally-relevant learning strategy.

Learning via perception versus learning from others

As part of a larger body of work focusing on children's learning from others, our group and others have found that both children and non-human primates prefer to learn novel information from a consensus over a single dissenter (Chen et al., 2013; Corriveau et al., 2009; Fusaro & Harris, 2008; Haun, Rekers, & Tomasello, 2012). On the one hand, this preference for the consensus makes sense, as it is far more likely that the information to be learned is robust if multiple people endorse it, rather than just one person. Indeed, such faithful conformity is important for social learning (Boyd & Richerson, 1988). Nevertheless, if children blindly rely on the relative frequency of others who endorse specific claims without considering epistemic information, it is likely that they will be led astray at times. Consider, as an example, the classic question put by parents to generations of children: "If all of your friends jumped off of a bridge, would you jump too?" Simply going along with the group without evaluating the group's actions or opinions is a risky endeavor.

To consider children's relative weighting of information provided by a consensus versus the child's available perceptual information, we devised an analogue of the Asch (1956) line length paradigm suitable for preschoolers (Corriveau & Harris, 2010). In a classic series of studies, Asch (1956) asked adults to weight two distinct sources of information—their own perceptual judgment and the reports made by other people. The task was a relatively simple match-to-sample task in which participants were asked to say which line from a set of three matched a target line. Left to their own devices, adults accurately selected the matching line. Yet, when they made their selection in the wake of several other people who had all agreed on a different choice, they were often swayed by this consensus. On about one-third of the trials, they agreed with the consensus, effectively making a 'mistake' that they would not ordinarily make.

In our setup, children were shown (via video) a set of three strips of foam-board (varying by 10% in height), and were asked to choose the "big one." In a pre-test, children were shown triplets of lines in the absence of a consensus. All 3- and 4-year-olds successfully identified the longest line. Then, in test trials, children made the same judgments after having watched a short video clip in which they saw three adults simultaneously point to a short strip when asked to choose the biggest—all three adults pointed to the medium-sized strip on some trials and the shortest on others. Thus, we were able to test the extent to which children would readily abandon their own previous assertion about which line was longest in order to privilege the opinion held by the most people. Note that because children were presented to the consensus via video, we thought it was possible that they might not be swayed at all by a consensus which displayed such blatant inaccuracies.

We found that preschoolers modified their own response to match the (incorrect) adult consensus on about one-quarter of the trials. Specifically, children who failed to choose the longest strip chose either the medium-sized or the smallest strip, depending on what the consensus had indicated moments before. Thus, they were modifying their response to defer to that of the consensus. This deference to the consensus has since been replicated in a live setup using children as informants and verbal responses instead of points (Haun & Tomasello, 2011). Taken together, the results from both of these studies indicate that children, like adults, are prone to yield to the consensus—even when they themselves had previously indicated the correct answer.

However, two other pieces of evidence suggested that children were doing something more than simply yielding to social pressure. First, at the end of the experiment children were invited to say whether the adults (in the video) had been "very good" or "not very good" at answering the questions. As compared to children who never conformed, children who conformed on one or more trials were more likely to judge the adults to be good at answering the questions. Second, when children were asked to say which line the adult consensus had picked out on a given trial, children who had sometimes conformed were likely to say that the consensus had picked out the correct strip: Thus, consistent with social psychological theory on the importance of avoiding cognitive dissonance when explaining one's own prior actions (Aronson, 1969; Cooper & Fazio, 1984; Festinger, 1957). Children explained their conformist responses by misremembering what the adults had done (and thus, remembered conforming to the adults' perceptually correct response), and portraying the adults in a more positive light (i.e., saying they were 'very good' at judging the length of lines). By contrast, children who responded autonomously were more likely to correctly remember the adults' incorrect actions as well as to characterize them negatively (i.e., saying they were 'not very good' at judging line lengths). Taken together, these data suggest that young children are developing a coherent theory to justify their conformist response.

We interpreted these findings to suggest that children were displaying "respectful deference" (Corriveau & Harris, 2010; Harris & Corriveau, 2011, 2013). They entertained the possibility that the consensus had provided accurate information. This interpretation fits well with the two observations made above. Children who sometimes agreed with the consensus were prone to say that its members were very good at answering the questions and had identified the biggest line correctly even if they had not actually done so.

However, children who displayed respectful deference were not fully convinced that the consensus was accurate—nor did such deference actually modify children's perception of the line lengths. To confirm this interpretation, we asked children to engage in a more pragmatic task immediately following their line judgment (Corriveau & Harris, 2010, Study 2). They were asked to choose one of the lines to help a bunny cross a bridge. Only the longest line would complete the bridge. If the child correctly chose the longest line, the bunny would cross the bridge and retrieve a high-value sticker. If the child incorrectly chose one of the two shorter lines, the bunny would not be able to cross the bridge, and would retrieve only a low-value sticker.

As before, we found that children did defer to the incorrect consensus in stating that one of the shorter lines was the longest. However, their responses to the more pragmatic task were quite different: all children correctly chose the longest line in order to receive a high-value sticker. Thus, our data do not support the strong claim that deference actually modifies perception—although our data do suggest that children engage in such socially prescribed deference in certain situations.

Note that although autonomous decision making is emphasized in Western educational systems, privileging autonomous decisions is not a culturally universal practice. For adults, the act of non-conforming is seen as 'deviant' in an East Asian cultural context, whereas it is 'unique' in a Western cultural context (Kim & Markus, 1999). Moreover, all children have access to a socially based learning strategy. Indeed, a large body of research has focused on children's imitation as a mechanism for the transfer of cultural knowledge. In some cases, children are prone to 'over-imitation'—they follow a demonstrated set of rules even if they are inefficient for achieving the perceived goal (Lyons, Damrosch, Lin, Simeone, & Keil, 2011; Lyons, Young, & Keil, 2007; Nielsen & Tomaselli, 2010). Such deferential imitation closely mirrors the pattern just described for children's deference to a consensus.

Conformity across cultures

In the study described above, the rate of conformity amongst Asian-American preschoolers was more than double that of Caucasian-American preschoolers (40% versus 18%, respectively, Corriveau & Harris, 2010). Whereas about 70% of Caucasian-American children were not swayed by the consensus on *any* trial (i.e., they made only correct perceptually based judgments), only about 40% of Asian-American children made only autonomous judgments in the face of a consensus. Although we had not anticipated this large variability based on ethnicity, such a finding is consistent with cultural differences in the development of social cognition (e.g., Wellman et al., 2006; Shahaeian et al., 2011) as well as adult cross-cultural differences in rates of conformity (Bond & Smith, 1996). Note that, in a sense, these data are all the more surprising because Asian-American children were asked to consider information from an out-group of (Caucasian) adult informants, whereas Caucasian-American children were asked to consider information from an in-group.

In a meta-analysis of replications of the Asch paradigm with adults, Bond and Smith (1996) found a robust relationship between the frequency of conformity and the level of collectivism established in survey studies of cross-national variation in values (e.g., Hofstede, 1983). For example, adults in collectivistic countries, where the emphasis is on the group over the individual (Triandis, 1995), had a stronger tendency toward conformist responses than the levels reported by Asch. Moreover, studies conducted in East Asian cultures such as Hong Kong and Japan revealed a greater conformist bias, which support findings that Asian adults are more likely to conform to a majority in various paradigms (e.g., perceptual judgments, opinions on controversial issues) than are Americans (e.g., Huang & Harris, 1973; Meade & Barnard, 1973; see also Frager, 1970; Williams and Sogon, 1984 for characteristics associated with conforming behavior among Japanese adults). These cross-cultural differences in conformity are evident in children as well (Chu, 1979).

Thus, our developmental data replicate and extend the cross-cultural differences shown in adults in the Asch line-length paradigm (e.g., Bond & Smith, 1996), as well as more general differences in social cognitive development described in the introduction. Nevertheless, one limitation of the data presented so far is that we did not collect any information about the families of our Caucasian-American and Asian-American participants. Thus, we do not know the extent to which these differences in deference are a function of socialization or acculturation. Below, we consider the role of socialization and parenting values in children's use of deference as a learning strategy. We then consider how socialization might lead to predicted differences in deference based on acculturation and social context.

Cultural differences in socialization

Given such striking cultural differences in children's deference to a consensus we might ask the extent to which collectivistic and individualistic cultures nurture such respectful deference in early childhood. As cultural and cross-cultural psychologists have demonstrated, human behavior and development, including the act of learning, are situated in sociocultural contexts (e.g., Rogoff, 1993; Vygotsky, 1978). Our review of the literature reveals significant cultural differences in parenting values, parental use of mental-state talk, children's developing understanding of belief, and children's early social referencing, all of which might influence children's approach to learning in novel situations. Such differences in socialization may influence children's relative weighting of social learning strategies versus more independent learning strategies. Below, we outline some cultural differences in socialization and discuss how these differences might lead to variability in learning approaches.

Parenting values

Adult values of conformity vary greatly across individualistic and collectivistic cultures. In the individualistic American culture, conformity is associated with relinquishing one's autonomy and giving in to collective pressure, and is therefore often viewed as a direct violation of Western core cultural ideals (Kim & Markus, 1999; Markus & Kitayama, 1994). Therefore, conformity is discouraged, and asserting individuality in response to group pressure is encouraged (Kim & Markus, 1999). On the other hand, in East Asian culture, which tends to be more collectivistic, asserting one's individuality and separating from the group is deemphasized (Kim & Markus, 1999). Individuals are expected to sacrifice their personal opinions when they conflict with the group and adjust to group norms in order to maintain group solidarity (Markus & Kitayama, 1994).

Given that parents are often children's first teachers and their first interaction with the social world, it is likely that parental sociocultural values will influence the socialization of children. Indeed, prevalent parenting practices in China differ in significant ways from those in North America. Specifically, practices that stress democratic participation, warmth, and acceptance are more pronounced in North American parents. By contrast, cooperative participation and training are more common in the parenting practices of Chinese parents (Chao, 2000; Wu et al., 2002). Similarly, parents of Asian descent (e.g. Taiwanese, Chinese) value conformity, power, and the encouragement of modesty more highly than do European mothers (Suizzo & Cheng, 2007).

Do these parenting values influence children's socialization and early learning? Recent developmental research suggests that parenting values may influence the amount of choice a child has in the learning process. European-American mothers are more likely to elicit and ask their child about emotions, preferences and thoughts, whereas Eastern mothers are more likely to focus on behaviors. This focus on behaviors in Eastern mothers is also reflected in more parent-directed behavior and fewer child-directed choices than Western parent-child dyads (Doan & Wang, 2010). By implication, Western children have more experience with child-directed autonomous decision-making in novel learning situations.

Given the influence of parenting on children's sociocultural learning, it is sensible that children in Eastern cultures might be more inclined to use conformity as a learning strategy because it is a mechanism that is fostered early on by their parents, and because there is a greater need among East Asian children and adults to 'fit in' (Kim & Drolet, 2003; Kim & Sherman, 2007). Thus, when parents adopt a more authoritarian parenting style that is likened to Eastern cultures one could expect that children will more readily conform. By contrast, parents who adopt a more authoritative parenting style might help their children to privilege individual learning strategies over conformity. Note here that although we focus on the difference between Eastern and Western cultures, parenting practices are also likely to be variable within a culture. Thus, it is somewhat misleading to think of conformity-based learning strategies as universally negative—indeed, as mentioned above, the act of non-conforming is seen by East Asian adults as 'deviant' (Kim & Markus, 1999). We suggest that parenting practices and values help children to determine the most efficient mechanisms to learn about the world. Conformity can be seen as a culturally privileged strategy for children's efficient learning about their world.

Mental-state talk

Not only do parenting styles influence parental behavior towards their children, but they also influence parental communication patterns. As previously mentioned, the majority of Eastern parenting styles have demonstrated a proclivity towards regulating children's behaviors (Tardif, Wang, & Olson, 2009). To accomplish this, in East Asian cultures—in particular, in China—parental language serves a regulative function in guiding behaviors and coordinating social interactions. As Hansen (1983) claims, in the Chinese context "the function of words is to engender and express attitudes with implications for action, rather than to express some 'content', such as the speaker's thought" (p. 61). Therefore, the focus of East Asian parent–child conversations is on behavior expectations and cultural norms. In contrast, in Western cultures, language often maps onto "belief psychology," with the function of language being descriptive or representative. That is, in the Western context, communicative language is used to convey meaning, including ideas, thoughts, and concepts (Doan & Wang, 2010). Recent research indicates that American mothers are more likely than Chinese-American mothers to use mental-state words such as 'think,' 'want,' 'know,' when engaging in conversation with their child (Doan & Wang, 2010). Thus, American mothers are more likely than Chinese-American mothers to use language to encourage curiosity and to foster independent thinking. Similarly, European-American mothers are more likely to modulate their assertions than Chinese-American mothers. For example, they are more likely to include words like 'might,' 'maybe,' 'perhaps,' 'possibly,' and so forth when making assertions (Doan & Wang, 2010). Such modulation is consistent with the idea that European-American mothers are more prone to signal the provisional or personal nature of their assertions as compared to Chinese-American mothers.

For this reason, when presented with information that conflicts with their perception or beliefs, children in Western cultures are less inclined than children in Eastern cultures to depend on conformity as a learning strategy. Rather than depend on conformity, children in Western cultures are more likely to focus on perceptually based, autonomous learning strategies.

In sum, although more research is needed to establish the link, it is plausible that European-American preschoolers conceptualize beliefs as personalized claims more readily than Chinese-American preschoolers because they are often involved in family conversations where individualized assertions are voiced and marked as such. Asian-American preschoolers, on the other hand, may be more prone to regard other people's assertions as statements of agreed fact, rather than individual assertions. We suggest that this difference in children's conceptualization of belief is likely to influence children's default learning strategies in novel situations.

Children's understanding of mental states

Children's understanding of mental states is directly related to parent–child talk about mental states. Indeed, such mental state language facilitates children's understanding of belief (Harris, de Rosnay, & Pons, 2005; Meins & Ferneyhough, 1999; Ruffman, Slade, & Crowe, 2002). Before we highlight cultural differences in children's understanding of belief, we first review universal developmental trends in children's understanding of mental states.

As children weight their own judgments against the testimony of others, their interpretation of the informants' psychological states plays a critical role in their decision to defer or not to defer to the consensus. This ability to understand mental states is referred to as Theory of Mind (ToM). Across all cultures examined thus far, research has shown that children fail in false-belief tasks at age 3, but succeed in those tasks by age 5 (Wellman, Cross, & Watson, 2001). Specifically, in comparing children from East Asian and Western cultures, Sabbagh, Xu, Carlson, Moses, & Lee (2006) found that Chinese and American preschoolers performed similarly on Theory of Mind tasks, suggesting a universal trend in the development of children's mental-state understanding.

Although children pass the standard false-belief tasks at similar ages across cultures (Wellman et al., 2001), we mentioned earlier that the acquisition of the precursor skills necessary to pass this task vary systematically across cultures. Specifically, Chinese and Iranian children are able to pass tasks focusing on Knowledge Access (people who perceive an event know about it) earlier than tasks focusing on Diverse Beliefs (different people have different ideas and opinions about the same thing). By contrast, children from Australia and the United States display the opposite developmental pattern: finding tasks requiring understanding of diverse beliefs easier than tasks requiring understanding of differing access to knowledge (Shahaeian et al., 2011; Wellman et al., 2006).

What are the implications of this developmental difference in cultural acquisition of mental-state understanding? As mentioned above, it may be the case that children develop a culturally specific understanding of how beliefs operate. Whereas Eastern children view beliefs as analogous to facts, Western children view beliefs as analogous to opinions. Accordingly, Chinese children, when provided with information—even information that conflicts with their own judgment—might perceive the informants' testimonies as statements of fact, and thus privilege the consensus over their own perception. By contrast, Caucasian-American preschoolers may be more likely to regard the informants' testimonies as expressions of opinions and understand that people can hold different ideas about the same thing.

Given the cross-cultural variation in the developmental progression of ToM, it is not surprising that we find cultural differences in how children understand and acquire knowledge. Whereas in more collectivistic cultures, learning is contextually based and testimonies are construed as knowledge involving a definite mind-to-world fit, in more individualistic cultures learning is much more individually based, relying on one's own logic, with beliefs construed as individualized and subjective.

Early social referencing

A precursor to understanding mental states is children's ability to understand emotional states. Emotion development and emotion regulation are often influenced by the child's social environment. Specifically, young children regulate a negative affect by turning to their caregiver (usually their mother) and referencing her reaction to events (Baldwin & Moses, 1996; Bowlby, 1982; Campos, 1983; Campos et al., 2004; Walden, 1991). Recent research indicates that children as young as 18 months weight the importance of social and perceptual information when deciding to descend a slope (Tamis-LeMonda, Adolph, Lobo, Karasik, Ishak, Dimitropoulou, 2008). They are more likely to privilege social information over perceptual information in situations where the information is uncertain or when they have little experience in similar tasks. Given the difference in parenting styles between Western and Eastern mothers, it is plausible that parental encouragement of autonomy might also lead to an increased trust in the child's own perception over the information from a social other (e.g., their mother). To our knowledge, no such study has explicitly looked at the relation between social referencing and motor development across cultures. This predicted difference in social referencing might be expected due to cross-cultural differences in attachment patterns by 12 months of age (van IJzendoorn & Sagi-Schwartz, 2008). Compared to the rates of attachment styles in the United States, a larger proportion of Asian infants are classified as insecure-ambivalent, which includes a heightened awareness of their mother.

Such cultural differences in the appropriateness of social referencing are also seen in the preschool years—in particular, in parents' perceptions of the appropriateness of their preschoolers' help-seeking behavior for regulating negative or unexpected emotions. Specifically, whereas East Asian, collectivistic mothers view preschoolers' need for reassurance in an emotionally distressing situation (meeting a new stranger) as acceptable, Western, individualistic mothers perceived their child as more problematic if the child clung to the mother or asked for reassurance while distressed (Mizuta, Zahn-Waxler, Cole, & Hiruma, 1996). Although the experimental task we have focused on here (judging the length of lines in the face of an incorrect consensus) may be perceived as less emotionally arousing, viewing a clear conflict between perceptual and adult information is most definitely unexpected. By implication, such emotional experiences with caregivers may lead East Asian children to be willing to resolve the conflict in favor of the adult, whereas American children might be more willing to resolve the conflict in favor of their own perception.

Conformity across generations

If the differences between European-American children and Asian-American children are due to cultural differences in early socialization practices, such as variation in parenting style and family discourse, we would expect these differences to gradually attenuate as parents and their children become more acculturated to American society following immigration. Alternatively, the differences between European-American children and Asian-American children could be due to the Asian-American children's minority status only. On this hypothesis, we might expect Asian-American children to be more deferential than their Caucasian-American counterparts, regardless of the amount of time the Asian-American children had spent in the United States.

To explore this question, we extended the Asch line-length study to consider the influence of acculturation by comparing deference rates among 1st generation Asian-American children (parents born in China and child born in the US), 2nd generation Asian-American children (parents and child born in the US), and at least 2nd generation Caucasian-American children (Corriveau, Kim, Song, & Harris, 2013). In addition to exploring the effect of acculturation on children's deference, we also asked whether the rate of deference depends on the type of setting in which a judgment is made. Half of the children made judgments privately (experimenter hid behind an occluder), whereas the other half made their judgments publicly in the presence of the experimenter, as in Corriveau and Harris (2010).

Two main findings emerged from this research. First, in the public condition, we replicated the difference in the rate of deference between Caucasian-American and Asian-American children found in Corriveau and Harris (2010). Whereas only about 30% of Caucasian-American children defer, about 70% of Asian-American children defer at least once. We had predicted that the reason for the difference in deference between Asian-American and Caucasian-American children would be due to differences in parenting—and thus, we expected to see a difference in deference between our first-generation and second-generation Asian-American participants. This was exactly what we found. Whereas about 55% of second-generation Asian-American children defer, 100% of first-generation Asian-American children defer at least once to the consensus, arguably because of increasing integration into US culture. Note that we do not consider children's deference to be simply social pressure or politeness. Rather, we suggest that children engage in 'respectful deference' by entertaining the possibility that the consensus was actually correct. As in Corriveau & Harris (2010), children's memory for the informant's line judgments and their judgments of the informant's actions were influenced by children's decision on whether or not to defer to the consensus. Thus, we suggest that children are developing a coherent theory to explain their own judgments.

Is it the case that Asian-American children are simply more deferential in general? It could be argued that the difference in deference rates between Asian-American and Caucasian-American children indicates that Asian-American children have a stronger proclivity to choose a consensus-based learning strategy across all situations. Given our hypothesis that parenting style is the mechanism parents use to foster culturally specific learning strategies, a bias towards consensus across all situations is certainly plausible.

An alternative possibility is that Asian-American children are more sensitive to the social aspect of situations, using a consensus-based strategy in a social context only. Indeed, the data from the private setting lend some credence to the second possibility. All three groups of children deferred at rates between 35 and 50%. Thus, whereas deference was related to cultural group in the public setting, this was not the case in the private setting. Moreover, when comparing the public setting to the private setting Caucasian-American and second-generation Asian-American children showed no significant difference in deference rates based on whether they made their judgments in a public or a private setting. By contrast, first-generation Asian-American children were significantly more deferential in the public setting than in the private setting. Thus, we suggest that Asian-American children, especially first-generation Asian-American children, are highly sensitive to the social context—at least when asked to engage in a perceptual task such as judging the length of lines.

To explore whether the difference in deference between first-generation Asian-American and Caucasian-American children is constrained to perceptual judgments only or found in a task where children were asked to evaluate functional information, we presented children with two tools to complete a novel goal (DiYanni, Nasrini, Nini, Kurkul, & Corriveau, under review). One of the tools was functionally efficient, whereas the other tool was functionally inefficient. Critically, prior to deciding which tool to use, children watched a movie where they saw other people making the tool choice. Half of the children watched as a single model chose the functionally inefficient tool (and acted on it three times). The other half watched three models each choose the functionally inefficient tool. Note that all models tried out both tools before ultimately choosing one, thus controlling for the amount of exposure to both tools. As in the Asch line-length setup, if children imitated the actions of the model(s), they would be privileging informant behavior over perceptual/functional behavior.

Our results lend support for the theory that even first-generation Asian-American children do not differ from Caucasian-American children in their global rate of deference. Rather, they selectively privilege the learning from others strategy based on social context. Both Asian-American and Caucasian-American children displayed the same imitation rate for the functionally inefficient tool when just one model had demonstrated it. By contrast, when Asian-American children had watched three informants demonstrate the tool, their rates of imitation were double that of the Caucasian-American participants. These data are consistent with an interpretation that early parent-child socialization may influence children's learning strategies across social contexts, although more research is needed to directly establish this link.

Conclusion

In this chapter, we aimed to highlight cultural differences in children's relative weighting of social information and perceptual information when learning about the world. We focused on the difficult situation of when perceptual and social information conflict and the child is asked to determine which information to weight more heavily. Based on social cognition research as well as cross-cultural research on parenting practices, we predicted that we might see cultural differences in children's strategy use when faced with uncertain situations. We found that Asian-American preschoolers were more likely than Caucasian-American preschoolers to weight social information over perceptual information—especially in situations where the informants were in agreement with one another, and when the child was asked to make decisions in public.

How should we interpret this cultural difference in the relative weighting of social information? We suggest that these differences are a result of distinct differences in parenting and socialization practices, which lead to measurable differences in social referencing, exposure to mental-state talk, and the development of mental-state understanding. Therefore, conformity as a learning strategy can be cultivated through culturally specific practices. Although conformity may have its drawbacks in some learning situations, on the whole, conformity and imitation have developed to allow children to learn culture-specific information.

References

Aronson, E. (1969). The theory of cognitive dissonance: A current perspective. In L. Berkowitz (Ed.), *Advances in experimental social psychology* (vol. 4). New York, NY: Academic Press.

Asch, S. E. (1956). Studies of independence and conformity. A minority of one against a unanimous majority. *Psychological Monographs, 70* (9, Whole No. 416).

Baldwin, D. A., & Moses, L. J. (1996). The ontogeny of social information gathering. *Child Development, 67,* 1915–1939.

Birch, S. A. J., Vauthier, S. A., & Bloom, P. (2008). Three- and four-year-olds spontaneously use others' past performance to guide their learning. *Cognition, 107,* 1018–1034.

Bond, R., & Smith, P. B. (1996). Culture and conformity: A meta-analysis of studies using Asch's (1952b, 1956) line judgment task. *Psychological Bulletin, 119,* 111–137.

Bowlby, J. (1982). *Attachment and loss. Vol. I. Attachment* (2nd ed.). New York, NY: Basic Books.

Boyd, R., & Richerson, P. J. (1988). An evolutionary model of social learning: The effect of temporal variation. In T. Zentall & B. G. Galef (Eds.), *Social learning: Psychological and biological approaches* (pp. 29–48). Hillsdale, NJ: Lawrence Erlbaum.

Campos, J. J. (1983). The importance of affective communication in social referencing: A commentary on Feinman. *Merrill-Palmer Quarterly, 29,* 83–87.

Campos, J. J., Frankel, C.B., & Camras, L. (2004). On the nature of emotion regulation. *Child Development, 75,* 377–394.

Chao, R. K. (2000). Parenting of immigrant Chinese and European American mothers: Relations between parenting styles, socialization goals, and parental practices. *Journal of Applied Developmental Psychology, 21,* 233–248.

Chen, E. E., Corriveau, K. H., & Harris, P. L. (2013). Children trust a consensus composed of out-group members—but do not retain it. *Child Development, 84,* 269–282.

Chu, L. (1979). The sensitivity of Chinese and American children to social influences. *Journal of Social Psychology, 109,* 175–186.

Cooper, J., & Fazio, R. H. (1984). A new look at dissonance theory. In L. Berkowitz (Ed.), *Advances in experimental social psychology* (pp. 229 –262). Hillsdale, NJ: Lawrence Erlbaum.

Corriveau, K., Fusaro, M., & Harris, P. L. (2009). Going with the flow: Preschoolers prefer non-dissenters as informants. *Psychological Science, 20,* 372–377.

Corriveau, K. H., & Harris, P. L. (2009). Preschoolers continue to trust a more accurate informant 1 week after exposure to accuracy information. *Developmental Science, 12,* 188–193.

Corriveau, K. H., & Harris, P. L. (2010). Preschoolers (sometimes) defer to the majority in making simple perceptual judgments. *Developmental Psychology, 46,* 437–445.

Corriveau, K. H., Kim, E., Song, G., & Harris, P. L. (2013). Young children's deference to a majority varies by culture. *Journal of Cognition and Culture, 13,* 367–381.

Corriveau, K. H., Kinzler, K. D., & Harris, P. L. (2013). Accuracy trumps accent in children's endorsement of object labels. *Developmental Psychology, 49,* 470–479.

DiYanni, C., Nasrini, J., Nini, D., Kurkul, K., & Corriveau, K. (under review). The role of consensus and culture in children's imitation of questionable actions. Boston University.

Doan, S. N., & Wang, Q. (2010). Maternal discussions of mental states and behaviors: Relations to emotion situation knowledge in European American and immigrant Chinese children. *Child Development, 81,* 1490–1503.

Festinger, L. (1957). *A theory of cognitive dissonance.* Evanston, IL: Row Peterson.

Frager, R. (1970). Conformity and anticonformity in Japan. *Journal of Personality and Social Psychology, 15,* 203–210.

Fusaro, M., & Harris, P. L. (2008). Children assess informant reliability using bystanders' non-verbal cues. *Developmental Science, 11,* 771–777.

Hansen, C. (1983). *Language and logic in ancient China.* Ann Arbor, MI: University of Michigan Press.

Harris, P. L., & Corriveau, K. H. (2011). Young children's selective trust in informants. *Philosophical Transactions of the Royal Society B, 366,* 1179–1187.

Harris, P. L., & Corriveau, K. H. (2013). Judging for yourself versus listening to others: Conformity revisited. In M. Banaji and S. Gelman (Eds.), *Navigating the social world: What infants, children, and other species can teach us. New York, NY:* Oxford University Press.

Harris, P. L., de Rosnay, M., & Pons, F. (2005). Language and children's understanding of mental states. *Current Directions in Psychological Science, 14,* 69–73.

Haun, D. B. M., Rekers, Y., & Tomasello, M. (2012). Majority-biased transmission in chimpanzees and human children, but not orangutans. *Current Biology, 22,* 727–731.

Haun, D. B. M., & Tomasello, M. (2011). Conformity to peer-pressure in preschool children. *Child Development, 82,* 1759–1767.

Heyman, G. D., Fu, G., & Lee, K. (2013). Selective skepticism: American and Chinese children's reasoning about evaluative academic feedback. *Developmental Psychology, 49, 543–553.*

Hofstede, G. (1983). Dimensions of national cultures in fifty countries and three regions. In J. Deregowski, S. Dzuirawiec, & R. Annis (Eds.), *Explications in cross-cultural psychology* (pp. 335–355). Lisse, The Netherlands: Swets & Zeitlinger.

Huang, L. C., & Harris, M. B. (1973). Conformity in Chinese and Americans: A field experiment. *Journal of Cross-Cultural Psychology, 4,* 427–434.

Kim, H. S., & Drolet, A. (2003). Choice and self-expression: A cultural analysis of variety seeking. *Journal of Personality and Social Psychology, 85,* 373–382.

Kim, H. S., & Markus, H. R. (1999). Deviance or uniqueness, harmony or conformity? A cultural analysis. *Journal of Personality and Social Psychology, 77*(4), 785–800.

Kim, H. S., & Sherman, D. K. (2007). "Express yourself": Culture and the effect of self-expression on choice. *Journal of Personality and Social Psychology, 92,* 1–11.

Kinzler, K. D., Corriveau, K. H., & Harris, P. L. (2011). Preschoolers' use of accent when deciding which informant to trust. *Developmental Science, 14,* 106–111.

Koenig, M. A., & Harris, P. L. (2005). Preschoolers mistrust ignorant and inaccurate speakers. *Child Development, 76,* 1261–1277.

Lyons, D. E., Damrosch, D. H., Lin, J. K., Simeone, D. M., & Keil, F. C. (2011). The scope and limits of overimitation in the transmission of artifact culture. *Philosophical Transactions of the Royal Society B, 366,* 1158–1167.

Lyons, D. E., Young, A. G., & Keil, F. C. (2007). The hidden structure of overimitation. *PNAS, 104,* 19751–19756.

Markus, H. R., & Kitayama, S. (1994). The cultural construction of self and emotion: Implications for social behavior. In S. Kitayama & H. R. Markus (Eds.), *Emotion and culture: Empirical studies of mutual influence* (pp. 89–132). Washington, DC: American Psychological Association.

Mascaro, O., & Sperber, D. (2009). The moral, epistemic, and mindreading components of children's vigilance towards deception. *Cognition, 112,* 367–380.

Meade, R. D., & Barnard, W. (1973). Conformity and anticonformity among Americans and Chinese. *Journal of Social Psychology, 89,* 15–25.

Meins, E., & Ferneyhough, C. (1999). Linguistic acquisitional style and mentalising development: The role of maternal mind-mindedness. *Cognitive Development, 14,* 363–380.

Mizuta, I., Zahn-Waxler, C., Cole, P. M., & Hiruma, N. (1996). A cross-cultural study of preschoolers' attachment: Security and sensitivity in Japanese and US dyads. *International Journal of Behavioral Development, 19,* 141–159.

Nielsen, M., & Tomaselli, K. (2010). Overimitation in Kalahari Bushman children and the origins of human cultural cognition. *Psychological Science, 21,* 729–736.

Pasquini, E. S., Corriveau, K. H., Koenig, M. A., & Harris, P. L. (2007). Preschoolers use past reliability in deciding which informant to trust. *Developmental Psychology, 43,* 1216–1226.

Rogoff, B. (1993). Children's guided participation and participatory appropriation in sociocultural activity. In R. Woxniak & K. Fischer (Eds.), *Development in context: Acting and thinking in specific environments* (pp. 121–153). Hillsdale, NJ: Lawrence Erlbaum.

Ruffman, T., Slade, L., & Crowe, E. (2002). The relationship between children's and mother's mental state language and theory of mind understanding. *Child Development, 73,* 734–751.

Sabbagh, M. A., Xu, F. Carlson, S. M., Moses, L. J., & Lee, K. (2006). The development of executive functioning and theory-of-mind: A comparison of Chinese and U.S. preschoolers. *Psychological Science, 17,* 74–81.

Shahaeian, A., Peterson, C. C., Slaughter, V., & Wellman, H. M. (2011). Culture and the sequence of steps in theory of mind development. (Paper submitted for publication).

Shutts, K., Banaji, M. R., & Spelke, E. S. (2010). Social categories guide young children's preferences for novel objects. *Developmental Science, 13,* 599–610.

Suizzo, M., & Cheng, C. (2007). Taiwanese and American mothers' goals and values for their children's futures. *International Journal of Psychology, 42,* 307–316.

Tamis-LeMonda, C. S., Adolph, K. E., Lobo, S. A., Karasik, L. B., Ishak, S., & Dimitropoulou, K. A. (2008). When infants take mothers' advice: 18-month-olds integrate perceptual and social information to guide motor action. *Developmental Psychology, 44*(3), 734–746.

Tardif, T., Wang, L., & Olson, S. L. (2009). Culture and the development of regulatory competence: Chinese-US comparisons. In S. L. Olson & A. J. Sameroff (Eds.), *Biopsychosocial regulatory processes in the development of childhood behavioral problems* (pp. 258–289). Cambridge, UK: Cambridge University Press.

Triandis, H. C. (1995). *Individualism and collectivism.* Boulder, CO: Westview Press.

Van IJzendoorn, M. H., & Sagi-Schwartz, A. (2008). Cross-cultural patterns of attachment: University and contextual dimensions. In J. Cassidy & P. R. Shaver (Eds.), *Handbook of Attachment: Theory, research, and clinical applications* (2nd edition). New York, NY: Guilford Press.

Vygotsky, L. S. (1978). *Mind in society: The development of higher psychological processes.* Cambridge, MA: Harvard University Press.

Walden, T. A. (1991). Infant social referencing. In J. Garber & K. A. Dodge (Eds.), *The development of emotion regulation and dysregulation* (pp. 69–88). Cambridge, UK: Cambridge University Press.

Wellman, H. W., Cross, D., & Watson, J. (2001). Meta-analysis of theory-of-mind development: The truth about false belief. *Child Development, 72*(3), 655–684.

Wellman, H. M, Fang, F., Liu, D., Zhu, L., & Liu, G. (2006). Scaling of theory-of-mind understandings in Chinese children. *Psychological Science, 17,* 1075–1081.

Wellman, H. M., & Liu, D. (2004). Scaling of theory of mind tasks. *Child Development, 75,* 523–541.

Williams, T. P., & Sogon, S. (1984). Group composition and conforming behavior in Japanese students. *Japanese Psychological Research, 26,* 231–234.

Wu, P., Robinson, C. C., Yang, C., Hart, C. H., Olsen, S. F., Porter, C. L., Jin, S., Wo, J., & Wu, X. (2002). Similarities and differences in mothers' parenting of preschoolers in China and the United States. *International Journal of Behavioral Development, 26,* 481–491.

8 Resolving conflicts between observation and testimony

The role of inhibitory control

Vikram K. Jaswal and Koraly Pérez-Edgar

Introduction

Throughout our lives, we are faced with conflicts between our own beliefs and those of other people. For example, we may believe that the earth is flat, that an uncle would prefer chocolate rather than carrot cake, or that the best way to get from A to B is via C. But these beliefs (formed on the basis of our own observations, inferences, and memories) can be contradicted by what other people tell us. How do we resolve these conflicts?

At one extreme, we could simply refuse to accept anything that did not match what we already believe. Perhaps we are, to borrow a phrase from Paul Harris (2002), "stubborn autodidacts." However, as Harris and others have pointed out, this cannot be the case because, of course, we do come to believe things that conflict with first-hand experience. For example, children eventually recognize that the earth is round even though it appears flat. At the other extreme, we could simply accept anything we were told. This is also unlikely (and ultimately foolish) because people sometimes provide us with information that is intentionally or unintentionally wrong. If we revised our knowledge base on the basis of all testimony, regardless of source or plausibility or coherence, our understanding of the world would be tenuous indeed.

As with many (most?) questions in psychology, the answer to how we resolve conflicts between personal experience and testimony is, "it depends." As adults, it depends on how confident we are in our initial belief, how confident we are in the source of the testimony, and how much discrepancy there is between our belief and the testimony (e.g., Jaccard, 1981). These factors are influenced by how much experience we have with the issue under dispute, as well as situational and personal variables that affect how readily we can "disbelieve" something we are told (e.g., Gilbert, 1991).

This chapter concerns how children resolve conflicts akin to the flat versus round earth example. What do children do when their own observations conflict with what they are told? As we will show, many young children cannot help but believe what they are told, even when there is an incentive to respond skeptically. We will argue that this credulity reflects a robust, specific bias children have to trust testimony. Indeed, responding skeptically requires *actively* inhibiting this bias. We will show that children who are better able to inhibit a prepotent response also tend to be more skeptical about testimony that conflicts with their beliefs. In addition, emerging evidence suggests that the ability to inhibit this prepotent response may be related to broader cognitive and socioemotional behavior patterns over time.

Observation versus testimony

Most people would probably consider beliefs formed on the basis of first-hand experience or personal observation to be superior to those formed on the basis of what someone tells them. Phenomenologically, first-hand experience somehow seems to be a more immediate, direct, and/or faithful source of knowledge than an account that has been filtered through another person. Indeed, John Locke (1690/1961) articulated just such a position when he wrote, "The floating of other men's opinions in our brains makes us not one jot the more knowing, though they happen to be true. What in them was science is in us but opiniatrety" (p. 58). When what someone says conflicts with what has been observed, it seems a reasonable intuition that information acquired through observation would be more compelling than information obtained through testimony (e.g., Gelman, 2009). And yet, as we alluded to above, we have found that children often weight the testimony of others more heavily than their own current beliefs.

Our earliest investigations asked what 2- to 5-year-olds did when an adult referred to an animal or artifact with a name that did not match what the thing looked like (Jaswal, 2004, 2006; Jaswal & Malone, 2007; Jaswal & Markman, 2007). For example, children were presented with a picture of an animal that looked a lot like a cat but had some dog-like features. Baseline trials showed that children spontaneously believed it was a cat. In our work, an adult would then unexpectedly refer to this hybrid animal as a "dog." Using a task designed by Gelman and Markman (1986), the children were asked to decide whether the animal chewed on bones (as dogs do) or drank milk (as cats do).

Two- and 3-year-olds tended to make the inference consistent with the label the adult applied to the animal rather than with its appearance. Older children were ambivalent, sometimes even rejecting outright the adult's testimony (e.g., "That's not a dog! That's a cat!"). Interestingly, we were able to turn believers into skeptics by having the adult hedge when providing the unexpected name ("I think this is a dog"). We could also turn skeptics into believers by having the adult explicitly acknowledge that children would find the unexpected label surprising ("You're not going to believe this, but this is actually a dog").

One question concerns whether children's label-based inferences actually reflected a belief in the unexpected labels the experimenter used, or whether children were simply complying with the pragmatic demands of the task. After all, they were playing an unfamiliar game with an unfamiliar adult authority figure. To investigate this possibility, we conducted another experiment in which we asked whether children would pass the experimenter's unexpected labels on to an ignorant third party (Jaswal, Lima, & Small, 2009). Our reasoning was that they would only do so if they actually believed the experimenter's unexpected labels; otherwise, they would use the perceptually obvious ones. Results showed that children did use the unexpected labels when in conversation with another person, suggesting that they actually believed the testimony even though it conflicted with what we knew their own beliefs would otherwise be.

In the next series of studies, we raised the stakes. Relying on testimony to learn about category membership is sensible because what something looks like is only a rough guide to the category to which it belongs (e.g., Gelman, 2003): Eels look like snakes, but they are actually fish, for example. In contrast, knowledge about the physical world—that, for example, two solid objects cannot pass through each other—is arguably less dependent on testimony from other people. Even non-human primates and 4-month-old infants, who obviously cannot understand testimony, seem to recognize the principle of solidity (Santos & Hauser, 2002; Spelke, Breinlinger, Macomber, & Jacobson, 1992). Whether this kind of knowledge about the physical world is innate or early developing, it clearly does not require input from other people in the way that, say, knowing that an eel is a fish does. Thus, we reasoned, children might not be deferential to testimony about the physical world in the way that they are deferential about category membership.

To investigate this possibility, we set up a situation in which 2.5-year-olds observed a physical event and then heard someone offer testimony that conflicted with what they had just seen (Jaswal, 2010). We used a large wood frame apparatus, originally designed by Hood (1995) to investigate the gravity bias. That is, young children expect that unsupported objects will fall straight down—even when their path is constrained by a visible, curved tube. Three "chimneys" were mounted at equal intervals into the top brace of the apparatus. Three opaque cups were placed in the lower brace of the apparatus, 47 cm beneath the chimneys. Each cup had several stickers with exemplars from a particular category on it (e.g., bears, birds, dogs). Each chimney could be connected to a non-adjacent cup using a tube—in this case, we used clear tubes. Thus, if an object were dropped through the right-most chimney, an observer could watch its trajectory as it traveled inside a clear tube until it fell into the left-most opaque (bird) cup. If someone claimed that it landed in a different cup (e.g., "It's in the bear cup"), this would present a conflict between first-hand experience and testimony. This was the situation that we repeatedly presented to children.

We asked this question of 2.5-year-olds because we knew that they would have the vocabulary to understand the testimony, and because children this age had participated in other studies using this apparatus (Hood, 1995). The procedure was as follows: On each of six trials, an adult experimenter sitting across the table from a child dropped a goldfish cracker down one of the tubes. Once it had fallen into an opaque cup, the experimenter invited the child to indicate (by naming or pointing to) the cup where it had landed. We called this the pre-testimony response of a given trial.

Next, the experimenter turned toward an adult confederate (who was sitting next to the child and who had witnessed the very same event), and she asked him where the goldfish cracker had landed. The confederate always claimed that the cracker had landed in one of the incorrect cups—this was the misleading testimony. At this point, the experimenter returned her attention to the child, and asked him or her to resolve the conflict by making a post-testimony response: "Where should we look?" The experimenter retrieved whichever cup the child indicated on the post-testimony response, and turned it upside down.

If a child identified the correct cup, the goldfish cracker would fall out and the experimenter would hand it to the child to eat. If a child identified an incorrect cup nothing would fall out when the experimenter turned it over. In this case, the child was invited to make another choice until the correct cup (and goldfish cracker) was located. Importantly, however, the child was only offered the gold-fish cracker to eat if his or her first post-testimony response was to the correct cup. Otherwise, when the correct cup was located, the goldfish cracker was put aside. Thus, there was an incentive to ignore or discount the confederate's testimony because it always directed children to an incorrect cup; deferring would result in the loss of a tasty treat. (All children were given several goldfish crackers at the end of the session.)

Children participated in six such trials, with the experimenter dropping the goldfish cracker through a different chimney each time. Our interest was in chil-dren's pre- and post-testimony responses on a given trial: Would those who made correct pre-testimony responses stick with that response even after they had heard the testimony from the confederate? Or, would they switch so that their post-testimony response aligned with the testimony from the confederate even though this conflicted with what they had just seen?

Over the course of the six trials, children's pre-testimony responses were cor-rect, on average, 75% of the time. This is to be expected because, as we have been emphasizing, the tubes were clear and children could track the goldfish's trajec-tory until the moment it fell into an opaque cup. When children were invited to make their post-testimony response after the confederate claimed the goldfish was in a different cup, they were correct just half as often—around 38% of the time. This drop in correct responses was accounted for almost entirely by a concomitant increase in selections of the (wrong) cup mentioned by the confederate.

One might have expected deference early on in the session (when children might not have understood the game), followed by skepticism later (once they realized that the confederate's testimony was consistently wrong). But in fact, we found that the level of deference remained high across all six trials—between 50 and 60%. Children did not become more skeptical as the session went on even though there was an incentive to respond skeptically—namely, finding (and get-ting to eat) the goldfish cracker. In fact, about one-quarter of the children were deferential on five of the six trials (another quarter were skeptical on most of the trials, a point to which we will return below).

Perhaps children were simply complying with the confederate's testimony? Because they did not know what the ramifications would be of contradicting the adult confederate, children may have felt obligated to make their post-testimony responses match his testimony. This seems unlikely for a few reasons. First, 2.5-year-olds are not particularly compliant. Second, the confederate's testimony did not direct children to indicate a particular cup in their post-testimony response. He simply made an assertion: "It's in the bear cup."

Finally, we conducted a control study in which we used exactly the same procedure, but this time, the cups the objects fell into were clear rather than opaque. Thus, children could see the item as it traversed the tube, as they made their responses, and as the confederate provided misleading testimony. Our reasoning was that if children's post-testimony responses in the earlier study reflected compliance, they should also comply in this situation as the social demands of the task also involved an unfamiliar adult offering misleading testimony. In fact, children in this control study did not defer: Both their pre- and post-testimony responses indicated the correct cup nearly 100% of the time. Thus, compliance alone cannot explain why many children in the earlier study so frequently deferred to the confederate's testimony. Instead, it would appear that many children in the earlier study believed the confederate's testimony, even though it conflicted with what they had just seen and with the location they had themselves just indicated in their pre-testimony response.

Biased to believe

Why were many children in Jaswal's (2010) study so credulous? Our hypothesis is that their credulity reflects a robust, default bias to trust testimony (see also Jaswal, 2013). Responding skeptically requires inhibiting the normally appropriate expectation that what people say is true—and as we know from a good deal of research in cognitive development, young children have difficulty with inhibitory control (e.g., Carlson, 2005). In this section, we will flesh out the notion that what people say is normally true, and describe a study that speaks to the specificity of the bias to trust testimony.

As a number of thinkers have pointed out, people normally say what they believe to be true. Sir Thomas Reid (1764/1997), for example, posited a principle of veracity, or "a propensity to tell the truth, and to use the signs of language, so as to convey our real sentiments" (p. 196). Grice (1975) described this particular implicit rule of conversation as the maxim of "quality," the notion that a speaker should not say what she or he believes to be false or make a statement without adequate evidence. In her seminal work on lying, Bok (1978) pointed out that societies institute strong sanctions against those who do not tell the truth. According to Dennett (1981), "The faculty of communication would not gain ground in evolution unless it was by and large the faculty of transmitting true beliefs" (p. 18). Of course, for a variety of reasons, including error, ignorance, and deception, people do sometimes say things that are false. However, this is a relatively rare occurrence. As Reid put it, even the greatest liars speak the truth a hundred times for every lie.

If we accept the proposition that testimony usually involves the transmission of true beliefs, then a bias to believe testimony would be sensible. It would save us the trouble of having to verify for ourselves everything we were told—a time-consuming and frequently impossible task. Indeed, a bias to believe testimony is arguably what allows us to so effortlessly take advantage of other people's knowledge and expertise.

Gilbert (1991) has suggested that in the very act of comprehending something, we as adults are disposed to believe it. We can go back to "unaccept" a piece of testimony, but this requires some cognitive effort. Indeed, Gilbert and his colleagues (e.g., Gilbert, Krull, & Malone, 1990) have shown that when adults' cognitive resources are taxed, they are more likely to misremember as true something they had earlier learned to be false than to misremember as false something they had earlier learned to be true. This asymmetry, Gilbert argued, suggests that the default setting is "believe." Our suggestion is that children, too, are biased to believe, and that responding skeptically to testimony is difficult because it requires inhibiting the normally reasonable expectation that what people say is true.

One important issue that needs to be addressed whenever a bias is invoked as an explanation for behavior is where such a bias would come from. Perhaps the bias to believe testimony reflects a general, undifferentiated trust children have in other people rather than anything specific about testimony. Children are, after all, dependent on other people for just about everything in their lives. Maybe their trust in testimony is a manifestation of the same presumably innate trust that allows them to, for example, accept food from a caregiver—a built-in expectation that others will be helpful or at least will not cause them harm (Baier, 1986).

To investigate whether children's willingness to believe what they are told represents a bias to trust testimony specifically, or a more domain-general bias to trust other people, we compared children's ability to resist misleading information presented via verbal testimony with their ability to resist misleading information presented in a non-testimonial way (Jaswal, Croft, Setia, & Cole, 2010). If children have difficulty responding skeptically regardless of how the misleading information is presented, then perhaps a domain-general bias can explain their sometimes surprising degree of credulity. If, on the other hand, they have more difficulty responding skeptically to testimony than the non-testimonial misleading information, then this would suggest that a more specific bias about testimony is at work.

Three-year-olds played a game in which an experimenter hid a sticker underneath one of two cups (outside the children's view) and invited children to search for it. The experimenter explained that if children found the sticker in the first cup they searched, they would get to keep it. If not, the experimenter would get to keep it. At various points throughout the session, another adult reminded children that the experimenter was being "tricky." Thus, we tried to be explicit from the very beginning that the game was a competitive one.

Children participated in one of two conditions: a testimony condition or an arrow condition. In the testimony condition, after the hiding event, the experimenter asserted that the sticker was in the cup opposite to the one where she had actually hidden it. For example, if the cups were red and blue, and if the experimenter hid the sticker under the red cup, she would say, "It's in the blue cup." The arrow condition was similar, but rather than asserting that the sticker was in the cup opposite to the one where she had hidden it, the experimenter placed a large cardboard arrow pointing downward on the empty cup. This sequence of events was repeated eight times, with pairs of differently colored cups, and the hiding location counter-balanced across trials.

Of the 16 children in the testimony condition, none found the sticker on the first trial. Even though the game had been set up as a competitive one, all children searched in the location indicated by the experimenter's testimony. On the subsequent seven trials, no more than four of the children found the sticker on any given trial. In fact, nine of the 16 children failed to find the sticker on any of the trials—they were misled by the testimony on each one! Much like in the Jaswal (2010) chimney study described earlier, it was almost as if many children could not help but search the location highlighted by the testimony, even though this prevented them from finding (and getting to keep) any stickers.

The 16 children in the arrow condition also all searched the location indicated by the experimenter on the first trial. They evidently expected that the experimenter would use the arrow in a conventional, helpful way (again, even though the game had been described as a competitive one). However, from the third trial on, most children in this condition searched in the location opposite to the one indicated by the arrow, which allowed them to find the sticker; only one of 16 children failed to find the sticker on any of the trials. Clearly, most had learned that a reverse contingency was in effect, that they should not interpret the arrow in the conventional way.

These data suggest that 3-year-olds do have a generic bias to trust insofar as children in both conditions searched in the location indicated by the experimenter on the very first trial. But on subsequent trials, children in the testimony condition clearly had more difficulty not searching the location indicated by the experimenter. This suggests that in addition to whatever undifferentiated trust children may have, they have a specific bias to trust testimony.

In short, responding skeptically in the testimony condition was challenging in Jaswal et al.'s (2010) study because it required inhibiting the normally reasonable expectation that what people say is true. Responding skeptically in the arrow condition was less challenging because children have less experience with arrows than with testimony and arrows are a more abstract representation of communicative intent. As a result, the expectation that people will use arrows in a veridical manner is much less entrenched.

Where would the bias to trust testimony come from? We suggest that it emerges from a generic bias to trust, as children repeatedly experience the correspondence between what they are told and what is the case. One reason to think that it may emerge from an undifferentiated trust is that there is some evidence to suggest that children have very strong expectations about another ubiquitous form of communication that also is also used in a primarily veridical manner—namely, pointing. People usually point to where things are rather than where they are not. Children have a great deal of difficulty not searching where they see someone point, even when there is an incentive not to do so (Couillard & Woodward, 1999), and even when the informant is actually ignorant (Palmquist, Burns, & Jaswal, 2012; Palmquist & Jaswal, 2012). With enough experience, children might very well develop a strong expectation that other communicative devices (e.g., arrows) will be used veridically.

Linking inhibition to skepticism

If responding skeptically to testimony requires inhibiting the expectation that what people say is true, then perhaps those who are better able to exert inhibitory control would also be better able to respond skeptically. We set out to investigate this possibility by replicating the chimney study described earlier (Jaswal, 2010), and examining how children's deference or skepticism on that task related to their ability to inhibit a prepotent response in an entirely different domain. Recall that, on average, 2.5-year-olds in the initial study were deferential to an adult confederate who claimed that a goldfish cracker had landed in a location different from where children had just seen it land. However, there were individual differences in performance on this task, with some children deferring on most of the six trials, and others rarely or never doing so.

In the replication, we recruited another sample of 58 children, and expanded the age range to include 2.5- to 3.5-year-olds (the average age was 35 months). Children participated in the chimney task as in Jaswal (2010), and also in several additional tasks that we had reason to believe could be related to individual differences in skepticism. Here, in keeping with the theme of this chapter, our focus will be on inhibitory control.

The inhibitory control task we used was computerized, presented on a touch-screen, and adapted from a spatial conflict task designed by Gerardi-Caulton (2000) and Rothbart, Ellis, Rueda, and Posner (2003). Children were told that they were going to play a game, the goal of which was to help various Sesame Street characters find their homes. In the lower left and lower right corners of the touchscreen, the outlines of two identical houses appeared. Inside each house was a different character—say, Bert on the left and Ernie on the right. On each of eight practice trials, either Bert or Ernie would appear, centered and above the two houses, and children were instructed to touch the character's house as quickly and as accurately as they could. When children made a correct response, the character in the house would bounce up and down for two seconds. When children made an incorrect response, the screen would go dark for two seconds. Children had no difficulty understanding the game (and indeed enjoyed the interactive nature of it—one reason we chose this particular task). All were able to move on to the test trials.

On test trials, the two houses appeared at the bottom of the screen, each with a different Sesame Street character inside as in the practice trials. This time, however, the target character appeared either above the matching house ("compatible trials") or above the opposite house ("incompatible trials"). The incompatible trials present what Rothbart et al. (2003) call a "natural conflict" because even adults have a strong tendency to make a response consistent with the side on which a stimulus appears (see Lu & Proctor, 1995). Responding correctly on incompatible trials thus requires inhibiting this prepotent response. Previous research has shown that children are less accurate at responding on the incompatible than the compatible trials (Gerardi-Caulton, 2000; Rothbart et al., 2003). (Previous research has also shown that children—and adults—are generally slower to respond to incompatible than compatible trials, but our reaction time data were unfortunately not reliable and so we will focus only on accuracy.) Children received 16 compatible trials and 16 incompatible trials. Trials were blocked such that children received four compatible and four incompatible trials, randomly ordered, within each of four blocks. Each block involved a different pair of Sesame Street characters.

On the chimney task, we found the same pattern of responses as in the Jaswal (2010) study described earlier: Children had no difficulty identifying the cup into which the goldfish cracker had fallen on their pre-testimony responses. But after hearing the adult confederate claim that it had landed in a different (incorrect) cup, many children claimed that it had landed in that cup, responding in a deferential way.

There was considerable variability, however, in how often children did this. Of the 58 participants, 20 never deferred to the misleading testimony on any of the six trials, and 15 deferred on all or all but one of the trials. Note that we are measuring deference conservatively here: "Deference" was defined as responding correctly on the pre-testimony choice and *then* switching to match the adult confederate on the post-testimony response of that trial. Trials on which children were wrong both pre- and post-testimony were not considered to represent deference even though the adult's incorrect testimony might have influenced them.

On the inhibitory control task, we found that, as a group, children were significantly more accurate on the compatible trials than on the incompatible ones, consistent with previous research (Gerardi-Caulton, 2000; Rothbart et al., 2003): they responded correctly, on average, to 12.5 of the 16 compatible trials, and 10.9 of the 16 incompatible ones. But our interest was in the relation between children's deference or skepticism on the chimney task and their performance on the inhibitory control task. Recall that our hypothesis was that responding skeptically might require actively inhibiting the expectation that what people say is true. Thus, children who are better able to inhibit a prepotent response might be better able to respond skeptically. Indeed, this is what we found.

First, we calculated for each subject an interference score, representing how much more difficult they found the incompatible trials to be compared to the compatible ones. This score was calculated by taking the difference between the number of compatible trials correct and the number of incompatible trials correct, and dividing by the number of compatible trials correct (Gerardi-Caulton, 2000). The difficulty score ranged from −1.0 to +1.0. Interference scores greater than 0 represent more difficulty on the incompatible trials than the compatible ones; interference scores less than 0 represent the reverse. Next, we split the children into two groups based on their performance on the chimney task: a "skeptical" group, children who deferred to the adult confederate on fewer than half of the trials (33 children); and a "deferential" group, children who deferred on three or more of the six trials (25 children). The two groups did not differ in age.

Results showed that children in the skeptical group had an interference score of, on average, 0.02, which of course does not differ from 0: They found the incompatible trials to be no more difficult (or easy) than the compatible ones. In contrast, children in the deferential group had an interference score of, on average, 0.19, which is significantly different from 0. They found the incompatible trials to be more difficult than the compatible ones. The average interference scores differed significantly between the two groups. Children who responded skeptically on the chimney task tended to be better able to manage the inhibitory control challenge involved in the spatial conflict task.

These data, then, lend support to the notion that one reason young children may be so credulous is because responding skeptically requires inhibiting the expectation that what people say is true. It's worth noting that the relationship between inhibitory control and skepticism could have gone in the opposite direction. At the start of this work, it seemed to us that a reasonable prediction could be that inhibitory control is required to respond deferentially on the chimney task—that the prepotent response would be responding on the basis of first-hand experience, in which case inhibition would be required to instead do so on the basis of testimony. In fact, however, that does not seem to have been the case: The thing that takes effort is ignoring the testimony, not ignoring personal observation. This may be particularly true when the testimony concerns something to which the child no longer has perceptual access (e.g., the cup that the child believed the ball was in was opaque). However, see chapter 6 for a null result.

Inhibitory control is a core component of a broader temperamental trait, effortful control, which, in turn, is defined as the ability to inhibit a dominant response in the service of performing a subdominant response (Rothbart & Rueda, 2005). Effortful control is also invoked when individuals must detect errors in the midst of performance or must engage in planning in anticipation of performance. It is seen as a core tool in the child's arsenal, needed to both self-regulate and integrate oneself as an adaptive member of the larger social environment. Thus, individual differences in effortful control have been associated with the development of theory of mind (Carlson, Moses, & Breton, 2002), the emergence of conscience and empathy (Kochanska, Murray, & Coy, 1997), levels of academic success (Checa & Rueda, 2011), and the quality and quantity of peer relationships (Valiente, Lemery-Chalfant, Swanson, & Reiser, 2008). Effortful control is often considered the regulatory component of temperament and can be contrasted with more reactive components such as surgency/extraversion and negative affect (Rueda, 2012).

Given our initial, intriguing finding that children who were more skeptical on the chimney task had less difficulty on the inhibitory control touchscreen task, we investigated whether performance on the chimney task was also related to changes in effortful control over time. We invited the children from our original study for a follow-up visit approximately one year later, and 40 of the original 58 were able to return to the laboratory. We did not repeat the chimney and touchscreen tasks at this second time point as they were no longer developmentally appropriate—children approaching age 4 perform so well that there is little observable variability.

To examine performance-linked changes in effortful control, we carried out a regression analysis using parental report on the Early Childhood Behavior Questionnaire (ECBQ; Putnam, Gartstein, & Rothbart, 2006), which parents completed at both time points. The ECBQ assesses temperament in toddlers and pre-school children. Designed as an "upward extension" of infant temperament measures, the ECBQ captures individual variation across 18 scales that encompass emotional (e.g., fear, frustration) and motoric (e.g., activity level, perceptual sensitivity) reactivity as well as regulatory mechanisms (e.g., attention focusing, soothability). These categories, in turn, create a three-factor structure that reflects broad profiles of reactivity and regulation: Negative affect, surgency/extraversion, and effortful control.

Within the analysis we looked to see if the child's level of skepticism on the chimney task at time 1 was associated with his or her level of effortful control at time 2, even after controlling for the profile at time 1. Skepticism scores from time 1 ranged from 0 (most skeptical, never deferred) to 6 (least skeptical, always deferred).

Parent report of children's levels of effortful control on the ECBQ at time 1 were highly predictive of their report of effortful control at time 2. Children's skepticism on the chimney task at time 1 did not directly predict effortful control at time 2. However, there was a significant interaction between skepticism and effortful control at time 1 when predicting effortful control at time 2.

To examine this interaction, we divided the children into the skeptical and deferential groups used to examine performance in the touchscreen task at time 1. (Skeptical children deferred 0–2 times on the chimney task at time 1; deferential children deferred 3–6 times.) Skeptical children had high levels of effortful control at time 1, which is consistent with their relatively good performance on the inhibitory control touchscreen task, and maintained those levels at time 2. In contrast, the deferential children's levels of effortful control increased from time 1 to time 2, reaching levels comparable to the level of effortful control shown by skeptical children a year earlier. This appears to be an important developmental progression as our data also suggest that over the course of the year as effortful control increased, the deferential children became less impulsive, less frustrated and less fearful, while also being more soothable and showing greater attentional control.

Thus, it appears that the ability to *judiciously* set aside the inherent bias to trust testimony, particularly when the testimony comes from a speaker who is repeatedly incorrect, may be an important marker for, or reflection of, a growing flexibility in the way children come to internalize outside information. This ability, in turn, may help the children navigate a broader social realm and regulate reactive or prepotent impulses.

Conclusion

Young children have an early emerging and robust predisposition to trust and rely on adult testimony. This bias serves as an efficient learning mechanism, allowing children to acquire new information indirectly, without having to experience everything for themselves. However, there are circumstances when children have to resolve conflicts between what someone says and what the children already believe. The studies summarized here suggest that responding skeptically to testimony can pose a challenge to young children, though there are considerable individual differences. One source of these differences seems to involve inhibitory control. Interestingly, a child's level of skepticism may help predict parent-reported change in effortful control over time. This research program represents an initial step toward understanding why it can be so difficult for children (and adults) to achieve a healthy balance between credulity and skepticism.

Acknowledgments

The research described here was supported by NICHD Grant HD-053403 to VKJ, NIMH grant MH-094633 to KPE, and by a grant from the Jacobs Foundation to VKJ and KPE. We thank the families who participated, as well as the research assistants and graduate students who helped to conduct the research described here.

References

Baier, A. (1986). Trust and anti-trust. *Ethics, 96,* 231–260.
Bok, S. (1978). *Lying.* New York, NY: Random House.
Carlson, S. M. (2005). Developmentally sensitive measures of executive function in preschool children. *Developmental Neuropsychology, 28,* 595–616.
Carlson, S. M., Moses, L. J., & Breton, C. (2002). How specific is the relation between executive function and theory of mind? Contributions of inhibitory control and working memory. *Infant and Child Development, 11,* 73–92.
Checa, P., & Rueda, M. R. (2011). Behavioral and brain measures of executive attention and school competence in late childhood. *Developmental Neuropsychology, 36,* 1018–1032.
Couillard, N. L., & Woodward, A. L. (1999). Children's comprehension of deceptive points. *British Journal of Developmental Psychology, 17,* 515–521.
Dennett, D. C. (1981). *Brainstorms: Philosophical essays on mind and psychology.* Cambridge, MA: MIT Press.
Gelman, S. A. (2003). *The essential child: Origins of essentialism in everyday thought.* Oxford, UK: Oxford University Press.
Gelman, S. A. (2009). Learning from others: Children's construction of concepts. *Annual Review of Psychology, 60,* 115–140.
Gelman, S. A., & Markman, E. M. (1986). Categories and induction in young children. *Cognition, 23,* 183–208.
Gerardi-Caulton, G. (2000). Sensitivity to spatial conflict and the development of self-regulation in children 24–36 months of age. *Developmental Science, 3,* 397–404.
Gilbert, D. T. (1991). How mental systems believe. *American Psychologist, 46,* 107–119.
Gilbert, D. T., Krull, D. S., & Malone, P. S. (1990). Unbelieving the unbelievable: Some problems in the rejection of false information. *Journal of Personality and Social Psychology, 59,* 601–613.
Grice, H. P. (1975). Logic and conversation. In P. Cole & J. L. Morgan (Eds.), *Syntax and semantics: Vol. 3. Speech acts* (pp. 41–58). New York, NY: Seminar Press.
Harris, P. L. (2002). Checking our sources: The origins of trust in testimony. *Studies in History and Philosophy of Science, 33,* 315–333.
Hood, B. M. (1995). Gravity rules for 2- to 4-year-olds? *Cognitive Development, 10,* 577–598.
Jaccard, J. (1981). Toward theories of persuasion and belief change. *Journal of Personality and Social Psychology, 40,* 260–269.

Jaswal, V. K. (2004). Don't believe everything you hear: Preschoolers' sensitivity to speaker intent in category induction. *Child Development, 75,* 1871–1885.

Jaswal, V. K. (2006). Preschoolers favor the creator's label when reasoning about an artifact's function. *Cognition, 99,* B83–B92.

Jaswal, V. K., (2010). Believing what you're told: Young children's trust in unexpected testimony about the physical world. *Cognitive Psychology, 61,* 248–272.

Jaswal, V. K. (2013). Biased to believe. In M. R. Banaji & S. A. Gelman (Eds.), *Navigating the social world: What infants, children, and other species can tell us* (pp. 241–244). New York, NY: Oxford University Press.

Jaswal, V. K., Croft, A. C., Setia, A. R., & Cole, C. A. (2010). Young children have a specific, highly robust bias to trust testimony. *Psychological Science, 21,* 1541–1547.

Jaswal, V. K., Lima, O. K., & Small, J. E. (2009). Compliance, conversion, and category induction. *Journal of Experimental Child Psychology, 102,* 182–195.

Jaswal, V. K., & Malone, L. S. (2007). Turning believers into skeptics: 3-year-olds' sensitivity to cues to speaker credibility. *Journal of Cognition and Development, 8,* 263–283.

Jaswal, V. K., & Markman, E. M. (2007). Looks aren't everything: 24-month-olds' willingness to accept unexpected labels. *Journal of Cognition and Development, 8,* 93–111.

Kochanska, G., Murray, K., & Coy, K. C. (1997). Inhibitory control as a contributor to conscience in childhood: From toddler to early school age. *Child Development, 68,* 263–277.

Locke, J. (1690/1961). In P. H. Nidditch (Ed.), *An essay concerning human understanding.* Oxford, UK: Oxford University Press.

Lu, C., & Proctor, R. W. (1995). The influence of irrelevant location information on performance: A review of the Simon and spatial Stroop effects. *Psychonomic Bulletin and Review, 2,* 174–207.

Palmquist, C. M., Burns, H. E., & Jaswal, V. K. (2012). Pointing disrupts preschoolers' ability to discriminate between knowledgeable and ignorant informants. *Cognitive Development, 27,* 54–63.

Palmquist, C. M., & Jaswal, V. K. (2012). Preschoolers expect pointers (even ignorant ones) to be knowledgeable. *Psychological Science, 23,* 230–231.

Putnam, S. P., Gartstein, M. A., & Rothbart, M. K. (2006). Measurement of fine-grained aspects of toddler temperament: The Early Childhood Behavior Questionnaire. *Infant Behavior and Development, 29,* 386–401.

Reid, T. (1764/1997). In D. R. Brookes (Ed.), *An inquiry into the human mind on the principles of common sense.* University Park, PA: Pennsylvania State University.

Rothbart, M. K., Ellis, L. K., Rueda, M. R., & Posner, M. I. (2003). Developing mechanisms of temperamental effortful control. *Journal of Personality, 71,* 1113–1144.

Rothbart, M. K., & Rueda, M. R. (2005). The development of effortful control. In U. Mayr, E. Awh, & S. Keele (Eds.), *Developing individuality in the human brain: A tribute to Michael I. Posner* (pp. 167–188). Washington, DC: American Psychological Association.

Rueda, M. R. (2012). Effortful control. In M. Zentner & R. L. Shiner (Eds.), *Handbook of temperament* (pp. 145–168). New York, NY: Guilford Press.

Santos, L. R., & Hauser, M. D. (2002). A non-human primate's understanding of solidity: Dissociations between seeing and acting. *Developmental Science, 5,* F1–F7.

Spelke, E. S., Breinlinger, K., Macomber, J., & Jacobson, K. (1992). Origins of knowledge. *Psychological Review, 99,* 605–632.

Valiente, C., Lemery-Chalfant, K., Swanson, J., & Reiser, M. (2008). Prediction of children's academic competence from their effortful control, relationships, and classroom participation. *Journal of Educational Psychology, 100,* 67–77.

9 Trust in others' versions of experience

Implications for children's autobiographical memory

Gabrielle F. Principe

Introduction

As indicated by the various strands of research in this volume, children's conceptualization of the world is markedly shaped by the testimony of others. Children can come to represent the location of a hidden object or classify a novel entity on the basis of what other people tell them. Their understanding of faraway places and historic events is driven by information supplied by others. In these cases, children are dependent on testimony because they lack firsthand experience. But this is not to say that direct experience plays no role. Children surely draw on knowledge gained from their experiences to represent phenomena they have never seen but only heard about. For example, when children learn about Disney World, they may use their memory of a neighborhood carnival to conjure up images of rides and other attractions. Similarly, when grandparents tell stories of one-room school houses, children may make use their current school experiences to generate a representation of their grandparents' classroom.

In these instances, information gained from others works to supplement existing knowledge in children's formulations. At other times, others' claims about the world can contradict children's experiences. When this happens, children either can stick to their existing representations or defer to the suggestions of others. There are a range of contexts in which children defer and rework their beliefs on the basis of newly gathered testimony. For instance, even though the earth appears flat and seems motionless, children accept that it is round and rotates (Siegal, Butterworth, & Newcombe, 2004). Likewise, despite no observable evidence for germs or dinosaurs, most children believe in their reality (Harris, Pasquini, Duke, Asscher, & Pons, 2006; see chapter 2). Children's willingness to hold such beliefs demonstrates that testimony can trump firsthand experience.

Just as children's formulations of the world are informed by testimony, children's memory for their experiences can be shaped by what others tell them. This may seem like a dubious claim because memory, in many respects, is an individual phenomenon. Children's memories of their lives exist within their own mental systems, and internal processes, such as personal expectations, goals, and emotions, shape children's representations and reports of experience. Yet memory is also social in nature. Talking about personal experiences with friends and family is a common social activity. Such discourse serves important social functions, such as building relational bonds, nurturing connectedness, and fostering a sense of shared history (see e.g., Nelson, 1993), but these interactions also can have mnemonic consequences. When children reminisce about the past, they are constantly encountering others' versions of experience. When these versions differ from their own—either because conversational partners have unwittingly misremembered the past or deliberately invented new details—children are faced with a dilemma similar to that experienced when they hear that the world is round or their hands are covered with germs. Children either can ignore the contrasting version of experience or update their existing representation to incorporate the newly gathered details. Similarly, knowledge gained from others before and during events can create expectations about children's experiences. When accepted, such expectations can influence how children interpret and encode what they see and hear.

This conceptualization of memory as shaped by the contributions of others is consistent with the constructivist view of memory originally articulated by Bartlett (1932). In this framework, memory is conceived of as a dynamic process in which internal factors, such as beliefs, feelings, and goals, and external factors, such as the testimony of others, combine with perception to build a representation of experience. Thus, event representations are imperfect representations of reality made up of more and different information than that available during the original experience. This perspective also characterizes the encoding process as extending beyond the generation of the initial representation (Baker-Ward, Ornstein, & Starnes, 2009). When individuals are exposed to new information that leads them to reconceptualize a past event, they revise the existing representation to conform to their current understanding. Consequently, memories of experience constantly are subject to condensations, embellishments, and distortions.

Much research into the mnemonic influence of others on children's memories has focused on the facilitative effects of memory-sharing conversations. For instance, event-relevant information supplied by more-knowledgeable others can help children formulate better organized and more elaborated representations of their experiences. To illustrate, when medical technologists helped children make sense of a novel radiological procedure by telling them what to expect, children were better able than others who received less preparation to later recall the details of their experience (Principe, Myers, Furtado, Merritt, & Ornstein, 1996). This boost in memory presumably occurred because the adult explanation improved children's ability to understand and represent this unfamiliar event. Other research has shown that dialogues that take place after events also can aid memory. For example, children who talked with an interviewer about a recent routine physical examination evidenced higher levels of spontaneous recall during a subsequent opportunity to discuss the procedure (Principe, Ornstein, Baker-Ward, & Gordon, 2000).

The facilitative effects of testimony on memory notwithstanding, knowledge gained from others also can lead to errors in remembering, especially when incorrect information is shared. Several lines of research in our lab demonstrate that children are surprisingly prone to recall misleading information gathered from others. Just as testimony can override observational data in children's formulations of the world, it also can trump firsthand experience in children's representations of personal events. This chapter offers a selective overview of three strands of work in which we explore conditions under which children's memories of experience can be swayed by the contributions of others. The first line focuses on how testimony that endorses the reality of mythical entities, such as the Tooth Fairy, can shape children's memory for certain types of events. The second area centers on how testimony in the form of rumors can contaminate children's memory for past events. Finally, the third set of studies examines how testimony from mothers can serve as a source of misinformation when they hold false beliefs about their children's experiences.

Testimony about myths

Most young children believe in the reality of culturally endorsed fantasy beings, such as ghosts and witches (e.g., Sharon & Woolley, 2004), and in event-related figures, such as Santa Claus and the Tooth Fairy (e.g., Harris, Brown, Marriott, Whittall, & Harmer, 1991; see also chapter 2). These myths are not generated by children themselves, but rather are presented ready-made by parents and widely endorsed by the community. The supernatural powers of these entities might seem too farfetched for acceptance (e.g., the Tooth Fairy knows when and where children lose teeth). But there often are strong demands to believe (e.g., a threat of no presents under the Christmas tree for disbelievers in Santa Claus) accompanied by seemingly tangible evidence of the reality of these beings, such as Easter baskets filled with candy or primary teeth replaced with prizes. Given the constructive nature of memory, not only might stories about a bunny that leaves candy or an elf who delivers toys encourage belief in mythical beings, they also might cause children to interpret and remember certain events in fantastical terms.

To examine this issue, we asked 5- to 6-year-olds with varying degrees of belief in the Tooth Fairy to recall their most recent tooth loss (Principe & Smith, 2008). We found that children who denied or only partially believed in the reality of the Tooth Fairy generally constrained their reports to mundane descriptions of their tooth loss and non-supernatural accounts of common Tooth Fairy rituals. By contrast, children who fully believed provided quite fantastic reports, embellished generously with accounts of events that could not have been real but that are consistent with the myth. For example, some described how the Tooth Fairy left money under their pillows and others recounted how she flew in through their bedroom windows.

Interestingly, many of these fantastic statements were triggered by actual occurrences that children interpreted in ways consistent with their fantastic expectations. To illustrate, consider the following exchange with 5-year-old Ben:

Int:	Tell me what happened when you lost your baby tooth?
Child:	The Tooth Fairy died.
Int:	She died? What? What happened?
Child:	Fluffy ate the Tooth Fairy.
Int:	Fluffy? Who's Fluffy?
Child:	My cat!
Int:	Your cat? Well, now how do you know that Fluffy ate the Tooth Fairy?
Child:	Because I saw him. He had fairy dust all over his mouth! Everywhere! His tongue, his teeth, his lips. My mom said it's not true, but I know Fluffy ate her.

We know that this and many other seeming fantastic stories were based on misinterpretations of actual experiences because parents provided independent accounts of their children's tooth loss and rituals in support of the myth. In this case, Ben's mother sprinkled glitter on his bed as evidence of the Tooth's Fairy's visit. Fluffy, who sleeps with Ben, somehow got glitter on its muzzle. So Ben's report of Fluffy eating the Tooth Fairy is not a fabrication based on pretense. Rather, expectations created by his parents regarding the Tooth Fairy led him to interpret a witnessed event, namely glitter on his cat's face, incorrectly, but in line with his beliefs.

One of the most intriguing findings is that the majority of full believers recalled actually seeing or hearing the Tooth Fairy on the night of their tooth loss. This subset of believers were exposed to especially high levels of concrete evidence in support of the Tooth Fairy (e.g., letter from the Tooth Fairy, window left open, glitter in bedroom), suggesting that testimony combined with seemingly tangible evidence puts children at risk for formulating memories of phenomenal experiences consistent with culturally endorsed myths.

Given that memories originating in experience usually include sensory details (Sluzenski, Newcombe, & Ottinger, 2004), the frequent claims of seeing and hearing the Tooth Fairy suggest that at least some of the children's descriptions of mythical experiences were due to genuine memory errors. By contrast, some may have construed the interview as an invitation to engage in pretense and deliberately reported their fantasies as real. To distinguish between these two alternatives, we altered the demands of the interview and asked some children to provide an exactly true report and others to give a fun account.

Most of the believers reported supernatural experiences consistent with the myth under both sets of recall instructions. By contrast, those who understood the myth's fictionality recalled mainly realistic experiences regardless of condition. Children with equivocal beliefs, however, evidenced a different pattern under the two sets of instructions—they described mostly realistic experiences in the truthful condition but fantastic events in the fun condition, suggesting that they were somewhat able to switch control from the make-believe to the real when motivated to do so. Given the inability of believers, but not uncertains, to modulate their reports on the basis of recall instructions, it seems that certainty in the existence of the Tooth Fairy led to genuine memory errors. Thus these data suggest that fantastic expectations engendered by the testimony of others can shape not only children's reports of experience, but also their underlying beliefs about what happened.

Rumors as testimony

In everyday life, one common means by which children encounter new information from others about their experiences is through rumor. There are several reasons to suspect that rumor has much potential to influence children's memory for the past. First, rumors have no definite factual basis but are passed along as if they do. Second, individuals generally assume that information exchanged during the course of conversations is true. To illustrate the potential impact of rumor, consider the following exchange with 4-year-old Emma:

Int: Tell me what happened when Magic Mumfry visited your school.
Child: Mumfry lost his rabbit. It runned away.
Int: Tell me more about that.
Child: The rabbit, it jumped out and Mumfry couldn't find it.
Int: Then what happened?
Child: Then we see it, the rabbit. We see it hiding under Miss Marie's desk and we screamed! It goes jumping out!
Int: Did anything else happen?
Child: Chewing, we heared it . . . chewing in the toybox, like on *our* toys. And I, so I, got a bucket to catch it and I said, "Good rabbit, come here rabbit" and it comes hopping out and hop hop hop out the window.

There are several noteworthy aspects of this conversation. First, Emma's account is coherent and well-organized. It shows that, like most children her age, she has mastered some of the fundamental narrative skills for recounting personal experiences. Second, none of the things that Emma reports actually happened. Her entire report is false. There was no rabbit in her school on the day of Mumfry's visit. Third, and most significant to this volume, Emma was a participant in a study in which some of her classmates heard an adult say that Mumfry's rabbit got loose in the school on the day of the show, so it is possible that they shared this information with Emma. But there is more to the story. The adult never said anything about the rabbit hiding under a desk, chewing on toys, or hopping out of a window. So how did these details become part of the story of what happened during Mumfry's visit? This next section of the chapter explores how rumor and the dialogue it prompts can engender such errors in children's memory.

In this investigation, 3- to 5-year-olds saw a scripted magic show in their preschools (Principe, Kanaya, Ceci, & Singh, 2006). During the show, a confederate magician, Magic Mumfry, tried to pull a live rabbit out of his top hat. After several unsuccessful attempts, Mumfry gave up and left the school. Next, some children overheard a scripted conversation between two adults in which one alleged that Mumfry's trick failed because his rabbit had got loose and was eating carrots in the classrooms rather than residing in Mumfry's hat. Other children, like Emma, did not overhear the adult rumor conversation but were the classmates of those who did. After the first group was exposed to the escaped rabbit rumor, they interacted naturally with the second group. We wanted to know whether the second group would learn about the alleged loose rabbit from their classmates who heard the rumor and whether details in line with the rumor might leak into their later reports.

Two weeks later, children were questioned about the show and instructed to tell "only about things that you remember happening to you—things that you really did or remember seeing with your own eyes." Emma's narrative is characteristic of those relayed by many of the children who either heard the loose rabbit rumor directly from the adult conversation or were their classmates. All but one child in these two groups reported that the rumored event actually occurred, and many claimed to have actually seen the loose rabbit with their own eyes (rather than merely hearing about it from someone). Further, the majority, like Emma, made false reports of the rumored event in response to open-ended probes and most embellished their accounts with compelling but non-occurring details. Importantly, a control group, who saw the magic show and the failed trick, but were not exposed to the rumor, made no false claims of a loose rabbit.

This investigation included a fourth group who actually experienced the event suggested by the rumor. Rather than hearing a rumor about a loose rabbit, these children saw a real loose rabbit following the failed trick. As expected, these children who witnessed a loose rabbit generated quite detailed narratives about this actual experience. However, both non-witness groups (i.e., those who overheard the adult conversation and those who were classmates of those who heard the adults) provided much more elaborate accounts describing a loose rabbit than those in first group who actually witnessed a rabbit. This pattern reveals that testimony in the form of rumor can engender false accounts that are more elaborate than true accounts of the very same event. Importantly, much of the elaborative detail relayed among the non-witnesses went beyond the verbatim rumor and included original constructions in line with its theme, demonstrating that testimony in the form of rumors can lead children to invent and relay novel and non-experienced details.

When experience conflicts with rumor

These findings prompted us to consider whether rumor might be less powerful in situations where it conflicts with the past rather than helps to explain an ambiguous event. This contrast was of interest because when rumors (or any form of testimony) merely fill a gap, heard information can be imported into memory without displacing or overwriting any experienced details. But when rumors conflict with the past, there is a contradiction between what was experienced and what was heard and children must resolve it.

To examine this question, after watching the magic show, some of the non-witness children experienced a real explanation for the failed trick, namely that the rabbit was sick and therefore was unable to perform the trick (Principe, Tinguely, & Dobkowski, 2007). These children saw Mumfry check his rabbit with medical instruments and give it "medicine." This manipulation made the subsequent loose rabbit rumor conflict with the explanation these children witnessed. When interviewed one week later, 5- and 6-year-olds were better able than 3- and 4-year-olds to resist the rumor when it conflicted with their experiences than when it merely filled a gap. By contrast, 3- and 4-year-olds were equally likely to be misled by the rumor in both contexts.

These age trends fit with findings in the source monitoring literature that suggest that older children's more sophisticated ability to reflect on the sources of their beliefs makes them better able than younger children to avoid confusing experienced information with contradicting testimony from others (Welch-Ross, 1999). This pattern is also consistent with what we know about children's developing understanding of representational processes. Researchers in the theory-of-mind tradition suggest a major transition between 3 and 6 years (e.g., Perner, 1991). Younger preschoolers have been characterized as assuming that the mind exactly copies the world and therefore everyone has the same true beliefs about it. In contrast, older children realize that representation is a subjective process and that different people can have different representations of the same experience. Younger children's "copy" theory-of-mind may have made it difficult for them to simultaneously consider their observed explanation and that derived from rumor, whereas the older children's more sophisticated understanding may have made it easier for them to resolve the contradicting representations of the failed trick.

Examination of false narratives supports this explanation. The younger children for whom the rumor conflicted based the majority of their false accounts on only one representation of the failed trick—the non-occurring rumor. By contrast, the older children more readily imported details consistent with the witnessed sick rabbit episode, suggesting they had more ready access to both representations and consequently drew from both in constructing their accounts. We also found that stronger performance on a series of standard appearance-reality and false-belief tasks was linked with reduced reports of the rumored event and lower levels of descriptive detail consistent with the rumor. This relation remained significant after controlling for age, further supporting the notion that understanding of mind may be important for resisting testimony that contradicts with children's experiences.

Child generated rumor

Given children's tendencies to make causal inferences under certain conditions (e.g., Schmidt & Paris, 1978), we wondered whether children would propagate causal inferences derived about their experiences in a manner that affects their own and their peers' reports. To examine this issue, we modified our magic show so that Mumfry failed at two tricks: pulling a rabbit out of his hat and producing a birthday cake from a baking pan (Principe, Guiliano, & Root, 2008). Following the show, some children saw two sets of clues (carrot ends with "teeth marks" and a plate with cake crumbs and a dirty fork) that were expected to induce inferences about the two failed tricks (the rabbit got loose in the school and someone ate the cake).

One week later, nearly 80% of children who saw the clues reported that Mumfry's rabbit had got loose or that someone had eaten the cake, indicating that the clue manipulations prompted the generation of inferences about the failed tricks that some later misattributed as part of the experienced show. Further, nearly 40% of children who were classmates of those exposed to clues reported that the rabbit had got loose or that someone had eaten the cake, indicating that children not only propagated their inferences but that their transmissions leaked into peers' reports. Interestingly, as in the (2006) study mentioned above, the classmates produced more elaborate false reports describing the non-events than those who saw the clues firsthand, suggesting children may be more likely to embellish information picked up from others than that derived from their own reasoning.

Social factors

Levels of false reports and accompanying narratives are larger in our rumor studies than in most suggestibility investigations where children are exposed to misinformation in interviews, such as when examiners ask questions that directly suggest that a non-event took place: "Tell me everything that you can remember about the time a man came into the daycare and stole something." (e.g., Bruck, Ceci, & Hembrooke, 2002) or other private contexts, such as when parents read storybooks that suggest body touch by an unfamiliar adult that never occurred (e.g., Poole & Lindsay, 2001). Given that children in our work interact freely following the rumor, it may be that it is this social experience, rather than the rumor itself, that drives the exceptionally high levels of errant accounts and fictitious elaboration.

To test this possibility, we replicated our usual procedure, in which some children overheard from adults the scripted loose rabbit rumor, but permitted only half of the children to interact with peers following the rumor (Principe, Daley, & Kauth, 2010). When questioned one week later, those children who heard the rumor and then interacted with peers made more false reports of the rumored occurrence, were more likely to admit to seeing this non-event, and described this non-occurrence in more detail than those who did not have the opportunity to converse with their peers following the rumor. These findings demonstrate that the opportunity for peer conversation following rumor amplifies its interfering effects. Further, more than one-third of the details reported by children who interacted overlapped with something a peer had uttered, whereas those who were denied an opportunity to interact evidenced only a 9% overlap in their reports (most of which were mere verbatim repetitions of the rumor). This group difference indicates that the testimony shared following the rumor had a powerful effect in shaping children's later reports. It also means that collaboration following exposure to a misinformation source such as rumor can lead to high levels of corroboration even when no members of the group are accurate.

In a follow-up study, we found that the rumor induced greater memory contamination if it was planted among familiar peers than if it was encountered among strangers. Further, familiarity led to greater overlap in the content of errant accounts, demonstrating that memory-sharing conversations with familiar peers as opposed to strangers more readily shape subsequent memory. Taken together, these two studies demonstrate the mnemonic impact of testimony via rumor differs as a function of how and with whom rumored information is shared.

Representational influences

As mentioned above, a consistent finding in our work is that children who recall seeing a loose rabbit offer more voluminous false narratives consistent with the rumor than those who did not admit to seeing it. This pattern suggests that when children generate detailed images of events they hear about from others, it may put them at risk for later mistaking them for real experiences. But there may be more to the story. We found that children who reported seeing a loose rabbit described this rumored event with relatively more perceptual (e.g., color and sound) and contextual (e.g., spatial location and temporal order) detail than those who were unable to say how they knew about the rabbit or who claimed another source (Principe, Haines, Adkins, & Guiliano, 2010).

These distinctions are important because according to Johnson and colleagues' source-monitoring theory (Johnson, Hashtroudi, & Lindsay, 1993), individuals evaluate the details of a memory in order to make decisions about its source, such as whether a memory for an event is based on direct experience or the secondhand testimony of another person. In this framework, experienced events are represented in memory with greater perceptual, contextual, semantic, and affective detail than imagined, suggested, or otherwise non-experienced events, and the differing profiles of these two classes of memories serve as cues to discriminate source. Given that perceptual and contextual details typically serve as cues to an experienced source, it may be that the generation of these qualities in children's representations of the rumored event interfered with the usually successful source judgment process and consequently led some to misattribute the rumor to a witnessed occurrence. This interpretation suggests that rumored events can come to be represented similarly to experienced events and that such representational changes put children at risk for wrongly attributing heard about events to an experienced source. The point is that children who erroneously recalled experiencing the rumored event might not have been engaging in faulty reasoning about source, but rather were dealing with a memory uncharacteristic of its class. These findings are consistent with other research showing that the usually successful source judgment process can go awry when representations of non-experienced events develop qualities typical of real experiences (e.g., Blandon-Gitlin, Pezdek, Lindsay, & Hagen, 2009) and suggest the importance of further exploring the conditions under which perceptual and conceptual cues may be generated on the basis of testimony from others.

Adult versus peer sources

In several studies, we have found that rumor is more mnemonically damaging when picked up from peers than when overheard from adults. To investigate whether conversational factors might underlie this trend, we recorded children's natural post-rumor discussions (Principe, Cherson, DiPuppo, & Schindewolf, 2012). Following our initial study, three groups were established. The overheard group overheard the loose rabbit rumor. The classmate group did not hear the rumor but were the classmates of those who did. The control group had no exposure to the rumor. For 20 minutes following the rumor, overheard and classmate children wore a small audio recorder that captured their conversations.

In line with prior findings, when interviewed one week after the show, nearly all of the overheard and classmate children, but none of the control children, reported that Mumfry's rabbit was loose. Likewise, many overheard and classmate children recalled seeing the alleged loose rabbit and generated high levels of constructive embellishments consistent with the rumor. As expected, classmate children made more frequent reports of seeing the rumored occurrence and offered more lengthy false narratives than overheard children.

Examination of children's natural exchanges in their classrooms on the day of the magic show revealed a remarkable amount of dialogue going on among those who heard the rumor directly from the adult as well as those who had picked it up secondhand from their peers. In fact, every child in both groups uttered at least one statement about the alleged loose rabbit, demonstrating that every overheard and classmate child was actively engaged, albeit in varying degrees, in circulating the rumor. Children's unanimous participation in the propagation of stories about a loose rabbit provides some insight into the basis of the near ceiling levels of later reports of the rumored event. Further, most of the information transmitted was made up of constructive utterances consistent with the theme of the rumor but beyond its literal content, demonstrating that the details children invented and shared generally were believable. This may be a key factor in producing the large mnemonic effects of rumor given that believability is necessary for rumors to be spread readily and widely (see Rosnow, 1991).

Comparison of overheard and classmate children's dialogue revealed that these two groups talked differently about the alleged occurrence. Not only did the classmate children utter more information in line with the rumor than their overheard peers, they also generated twice as many original transmissions. Further, classmate children were more affected than overheard children by what went on in the classrooms on the day the rumor was planted. They evidenced greater overlap between things they themselves said as well as things their classmates uttered and their subsequent interview reports. These patterns suggest that rumors gleaned from peers are particularly potent because they lead to deeper and more inventive rumor mongering than rumors picked up from adults. Thus consistent with other findings in the testimony literature, not all overheard information is treated the same—its influence, at least in part, is dependent on qualities of the informant.

Testimony from parents

Much research documents the importance of parent/child memory-sharing conversations in fostering the development of children's autobiographical remembering skills (see e.g., Ornstein, Haden, & Hedrick, 2004). Little attention, however, has been directed towards exploring what happens when parents share false information during such exchanges. To examine this issue, we interviewed 3- to 5-year-olds one week after our usual magic show (Principe, DiPuppo, & Gammel, 2013). On the morning of the interview, children's mothers were given a voice recorder and asked to talk with their children in natural manner about their memory for the show. In written directions to mothers, some received a false suggestion that the magician's rabbit may have got loose in the school on the day of the show and asked mothers to question children about this possibility.

During the interview, 60% of children whose mothers were misinformed reported a loose rabbit. Other research has shown that parents can be a source of memory error when they parrot experimenter-provided scripted suggestions (e.g., Poole & Lindsay, 2001), but this is the first demonstration that misinformation encountered by parents can leak into children's later accounts when they are not asked to suggest non-events but merely to talk with children in a natural manner.

To explore factors that might be associated with false reports when mothers have been misinformed, we focused on maternal style. Mothers naturally take on a high- or low-elaborative style when remembering with their children (see e.g., Ornstein et al., 2004). In contrast to low-elaborative mothers, high-elaborative mothers encourage extended conversations by asking many open-ended –*wh* questions, providing new information to cue memory, and following in on children's leads. Consequently, children with high-elaborative mothers describe experiences in a more narratively sophisticated manner than those with low-elaborative mothers. Despite this usual positive association between maternal elaborativeness and memory, we found that children of high-elaborative mothers were twice as likely as those of low-elaborative mothers to make false reports and generously embellish their accounts with non-occurring details.

Why would the high-elaborative style usually associated with more skilled remembering be linked with greater memory error? Examination of mother–child dialogues revealed that the high-elaborative mothers were more persistent and more inventive in their use of the misinformation to structure their discussion. In particular, high-elaborative mothers provided more than three times the elaborations consistent with the theme of the suggestion than those who were low-elaborative. Examples of typical elaborations are: "Where did the rabbit go?" "Did you get carrots for the rabbit," and "Maybe the rabbit was hiding in Mumfry's cape."

Given that a high-elaborative style is composed of several elements, we next explored which features of this style might put children most at risk when mothers have been exposed to misinformation (Principe et al., 2013). We focused on the independent contributions of natural variations in mothers' elaborative questioning and their tendencies to support children's autonomy in conversational remembering because causal examination of mothers' speech in our first study revealed that these two features do not always co-occur. For instance, some high-elaborative mothers regularly followed in on children's conversational leads (e.g., Child: "Mumfry lost his rabbit." Mother: "Oh no! What do you think happened to the rabbit?"), whereas others pushed for a specific agenda in their children (e.g., Child: "There was no rabbit. We didn't see it" Mother: "Maybe it was hiding. Did you see it hiding somewhere? In the toybox?").

We classified mothers as high or low on each on the basis of a median split and formed four post-hoc groups: high-elaborative/autonomy-supportive, low-elaborative/autonomy supportive, high-elaborative/controlling, and low-elaborative/ controlling. Mothers' use of elaborative questioning and maternal autonomy support was not correlated and relatively equivalent numbers of mothers fell into each group.

Examination of the mother/child conversations revealed that high-elaborative/ controlling mothers provided more questions and statements in line with the theme of the suggestion than did high-elaborative/autonomy supportive mothers, who in turn offered more elaborations consistent with the loose rabbit misinformation than did mothers in either low-elaborative group. We also found that children of high-elaborative/controlling mothers acquiesced to a higher proportion of their mothers' questions and statements about the suggested-but-non-occurring loose rabbit compared to the other three groups, indicating that these children were particularly likely to defer to their mothers' suggestions.

Mothers' stylistic differences also were met with variation in children's interview performance. Compared to the other three groups, children of high-elaborative/ controlling mothers were more likely to wrongly report a loose rabbit and embellished their reports describing this non-event with more narrative detail. Further, children of high-elaborative/controlling mothers evidenced the highest level of overlap between things mothers uttered during the mother/child conversation and things children themselves said during the interview, demonstrating that they were particularly prone to let pieces of their mothers' contributions leak into their subsequent reports. Thus it is not merely a high elaborative style that makes misinformed mothers suggestive, but rather the combined tendencies to provide high structure in the form of elaborative questions and control the memory sharing agenda.

These patterns suggest that the high-elaborative/controlling mothers unwittingly created a particularly coercive memory sharing environment and their persistence in offering new information consistent with the misinformation and controlling the direction of the conversation may have led to more acquiescences in the mother/child conversations and consequently more errors during the interview. Further, the willingness of children of high-elaborative/controlling mothers to accept their mothers' suggestions during the mother/child conversations and later relay similar information during the interview suggests that these children also may behave in ways that facilitate the conversational shaping of their memory reports. Indeed, these seemingly linked maternal and child patterns are consistent with arguments made by Ornstein and colleagues (2004) that it is not merely maternal style that causes certain child behaviors but rather the interaction of tendencies of mothers and children that produces specific mnemonic outcomes. Thus characteristics of children as well as their informants are important factors in considerations of the impact of testimony from others on event memory.

Extant work shows that mothers focused on the goal of helping children remember correctly are more controlling and less autonomy-supportive than those centered on learning their child's perspective on an event (Cleveland, Reese, & Grolnick, 2007). We wanted to know what happens when you put maternal mis- information into the mix. If a focus on children's memory performance leads to more maternal control, then such a focus may more often steer the conversation and children's subsequent memory in the direction of misinformation. We estab- lished two experimental groups: the mothers in the outcome-oriented group were given the goal of helping their children accurately remember the magic show and the mothers in the process-oriented group were given the goal of learning their children's perspective on the event (Principe et al., 2013). As expected, we found no group differences in maternal elaborative questioning. However, mothers in the outcome-oriented group were more controlling and offered more suggestions consistent with the misinformation than mothers in the process-oriented group.

During the interview, children in the outcome-oriented group were more likely to wrongly report a loose rabbit and offered more fictitious elaborative detail in line with the maternal misinformation than children in the process-oriented group. These finding suggest that a focus on the goal of "getting the memory right" in conversations with their children can lead mothers to be more controlling and more often suggest false information about their children's experiences in such a manner that can lead to errors in children's later remembering. An important insight that comes from this research for understanding the impact of testimony is that parents' conversational tendencies and goals can have an impact on chil- dren's acceptance of misinformation about their experiences.

Conclusions and implications

Consistent with the theme of this volume, our studies show that children often trust what others tell them—especially when that new information aids in understanding, but sometimes even when it conflicts with current ideas. Our original contribution to this literature is that children's tendency to trust others not only has an impact on their beliefs about the world, but also can shape their memories of experience.

This view of memory as shaped by others is consistent with theories of collec- tive memory (e.g., Reese & Fivush, 2008) that characterize event representations as dynamic entities that are modified by conversational processes. In this framework, through the recounting of experience, tellers and listeners co-construct a shared ren- dering of the past. As a consequence, individual memories are revised in the direction of the collaborative narrative, becoming an amalgam of originally encoded informa- tion and new content derived from others' contributions. Our findings demonstrating that pre-event conversations can have similar representation-shaping effects suggest expansion of the collective memory framework to include consideration of the mne- monic impact of expectations created in conversation with others *before* events occur.

Our research also provides unique insight into why the contributions of others can have such a profound effect on children's memory. Not only do peers and parents nat- urally share information with children about experience, they also improvise embel- lishments that go above and beyond reality. Further, certain qualities of the informer, such as age, familiarity, and conversational style and goals, can affect the nature of information delivery in such a manner that has implications for later accuracy. Taken together, these patterns show that it is not testimony per se that affects children's remembering, but rather how testimony is encountered and shared with others.

On a broader level, one possibility is that the sorts of conversational negotiations elicited by the procedures we used—where children and their conversational partners hold different versions of experience—might serve important developmental functions, such as fostering children's understanding that people can have differing beliefs. In future work, a more fine-grained analysis of the conversation stream under the sorts of conditions engineered in our research may provide some insight into how memory sharing might serve as a primary means through which young children learn that others can represent the past differently and that memory is a subjective and fluid process rather than a static product.

Acknowledgment

This research was supported by Grants MH12619 and MH076811 from the National Institutes of Health.

References

Baker-Ward, L., Ornstein, P. A., & Starnes, L. P. (2009). Children's understanding and remembering of stressful experiences. In J. A. Quas & R. Fivush (Eds.) *Emotion in memory and development* (pp. 28–59). Oxford, UK: Oxford University Press.

Bartlett, F. C. (1932). *Remembering: A study in experimental and social psychology.* London, UK: Cambridge University Press.

Blandon-Gitlin, I., Pezdek, K., Lindsay, D. S., & Hagen, L. (2009). Criteria-based content analysis of true and suggested accounts of events. *Applied Cognitive Psychology, 23,* 901–917.

Bruck, M., Ceci, S. J., & Hembrooke, H. (2002). The nature of children's true and false narratives. *Developmental Review, 22,* 520–554.

Cleveland, E. E., Reese, E., & Grolnick, W. S. (2007). Children's engagement and competence in personal recollection: Effects of parents' reminiscing goals. *Journal of Experimental Child Psychology, 96,* 131–149.

Harris, P. L., Brown, E., Marriot, C., Whittall, S., & Harmer, S. (1991). Monsters, ghosts, and witches: Testing the limits of the fantasy-reality distinction in young children. *British Journal of Developmental Psychology, 9,* 105–123.

Harris, P. L., Pasquini, E. S., Duke, S., Asscher, J. J. & Pons, F. (2006). Germs and angels. The role of testimony in children's ontology. *Developmental Science, 9,* 76–96.

Johnson, M. K., Hashtroudi, S., & Lindsay, D. S. (1993). Source monitoring. *Psychological Bulletin, 114,* 3–28.

Nelson, K. (1993). The psychological and social origins of autobiographical memory. *Psychological Science, 4,* 7–14.

Ornstein, P. A., Haden, C. A., & Hedrick, A. M. (2004). Learning to remember: Social-communicative exchanges and the development of children's memory skills. *Developmental Review, 24,* 374–395.

Perner, J. (1991). *Understanding the representational mind.* Cambridge, MA: MIT Press.

Poole, D., & Lindsay, D. S. (2001). Reducing child witnesses' false reports of misinformation from parents. *Journal of Experimental Child Psychology, 81,* 117–140.

Principe, G. F., Cherson, M., DiPuppo, J., & Schindewolf, E. (2012). Children's natural conversations following exposure to a rumor: Linkages to later false reports. *Journal of Experimental Child Psychology, 113,* 383–400.

Principe, G. F., Cherson, M., DiPuppo, J., Schindewolf, E., Robinson, A., & Van Horn, E. (2013, April). Effects of mothers' memory sharing style and goal orientation on children's memory and suggestibility for a post event. In A. Greenhoot (Chair), *The goals and functions of memory sharing: Contributions to children's memories for their experiences.* Symposium poster presented at the meetings of the Society for Research in Child Development, Seattle, WA.

Principe, G. F., Daley, L., & Kauth, K. (2010). Social processes affecting the mnemonic consequences of rumors on children's memory. *Journal of Experimental Child Psychology, 107,* 479–493.

Principe, G. F., DiPuppo, J., & Gammel, J. (2013). Effects of mothers' receipt of misinformation and conversation style on children's event reports. *Cognitive Development, 28,* 260–271.

Principe, G. F., Guiliano, S., & Root, C. (2008). Rumormongering and remembering: How rumors originating in children's inferences can affect memory. *Journal of Experimental Child Psychology, 99,* 135–155.

Principe, G. F., Haines, B., Adkins, A., & Guiliano, S. (2010). False rumors and true belief: Memory processes underlying children's errant reports of rumored events. *Journal of Experimental Child Psychology, 107,* 407–422.

Principe, G. F., Kanaya, T., Ceci, S. J., & Singh, M. (2006). Believing is seeing: How rumors can engender false memories in preschoolers. *Psychological Science, 17,* 243–248.

Principe, G. F., Myers, J. T., Furtado, E. A., Merritt, K. A., & Ornstein, P. A. (1996, March). The relationship between procedural information and young children's recall of an invasive medical procedure. In L. Baker-Ward (Chair), *The role of individual differences in young children's reports of salient personal experiences.* Symposium paper presented at the meetings of the Conference on Human Development, Birmingham, AL.

Principe, G. F., Ornstein, P. A., Baker-Ward, L., & Gordon, B. N. (2000). The effects of intervening experiences on children's memory for a physical examination. *Applied Cognitive Psychology, 14,* 59–80.

Principe, G. F., & Smith, E. (2008). Seeing things unseen: Fantasy beliefs and false reports. *Journal of Cognition and Development, 9,* 1–23.

Principe, G. F., Tinguely, A., & Dobkowski, N. (2007). Mixing memories: The effects of rumors that conflict with children's experiences. *Journal of Experimental Child Psychology, 98,* 1–19.

Reese, E., & Fivush, R. (2008). The development of collective remembering. *Memory, 16,* 201–212.

Rosnow, R. L. (1991). Inside rumor: A personal journey. *American Psychologist, 46,* 484–496.

Schmidt, C. R., & Paris, S. G. (1978). Operativity and reversibility in children's understanding of pictorial sequences. *Child Development, 49,* 1219–1222.

Sharon, T., & Woolley, J. D. (2004). Do monsters dream? Young children's understanding of the fantasy/reality distinction. *British Journal of Developmental Psychology, 22,* 293–310.

Siegal, M., Butterworth, G., & Newcombe, P. A. (2004). Culture and children's cosmology. *Developmental Science, 7,* 308–324.

Sluzenski, J., Newcombe, N. S., & Ottinger, W. (2004). Changes in reality monitoring and episodic memory in early childhood. *Developmental Science, 7,* 225–245.

Welch-Ross, M. K. (1999). Preschoolers' understanding of mind: Implications for suggestibility. *Cognitive Development, 14,* 101–131.

10 Commentary I: Developing dimensions of deference

The cognitive and social underpinnings of trust in testimony and its development

Frank Keil

Introduction

The surge of work on trust in testimony in recent years, as exemplified by the chapters in this volume, raises a central question. There seems to be something obviously childlike about how younger humans deal with information that they learn through other minds and yet they also seem to show a precocious and extraordinary array of cognitive skills that they use to tune their interpretations of testimony. What changes over the course of development? By considering different views of how children may differ from adults with respect to their understanding of testimony, a more elaborated account of the cognitive and social underpinnings of testimony starts to emerge, one that not only shows several distinct dimensions that bear on how we grasp and use testimony but also shows how it is connected far more deeply to other facets of our folk beliefs than might seem at first glance. In short, there is no single cognitive skill that is the basis for developmental change with regard to understanding and use of testimony, but rather a rich constellation of intersecting abilities that extend far beyond testimony narrowly construed. In addition, it is striking how rudimentary versions of almost all these skills have very early origins, making all the more interesting questions of what factors develop and their role in the young child.

The core phenomenon that needs explanation concerns how distrust develops and why younger children seem to be so trusting. To understand this pattern of change, we will consider six ways in which younger children might differ from older children and adults, namely by being more unrealistic, more unquestioning, more ignorant, more clueless, more impulsive, or more uncultured. In all cases, the research on each dimension tends to point towards gradual developmental change and shows considerable cognitive challenges remaining in adults in each case; yet some dramatic shifts may also arise from interactions between these dimensions.

Young children do tend to trust second party information more than older participants. This is a consistent theme through most of the research on testimony and is the clear message in several chapters of this volume. For example, Heyman (chapter 6) repeatedly illustrates how preschoolers have a tendency to trust what they hear even when lies may have been quite salient in a speaker's past. Similarly, Mascaro and Morin (chapter 5) point out how young children can be strikingly tolerant of deceptive behavior and will continue to put their trust in others.

Yet, just as the overall pattern of greater trustfulness seems clear, it is equally evident that young children do not always trust informants. As seen in several of the chapters in this volume, quite young preschoolers can be especially attentive to prior competence to judge informants as well. They cannot be simply bullied into believing whatever they hear, no matter what. Equally obvious from the broader literature is the persistent finding of gullibility in many adults, who often trust when they should not. On a daily basis, one can find news reports of young and old adults naïvely believing quite astonishing things, whether it be claims about investment opportunities, terrorist plots, or healthy diets. How do those cases of gullibility in adults different from those in young children? In many cases, they may not be that different. Thus, as Harris and Corriveau (chapter 2) point out, far too many adults seem to evaluate science on grounds that might be more properly reserved for religion.

To gain a better sense of what is different about children, consider in a bit more detail six underlying dimensions that may influence deference. Each one is posed as a question about whether children differ in a largely qualitative manner from adults. In particular are children: unable to appreciate the value of direct real world evidence, unquestioning of those around them, so ignorant as to have little grounds for doubt, missing critical clues to poor testimony, incapable of dealing with information conflicts, and culturally unaware of good reasons to doubt others? In all cases, the story is far more interesting than simple deficits in younger children.

The unrealistic child?

Are children more trusting because they are unable to look for real world evidence to support their beliefs and instead acquire all knowledge in the ways they develop religious beliefs? They do at times seem to believe fantastic things, which older children and adults know to be clear fictions, but as Harris and Corriveau point out, in many respects, adults can also reason about religion and science in similar ways. Their justifications for both scientific and religious beliefs often seem to ignore basic rules of empirical evidence. At all ages they seem ready to embrace discourse about invisible agents and may excessively use heuristics such as appeals to authority and consensus. It is especially discouraging that so many adults seem to never get very far beyond using consensus and authority as reasons for adopting beliefs about scientific issues with huge public policy implications (Kahan, 2012). Harris and Corriveau see science as a late emerging cultural invention that is assimilated into the more cognitively foundational ways of taking things on faith that are intrinsic to religion. That conclusion seems warranted in many cases, but in other respects, both adults and children can be very attentive to real world evidence and use it to adjust their beliefs.

Even young children can recognize a special role for invisible mechanisms and indeed they have hunches about what sorts of hidden processes matter. Thus, even infants assume that the colors of insides of animated animals matter more to predicting their behaviors than the colors of their hats (Newman, Herrman, Wynn, & Keil, 2008). To be sure, they continue to make errors in thinking about insides well into childhood (Newman & Keil, 2008), but they do know that unseen elements can matter greatly and that one should look for evidence for the invisible (Buchanan & Sobel, 2011). Mechanism matters at all ages including unseen mechanisms; and mechanistic plausibility can override mere correlational evidence (Ahn, Kalish, Medin, & Gelman, 1995; Bes, Sloman, Lucas, and Raufaste, 2012; Gelman & Wellman, 1991). Thus, children can show some of the hallmarks of scientific thought well before the start of schooling (Gopnik & Wellman, 2012). Moreover, even young children are aware that causal-explanatory frameworks vary in systematic ways across domains and do not simply use domain-general rules of thumb (Gottfried & Gelman, 2005).

The problem, then, may not be an inability to think about the unseen and to have some crude sense of mechanisms that are linked to the unseen, even as these senses are very crude and incomplete (Keil, 2012; Lawson, 2006; Rozenblit & Keil, 2002). Instead, the problem seems to be a tendency to surrender beliefs, often empirically based ones, in the face of testimony. Even young children show signs of treating the real world as distinct from the fantasy world and understand what counts as evidence, but they are especially willing to defer even when it may be counterproductive to do so.

Children clearly have many cognitive skills that enable them to track evidence and evaluate its value, but for some reason they have much more difficulty incorporating testimony in a fully appropriate manner. This difficulty can be seen as a deep failing given just how much information is acquired indirectly; but it may also be an adaptive strategy for dealing with information overload. That is, from the standpoint of gathering information as rapidly as possible about the real world, it might be cognitively optimal early in development to simply take most things on faith except in the face of egregious informant incompetence. As children get older, they may get increasingly misled by this form of blind deference as they potentially encounter more malicious informants, but such pitfalls may not be inevitable if a culture appropriately teaches older children more sophisticated ways to use testimony, methods that range from learning more about internal motivations to knowing how to better interrogate informants. If this account is correct, and it is suggested by several of these chapters, it illustrates the need to know if testimony that children of different ages receive changes in its truth content. Do older children and adults hear more testimony from deliberately deceptive people? Or do they hear more claims that are influenced by unconscious biases? Do the topics of testimony change, perhaps from simple labels and property ascriptions to more evaluative and emotionally charged claims? Extensive analyses of natural language data between various dyads at different ages would provide an extremely useful basis for making stronger claims about optimal trust strategies at each age.

In short, if younger children are more trusting especially of such cues as consensus, and if they are especially unable to justify science and religion in different ways, such differences may not arise from an inability to take into account real word evidence nor from an inability to look for ways that even the invisible might be discounted or supported by observable facts. Very young children can be remarkably sophisticated in trying to discern the causal structure of the world at all levels from the seen to the unseen; but they seem to have also adopted a strategy, perhaps even a highly adaptive one, to let these considerable skills of causal discovery be overridden by testimony. Adults may also be adaptively prone to do so in certain structured contexts as well, such as being a patient in the emergency room.

The unquestioning child?

Are children so trusting because they are unquestioning, or at least very unskilled at asking the right questions? Does the art of interrogating simply exceed altogether the abilities of younger children and is it so intricate to be used only crudely by adults? Here, the evidence is complex. If there is a developmental change here, it is not so much in being able to ask questions, but perhaps in knowing how to carefully calibrate those questions and make appropriate decisions about relevance. But both of these skills are multi-layered ones that can be refined for much of a lifetime; indeed many professionals in the law, investigative reporting, and medical diagnosis continually work on honing those skills.

Children ask questions naturally and frequently (Callanan & Oakes, 1992; Chouinard, 2007). At the same time, as Mills & Landrum (chapter 4) illustrate, there are at least four components to question asking that are cognitively challenging and take time to develop: knowing when you need help, knowing whom to ask, knowing what to ask, and knowing when you have enough information. My sense is that children do not start from ground zero on any of these four components and instead have at least very crude skills in each area, and sometimes quite a bit more. Indeed, it is hard to understand how questioning could ever even get off the ground without some basic skills in place when even the first episodes of questioning begin. The very act of posing questions may have to presuppose some primitive versions of each of these skills.

But it is also obvious that each of these four skills continue to pose challenges for even the most sophisticated adults, especially outside their areas of expertise. Moreover, mastery of these skills starts to bring in many other areas of cognitive competence: theory of mind skills, metacognitive skills, social skills, real world causal understandings, among others. Children may be especially poor at one or more of these components, such as knowing when one needs cognitive support, but the limitations do not seem to be strict absolutes at any age and it is hard to see how they could be.

The subtleties of asking the right questions bear on the kinds of information one tracks. Thus, as these skills develop one would expect some divergence of questions about religion versus science as well as about episodic versus semantic knowledge. Principe (chapter 9) shows how collaborative memories and conversational skills, of which questioning is a part, can modify the nature of our memories, especially shifting towards more common shared memories. Similarly, Koenig and Stephens' chapter suggests that younger children are less vigilant about informant errors related to episodic memories than those related to semantic memories. Increasingly sophisticated questioning skills should start to incorporate different lines of questioning depending on the kinds of memories involved and accordingly should yield more powerful results for the questioner. Matching questioning strategies to informational content types is an important area for future work as is the question of how such strategies might be facilitated through instruction, culture, and expertise.

In sum, young children are not unquestioning acceptors of everything they encounter, but the art of good questioning is enormously rich and hardly stops developing in childhood. It also connects broadly with many other cognitive skills ranging from cultural norms of polite levels of querying to metacognitive insights into one's own knowledge states. The seemingly simple act of questioning is in fact far more complex than it appears.

The ignorant child?

Perhaps children are so trusting simply because they know so little that they can use as a basis for assessing testimony. If one knows no facts and has no sense of why things are the way they are and or how things work, it would hardly be possible to evaluate claims made by others. In one sense, this is surely a major source of children's trustfulness. To be sure, in some cases children hear things that conflict with their own experiences (Jaswal & Pérez-Edgar, chapter 8); but in many other cases they simply do not know enough to pose a conflict. Even worse, when they do have conflicts, younger children often have more difficulty dealing with those conflicts and appropriately weighing the two forms of information (Jaswal & Pérez-Edgar, chapter 8).

But is their ignorance so overwhelming as to never be useful in guiding young children's judgments of informants? Even quite young preschoolers will pick plausible mechanisms over less plausible ones (Bullock, Gelman, & Baillargeon, 1982; Schulz, Goodman, Tenenbaum, & Jenkins, 2008) and will reject demonstrations of how to operate devices when the demonstration breaks fundamental laws of physical mechanics (Lyons, Damrosch, Lin, Simeone, & Keil, 2011). Such rejections of adult demonstrations of how to use devices do constitute denials of adult non-verbal "testimony." It would be odd if young children actually do have somewhat developed skills at assessing plausible versus implausible mechanisms, as well as at judging plausible versus implausible explanations and yet always completely capitulate in the face of conflicting testimony. Part of the reason they often capitulate in experiments may be that, in real life they are rarely presented with such explicitly conflicting pieces of information. This remains a question of important empirical investigation. How often do young children, let alone adults, directly confront cases where testimony directly conflicts with what they know? Perhaps much more often, they hear statements that create "truth tensions," in which they create oblique challenges to knowledge that are open to alternative explanations or rationalizations. It is useful in this regard to speculate on how often in our daily lives we encounter clear instances of unambiguous testimonial conflicts with what we think we know first-hand.

A second issue concerns the ways in which people of all ages are remarkably ignorant about the detailed causal mechanisms that explain their natural, artifactual and social worlds (Fernbach, Rogers, Fox, & Sloman, 2012; Keil, 2012; Lawson, 2006). This mechanistic ignorance is especially strong in young children (Mills & Keil, 2004); but it does not mean that they are not tracking causal patterns at more abstract levels and using more abstract information than that to assess plausibility (Keil, 2012). Such abstract levels of knowledge, however, may rarely pose strong tensions with most naturalistically encountered testimony. How often does a child hear testimony that contradicts abstract patterns? For example, if a child believes that common cause patterns are especially prominent in a domain such as disease causation, but does not know many mechanistic details, how likely is she to encounter direct conflicts with that hunch? Children do track a great deal of information about abstract causal patterns that are specific to domains such as living things, intentional agents, and simple bounded physical objects but these are not the same as having clockwork mental models of how things work even though such models are where conflicts would be most salient.

Children may often hear novel labels for things that do not directly contradict how they think the world works, but that do create a tension with known category boundaries, such as learning that whales are not fish. But category labeling may only be a small part of all the ways that their knowledge interacts with the contents of other minds. Broader skeletal folk science understandings may constrain hunches and ad hoc explanations but may rarely encounter strong testimonial challenges.

Thus, there are very different forms of ignorance: those about isolated facts and labels, those about more connected facts, those about concrete mechanisms, and those about broad domain specific casual patterns (such as action at a distance being more common in the social domain). Each plays a different role in how it interacts with testimony. For the most part, people do not hear detailed claims about mechanisms nor anything about abstract causal patterns. Instead, they may tend to hear categorization judgments and global pronouncements of effects or relations (e.g., cigarettes are bad for you; dogs are smarter than cats). In such cases, children's relative ignorance compared to adults may only play a minor role in evaluating testimony. We are only beginning to understand the levels at which the folk sciences cognitively operate and these may be gradually influenced by testimony in a cumulative manner, but perhaps very rarely in terms of perceived contradictions.

The clueless child?

Young children do seem to miss many clues to questionable testimony. As Koenig and Stephens (chapter 1) point out, they seem to be much more swayed by benevolence and competence than other presumably useful clues. Thus, cues such as informant age and cultural or experiential background are often ignored relative to competence. Warmth and moral status are also weighed heavily in attempts to detect deception. More subtly, young children may also neglect some departures from relevance. Thus, it can be a challenge to assess that testimony should be doubted simply because it is not wrong, but simply beside the point. In our lab, we find that navigating relevance can be a challenging exercise even for adults evaluating intricate explanations (Rottman & Keil, 2011). Relevance is also a critical facet of using the right questions (Mills & Landrum, chapter 4). One can ask a stream of successive questions to little benefit if they are not relevant to the goals at hand and do not build on each other in a logical fashion. This is not an easy art and indeed it is striking how many adults fail to use optimal questioning strategies in games such as 20 Questions.

Children, even very young ones, are not clueless with respect to tricks for evaluating testimony, but they do seem to weigh quite heavily two very simple cues: gross incompetence and some sense of ill will. But how often do people of any age go beyond such heuristics when evaluating testimony? Especially when under speeded conditions, cognitive load, or when dealing with multiple messages, it may be difficult to override such snap judgments. One emerging strategy that could help this problem is learning how to partition out certain bodies of information as part of legitimate areas of expertise and using heuristics for identifying both those areas and the best experts in those areas. Navigating the division of cognitive problem is a major challenge that takes many years to even solve (Danovitch & Keil, 2004; Keil, Stein, Webb, Billings, & Rozenblit, 2008; Lutz & Keil, 2002). As pointed out by Robinson, Nurmsoo, & Einav (chapter 3), we are just beginning to see the many links between how we understand and use areas of expertise and how we evaluate and use testimony on a daily basis both from experts and other specialized groups. In addition, there remain important questions about degrees of expertise, transient expertise, and even different forms of expertise (Danovitch & Keil, 2004). It seems plausible that once one decides that one is in the presence of a well-grounded expert, one shifts dramatically in one's evaluation of testimony and in terms of which clues to monitor. Similarly, depending on the form of expertise, one might deploy very different clues as to when an informant has exceeded either their depth or breadth of quality knowledge. A sense of these different facets of expertise may emerge quite early and may moderate use of testimony accordingly.

In terms of using clues to good and bad testimony it is striking that young children can have such difficulty with lies (Heyman, chapter 6). This particular difficulty may revolve around the challenges of discerning ulterior motives more than it does with simpler moral assessments. Thus, young children may use a simple ill-will detector strategy for inferring unreliable sources while not engaging in more subtle analyses of hidden agendas, mixed messages, and the like. As Heyman points out, lie detection can be notoriously hard even for adults in some circumstances, so children's difficulties may not be so completely surprising.

A different set of clues that may come to bear more and more on testimony concerns the ability to assess the complexity of a situation and to know when testimony is needed. There are several ways in which younger children have biased assessments of complexity and there are vestiges of these biases in adults as well (Keil, Lockhart, & Schlegel, 2010; Lilienfeld, 2012). Clues to the complexity of a domain, a device, or a situation are critical to knowing whether one even needs to defer or rely on testimony. Thus, it usually makes little sense to seek out confirmation by others on questions concerning small numbers, simple shapes, or how simple devices (e.g., a door stop) work. Countless times every day, we triage out certain problems as not likely to need or be helped by testimony. Much of this process involves rapid assessments of complexity and if the level is within our own cognitive grasp or whether we are likely to be over our heads. We all make systematic errors concerning complexity, but ongoing work in our lab indicates that our perceived levels of complexity of various phenomena do drive our intuitions about the need to defer.

One potentially large developmental difference concerning clues may involve more sophisticated computations about hidden agendas (see Heyman, chapter 6). Thus, distrust in the form of cynicism may be hard for young children because it requires an ability to understand how motivated reasoning works (Mills & Keil, 2005, 2008). But even here more subtle cognitions about mental states may evade many adults. For example, the phenomenon of "self-handicapping" might be a basis for distrusting a person's claims, but it is a subtle effect that might evade most adults. Similar claims might be made about using clues to cognitive dissonance and many other biases. Particularly perceptive adults might be able to discern such subtle mental cues including many forms of self-deception, but most continue to make mistakes as is especially evident in the challenges of detecting lies.

The impulsive child?

Perhaps children differ with respect to testimony by not being able to effectively manage competing bodies of information, that is to inhibit information that they should regard as less important. A long history in developmental psychology documents that younger children can have more difficult inhibiting certain prepotent responses and this factor also appears to come into play in cases where children believe one thing and an informant says another. In such cases, the bias to trust what others say can even overrule one's own first-hand beliefs. This bias to trust is remarkable in its ability to thwart what might be appropriate levels of skepticism and the question arises as to whether children are dramatically different from adults in this respect. The answer to that question is complex. As Jaswal & Pérez-Edgar (chapter 8) note, individual differences may be just as salient here as developmental differences. Across a range of ages one's level of inhibitory control is closely linked to degrees of skepticism. More broadly, one wonders if even relatively uninhibited children might be able to be skeptical when their knowledge is more heavily grounded by a rich knowledge base and ample experience. Cognitive load might be reduced in such cases, freeing up resources to weigh one's own beliefs against those of others. This seems plausible given that children's metamemorial skills are often better in domains of high local expertise such as chess skill (Chi, 1976).

Beyond the question of whether the bias to prefer testimony can be overridden in young children with more familiar knowledge, by other situational supports or even by cultural norms (see below), the question remains as to why this bias exists. As noted in other chapters in this volume, for the young children such a strategy of high deference may be adaptive given the information that children typically encounter and the low odds that deferring will lead them astray when they are young. This bias might also be seen as a System 1 strategy (Kahneman, 2011) that is difficult to override without slower reflective thought.

A testimony-favoring bias may also be an adaptive strategy in rapid processing of adult communications. Most of the information we encounter is not delivered in well-demarcated snippets that are set pieces awaiting careful deliberative evaluation. Instead, information streams by in rapid discourse and must be quickly integrated into prior knowledge. In such cases, the pro-testimony bias may be very much in force.

In ongoing research we have evidence supporting this interpretation. We have focused on cases where informants make claims with great certainty. In most cases, high certainty should be taken as evidence that the informant's statement is more likely to be true. But even excluding cases of deception, there are cases where high certainty may actually be reason for increased doubt, namely where it is blatantly implausible that anyone could have certainty about the claimed area of knowledge. Thus, if a person says with completely sincere certainty that there are xx many grains of sand in Hawaii or that the US President's spouse in 2064 will have red hair, that person's credibility is far lower than one who expresses doubt. We find that younger children are more strongly swayed by such certainty expressions and have difficulty inhibiting the certainty clue even when they also realize that it is utterly implausible that one could have the alleged knowledge. Moreover, when adults are put under load, they too start to be more influenced by certainty even in the face of high implausibility. This may be just one of several cases where adult cognitive load makes the pull of quick testimony evaluation heuristics more compelling.

An increased reliance on quick surface heuristics may also occur with more emotionally charged content. We have seen that younger children may be more swayed by informant warmth (Heyman, chapter 6) but this may be just the one part of a much more complex set of ways in which emotional loadings on speakers and messages cause one to process information more superficially. In a related vein, we have evidence that people have more difficulty assessing the quality of their abilities to justify arguments when they care more about an issue (Fisher & Keil, in press). Thus, emotion and cognition may be heavily intertwined in accounts of what changes in the developing child's use of testimony.

The uncultured child?

Are preschool children more trusting because they are essentially "pre-cultural" beings who have not yet learned their culture's admonitions to doubt what others say? Such an account seems to oversimplify as well. To be sure, younger children will not be as fully versed in their culture's norms as older children and adults, but nor are they culture-free by the time they are able to understand testimony at even the crudest level. Moreover, even if they are more trusting, that increased trust may reflect a culture's views of appropriate epistemic stances in younger members of their culture. As Mascaro and Morin (chapter 5) point out, younger children are more often hearing testimony from caregivers who might be expected to provide more veridical information than peers, so higher levels of trust may reflect an embedding culture's expectations about what younger children are likely to hear. Alternatively, younger children may have simply learned through experience that testimony of adults is quite reliable while older children, who enter wider communities of informants, learn that some degree of doubt is more appropriate. It may well be that both factors are at play, but it seems quite plausible that increased doubt about what one learns from peers does not occur so much because of negative feedback about testimony but rather because the culture at large has communicated that testimony from caregivers, and perhaps more broadly from certain adults, is more likely to be trustworthy than that from peers. As noted earlier, however, there is a clear need for systematic large-scale data on the quality of testimony that is delivered in different communicative settings at different ages.

We also see that the ways we weigh information seem to be strongly influenced by culture from an early age and that there are striking differences across cultures. For example, Corriveau, Min, and Kurkul (chapter 7) show how deference to consensus varies dramatically in preschoolers who are Asian-American as opposed to Caucasian-American, revealing that well before the start of formal schooling, one's local culture can strongly shape one's patterns of trust, such as the influence of consensus. This in turn may be related to quite specific parenting practices. Moreover, it seems to be a graded process with first generation Asian-American children showing consensus deference more strongly than second generation Asian-American children, who in turn show it more strongly than Caucasian-American children. This graded effect demonstrates quite subtle levels of cultural influence on doubt that happen early on.

Such cultural influences are likely to extend far beyond those related to consensus. Thus, some cultures may attach more importance to public images and impression management and if, so, may foster earlier awareness of reasons to doubt those who are motivated by desires to impress others. As Heyman (chapter 6) notes, an increasing awareness of ulterior motives during the school years is a strong factor in coming to have less trust in those who appear to be engaging in impression management and, indeed, Heyman reports higher levels of such skepticism in Chinese children opposed to U.S. children. More broadly, this contrast is related to greater awareness in some cultures of ulterior motives and how they might cause one to adjust trust in a message.

Just as young children are influenced more by culture than might be apparent at first, cultures can continue to have more and more subtle influences well into adulthood. One intriguing example may occur in that apparent minority of people in certain subcultures who come to understand that religion and science are to be understood in different informational terms. Harris and Corriveau (chapter 2) argue that science, with its focus on evidence-based assessments of information, may be rare and a recent cultural phenomenon in contrast to millennia of religious beliefs. As evidence mounts that some cultures (such as the UK and China) have moved away from religious orientations, the possibility arises for expanding circles of awareness of different explanatory foundations for science. Alternatively, other forms of religious-like beliefs, such as in astrology, may insert themselves into the gap.

In short, testimonial practices may be heavily influenced by cultures and there may even be ways in which all cultures suggest to younger children that they be more trusting than older ones; but even before children are really able to understand spoken testimony it seems likely that their views on what to believe about informants are very much colored by their cultures and that even adults may continue to revise such testimony-related attitudes as their cultures shift and their roles in a culture change. In addition, as noted earlier, cultures may convey different values on what sorts of questioning strategies are acceptable and may even communicate different strategies as a function of social status and gender.

One intriguing facet of cultural influences may be that children and adults alike may be blind to the degree to which they do depend on testimony. This has been called the "individualism bias" (Gelfert, 2011) and may manifest itself in all the ways that we do depend on other minds to support our beliefs. For example, in work with Kominsky, we showed that both adults and children think that they personally know the critical features that distinguish natural kinds such as ferret and weasel when in fact they only know about such differences through deference pathways (Kominsky & Keil, in press). Even as we may profoundly outsource many of our beliefs through chains of testimony, we may greatly underestimate the extent to which we do so.

Pluralism and integration

Two themes emerge robustly from our consideration of the different facets of testimony and the developmental trend of increasing distrust with age. First, several distinct factors govern the extent to which we trust an informant, each of which has surprisingly early roots as well as surprisingly long developmental trajectories. In no case that we have considered are very young children completely incompetent. They have some appreciation of real world patterns and evidence, and use that information to assess information. They are therefore not operating out of complete ignorance. They ask questions and gain information benefits from the answers they receive. They can use at least some clues to reliable testimony. They are not invariably unable to deal with information conflicts, and they learn early on from their culture ways to construe what others say. At the same time, each of these dimensions, along with several possible others, is a rich cognitive skill in its own right that continues to develop right on into adulthood. Moreover, it seems likely that each dimension can leave developmental legacies in adult functioning, especially when adults are under various forms of cognitive load.

Second, in addition to increasing distrust happening as a result of gradual change in all these dimensions, more dramatic changes may occur as a result of interactions between these dimensions and this may be one of the most important areas for future research. Every dimension considered here is likely to interact with all the others and amplify the effects on trust. For example, the degree to which one is impulsive will surely influence when one asks questions and what types of questions one asks just as the questions one asks and receives may influence the extent to which one impulsively lets consensus trump other forms of information. We have seen how cultural values and norms might influence each of the other dimensions, such as degrees of ignorance or the contrast between religion and science. If there are more dramatic developmental discontinuities with respect to trust in testimony, they may well occur when these various dimensions interact.

A final point that emerges from this pluralistic perspective is how much trust in testimony as a whole is intimately connected to the rest of cognitive science. Thus, a full account of trust in testimony and how it develops must bring in numerous aspects of a developing theory of mind, the insights of both folk science and more formal sciences, emotion regulation skills, social influence, and causal reasoning, among many others. The chapters in this volume clearly demonstrate that the act of trusting others is a remarkably rich and diverse process.

References

Ahn, W., Kalish, C. W., Medin, D. L., & Gelman, S. A. (1995). The role of covariation versus mechanism information in causal attribution. *Cognition, 54,* 299–352.

Bes, B., Sloman, S., Lucas, C. G., & Raufaste, E. (2012). Non-Bayesian inference: Causal structure trumps correlation. *Cognitive Science, 36,* 1178–1203.

Buchanan, D. W., & Sobel, D. M. (2011). Mechanism-based causal reasoning in young children. *Child Development, 82,* 2053–2066.

Bullock, M., Gelman, R., & Baillargeon, R. (1982). The development of causal reasoning. In W. J. Friedman (Ed.), *The developmental psychology of time* (209–254). New York, NY: Academic Press.

Callanan, M. A., & Oakes, L. M. (1992). Preschoolers' questions and parents' explanations: Causal thinking in everyday activity. *Cognitive Development, 7,* 213–233.

Chi, M. T. (1976). Short-term memory limitations in children: Capacity or processing deficits? *Memory & Cognition, 4,* 559–572.

Chouinard, M. (2007). Children's questions: A mechanism for cognitive development. *Monographs of the Society for Research in Child Development, 72* (Serial No. 286).

Danovitch, J. H., & Keil, F. (2004). Should you ask a fisherman or a biologist? Developmental shifts in ways of clustering knowledge. *Child Development, 75,* 918–931.

Fernbach, P. M., Rogers, T., Fox, C. R., & Sloman, S. A. (2012). Political extremism is supported by an illusion of understanding. *Psychological Science, 24,* 939–946.

Fisher, M., & Keil, F. C. (in press). The illusion of argument justification. *Journal of Experimental Psychology: General.*

Gelfert, A. (2011). Expertise, argumentation, and the end of inquiry. *Argumentation, 22* (July), 1–16.

Gelman, S. A., & Wellman, H. M. (1991). Insides and essence: Early understandings of the non-obvious. *Cognition, 38,* 213–244.

Gopnik, A., & Wellman, H. (2012). Reconstructing constructivism: Causal models, Bayesian learning mechanisms and the theory theory. *Psychological Bulletin, 138,* 1085–1108.

Gottfried, G. M., & Gelman, S. A. (2005). Developing domain-specific causal-explanatory frameworks: The role of insides and immanence. *Cognitive Development, 20*, 137–158.

Kahan, D. M. (2012). Cultural cognition as a conception of the cultural theory of risk. In *Handbook of risk theory* (pp. 725–759). Dordrecht, The Netherlands: Springer.

Kahneman, D. (2011). *Thinking, fast and slow*. New York, NY: Farrar, Straus and Giroux.

Keil, F. C. (2012). Running on empty: How folk science gets by with less. *Current Directions in Psychological Science, 21*, 329–334.

Keil, F. C., Lockhart, K. L., & Schlegel, E. (2010). A bump on a bump?: Emerging intuitions concerning the relative difficulty of the sciences. *Journal of Experimental Psychology: General, 139*, 1–15.

Keil, F. C., Stein, C., Webb, L., Billings, V. D., & Rozenblit, L. (2008). Discerning the division of cognitive labor: An emerging understanding of how knowledge is clustered in other minds. *Cognitive Science, 32*, 259–300.

Kominsky, J., & Keil, F. C. (in press). Overestimation of knowledge about word meanings: The "misplaced meaning" effect. *Cognitive Science*.

Lawson, R. (2006). The science of cycology: Failures to understand how everyday objects work. *Memory and Cognition, 34*, 1667–1675.

Lilienfeld, S. O. (2012). Public skepticism of psychology: Why many people perceive the study of human behavior as unscientific. *American Psychologist, 67*, 111.

Lutz, D. R., & Keil, F. C. (2002). Early understanding of the division of cognitive labor. *Child Development, 73*, 1073–1084.

Lyons, D. E., Damrosch, D., Lin, J. K., Simeone, D. M., & Keil, F. C. (2011). Automatic causal encoding and the scope of overimitation. *Proceedings of the Royal Society B: Biological Sciences, 366*, 1158–1167.

Mills, C., & Keil, F. C. (2004). Knowing the limits of one's understanding: The development of an awareness of an illusion of explanatory depth. *Journal of Experimental Child Psychology, 87*, 1–32.

Mills, C. M., & Keil, F. C. (2005). The development of cynicism. *Psychological Science, 16*, 385–390.

Mills, C. M., & Keil, F. C. (2008). The development of (im)partiality. *Cognition, 107*, 528–551.

Newman, G., Herrmann, P., Wynn, K., & Keil, F. C. (2008). Biases towards internal features in infants' reasoning about objects. *Cognition, 107*, 420–432.

Newman, G., & Keil, F. C. (2008). 'Where's the essence?': Developmental shifts in children's beliefs about the nature of essential features. *Child Development, 79*, 1344–1356.

Rottman, B. M., & Keil, F. C. (2011). What matters in scientific explanations: Effects of elaboration and content. *Cognition, 121*, 324–337.

Rozenblit, L. R., & Keil, F. C. (2002). The misunderstood limits of folk science: An illusion of explanatory depth. *Cognitive Science, 26*, 521–562.

Schulz, L. E., Goodman, N. D., Tenenbaum, J. B., & Jenkins, A. C. (2008). Going beyond the evidence: Abstract laws and preschoolers' responses to anomalous data. *Cognition, 109*(2), 211–223.

11 Commentary II: "If you've seen it before, then you know"

Physical evidence and children's trust in testimony

Christine Howe

Introduction

As the editors signal in their introduction, the research presented in this volume addresses an identifiable sub-field of the vast literature concerned with social influences upon children's learning, specifically the sub-field concerned with children's criteria for acceptance or rejection of verbal information from others. As the chapters unfolded, it will have become clear that by the end of the preschool period these criteria already cover a multitude of factors. In particular, preschool children show sensitivity to the presence or absence of linguistic markers of uncertainty, the speaker's access to directly relevant information, the speaker's past history of accuracy within the specific domain, the speaker's general history of competence (and perhaps also of benevolence), and the culture's emphasis upon deference compared with personal autonomy. Sensitivity to these factors signifies impressive facility with both the epistemic and social dimensions of verbal communication, and in demonstrating this facility the preceding chapters have offered a significant (and in many respects novel) perspective upon the pragmatics of human communication.

However, construed as a sub-field of research concerned with social influences on learning, the studies covered in this volume are not merely intended to advance pragmatic analysis; they are meant also to inform theories of learning. There is in fact close alignment in the literature that the chapters represent between children's acceptance of testimony and their so-called "selective learning": children are believed to learn from testimonies they trust. Generally though, learning seems to have been interpreted as the short-term retention of some specific pieces of information, for instance the names or locations of individual objects. There appears to have been less emphasis upon longer-term retention, let alone upon consequences for whole knowledge systems. Yet as the chapter from Elizabeth Robinson and colleagues (chapter 3) makes clear, there ought to be connections between results from the sub-field and our understanding of how entire domains are mastered. Moreover, the sub-field has been construed elsewhere as carrying "a distinctly Vygotskyan spirit" (Koenig & Sabbagh, 2013, p. 399), and Vygotsky was most definitely concerned with knowledge acquisition in a very broad sense. His focus was the mastery of "scientific concepts," by which he meant the sum total of culturally accepted understandings.

For purposes of this commentary, I have decided to focus upon learning in this wider sense, meaning that inevitably I shall be integrating the sub-field (and the preceding chapters) with studies that the chapters do not cover in depth. In particular, I shall make links with research into children's understanding of physical relations, a topic that has been one of my personal interests over the past 25 years. Understanding in the physical domain is multi-level, and it is unlikely that any two adults hold identical representations within or across levels. Thus, the sum total of culturally accepted knowledge means commonly held views rather than perfect consensus. At the lowest level are the representations that individuals use to differentiate natural relations from non-natural, for instance to recognize that levitating magicians are behaving in a very strange fashion. At the next level are the representations that they use in everyday reasoning about the physical world, albeit attempting to explain levitation at a magic show or more prosaically to predict whether laundry will dry before it starts to rain. At the highest level are the representations that are currently used in formal science, and that children are expected to master in school. In my commentary, I shall call upon research relating to all three levels.

I shall in particular consider the relations between levels, for these have been a source of challenge for both theory and practice. Starting with the relation between the first and second levels and moving to the relation between the second and third, I shall make proposals about the respective roles in knowledge building of verbal communication about physical events and direct physical experience. I shall argue that while research reported in this volume is generally consistent with each specific proposal, the proposals as a totality require a more nuanced perspective on the trust-learning relation than, as indicated above, is currently adopted. Because it is based on the proposals as a totality, the conclusion also implies that there has been mileage as regards theoretical understanding in the focus upon a broad domain of knowledge rather than specific pieces of information. This, I shall suggest, is a message that may prove helpful for future research.

Recognition and everyday reasoning

Starting then with the lowest of the three levels outlined above, there is now a substantial body of research monitoring children's reactions to physical events that unfold or do not unfold in the normal fashion. With very young children, monitoring usually focuses on surprise reactions, as revealed in, say, increased eye gaze or heart rate. With older children and adults, judgments are often solicited, via for instance requests to press yes/no buttons to indicate whether or not events appear natural. Regardless of method, results suggest recognition skills at high levels of accuracy, at least in the context of object motion.

For example, differential patterns of gaze show that before their first birthday, children recognize that acceleration when rolling down slopes is natural while deceleration is non-natural (Kim & Spelke, 1992), falling when support is removed is natural but hovering is non-natural (Needham & Baillargeon, 1993), and direct proportionality between force and distance rolled is natural while inverse proportionality is non-natural (Kotovsky & Baillargeon, 1998). In my own research involving computer-simulated scenarios where balls fall from a hot-air balloon (Howe, Taylor Tavares, & Devine, 2012), differential judgments show that 6- to 10-year-olds recognize that acceleration during fall is natural while deceleration is non-natural, and that when the balloon is moving the only natural trajectory is a parabolic path in the direction the balloon is traveling. Results with judgment tasks reported in Kim and Spelke (1999) indicate that preschoolers may also recognize the naturalness of parabolic fall from a moving carrier.

Moving now to everyday reasoning about physical relations, the second of the three levels indicated above, this too is also typically studied via two types of task. The first type involves displaying events and inviting explanation, for instance asking why boats float. The second type involves predicting outcomes, for example deciding whether an empty metal box will float or sink when immersed in water. Both types of task have been widely used: studies that deploy them in relation to physical events comprise the bulk of the c.8000 entries in Duit's (2007) bibliography. Repeatedly, the results indicate widespread misconceptions, which are often reported with adults as well as with children. For instance, water boiling in large pans is frequently regarded as hotter than water boiling in small pans, inflated balloons are often expected to weigh less than flat ones, and motion is widely seen as contingent upon continuous forces in the relevant direction. Indeed, misconceptions have been detected with the events that feature in the recognition tasks, sometimes with the same participants.

For instance, in addition to completing recognition tasks in the research of mine that was outlined above (Howe et al., 2012), the 6- to 10-year-old participants were also asked to make predictions about speed and direction of fall. The recognition and prediction tasks were presented in counter-balanced orders two weeks apart, and used scenarios that were identical up to the point of fall. Thereafter the scenarios either continued naturally or non-naturally (recognition task) or froze to permit decisions about what would happen next (prediction task). Far from replicating the high levels of accuracy observed with the recognition task, only 31% of responses during the prediction task indicated acceleration during fall and only 3% indicated forward parabola during fall from a moving balloon. Equivalent results were obtained by Hast (2010) in research where 6- to 11-year-olds observed light and heavy balls rolling horizontally, rolling down slopes, and falling through air. Seventy-five percent of responses were correct on a recognition task, involving the balls moving naturally with the same speed or non-naturally with one ball faster than the other. However, only 6% of responses were correct on a prediction task, which deployed the same events but asked whether the balls would travel at the same speed or one would be faster.

Noting the discrepancy between recognition of object motion and everyday reasoning, some theorists have suggested that they may rest upon two entirely separate conceptual systems (see, e.g., Fodor, 1980; Hogarth, 2001; Plessner & Czenna, 2008). However, separation seems implausible when recognition of naturalness must be the first step in reasoning: whatever else, recognition must involve relating events to background representations, while reasoning must proceed through relating to background representations, reflecting on relations, and drawing inferences. At the same time, it is also unlikely that recognition and reasoning depend upon exactly the same body of knowledge as theorists such as Kim and Spelke (1999) have suggested, with their relative difficulty stemming from the fact that while recognition can be accomplished in one step (relating), reasoning involves a minimum of three (relating, reflecting, and inferring). If the underlying knowledge systems were identical, the only way in which the conceptions called upon when reasoning could differ from the conceptions used in recognition would be through being partial versions. However, the conceptions used in reasoning sometimes embellish the conceptions used in recognition rather than reduce these.

For instance, when the 6- to 10-year-olds in the Howe et al. (2012) research failed to predict accelerating speed of fall, this was not because they ignored speed change: 95% of errors occurred because deceleration was anticipated. Likewise, the failure to anticipate the trajectory of fall from a moving balloon was not because the motion was ignored. The modal trajectory was in a backward direction, not vertical fall as was typically predicted during fall from rest. Moreover in a further study where 6- to 10-year-olds observed computer-simulated billiards scenarios (Howe, Taylor Tavares, & Devine, 2013), sequences where a rolling ball struck a stationary ball and then bounced back in its original direction were widely recognized as non-natural. Yet bouncing back was precisely what the children typically predicted.

Following Carey (2009), it is tempting to interpret results such as these in hybrid terms, involving neither separate nor identical systems of knowledge. In particular, it might be argued that when faced with reasoning tasks, children do indeed start by calling upon the knowledge that underpins recognition. Moreover, they elevate some part of this knowledge into consciousness (not necessarily the same part on every occasion) as a prelude to drawing inferences about how (in prediction) and why (in explanation) scenarios unfold. At the same time, it might also be suggested that subsequent inferences can utilize elements from anywhere in the conceptual system that, on reflection, appear to be relevant, that is elements that can be linked with the partial representations drawn from recognition knowledge but lie outside of this knowledge. This is the line taken in Howe et al. (2012, 2013), but while it fits with the data, it also presupposes willingness amongst children to go beyond the "evidence of their eyes," namely the largely accurate representations that they use in recognition and partially access in reasoning.

It is over willingness to go beyond physical evidence that links can begin to be made with research discussed in this volume, for the research indicates that during the preschool years such willingness is ubiquitous. A pivotal theme in the chapter from Paul Harris and Kathleen Corriveau (chapter 2) is children's openness to invisible entities. Moreover pointing out in a subsequent chapter that Asch's (1956) classic judgment of lines task once persuaded adults to go beyond the physical, Corriveau and her colleagues (chapter 7) describe a version of the task that they have used with children. Paralleling Asch (1956), they have found that preschoolers, who had no difficulty in identifying which of three lines was of equal length to a standard when judging independently, often made erroneous decisions after witnessing errors from adults. Likewise, Vikram Jaswal and Koraly Pérez-Edgar (chapter 8) report that preschoolers can be persuaded to refer to a cat-like animal as a dog when they hear adults doing this. Moreover, in research that addresses object motion and therefore links directly with material presented above, they find that children who anticipate correctly where falling objects will land when judging independently often respond incorrectly after hearing adult errors.

The key point made by Harris, Corriveau, Jaswal and their various colleagues is that it is trust in adult testimony that leads children to discount physical evidence, a tendency that Jaswal and Pérez-Edgar describe as a "robust, default bias" which may stem from children's initial state of dependency. This makes me think that adult talk about object motion may be a major source of the misconceptions that appear in children's reasoning. As noted already, misconceptions are found at all ages, including amongst adults. Thus, like the children discussed above, adults seldom expect balls to accelerate as they fall through air, while also anticipating that mass makes a difference to how quickly balls reach the ground (Cahyadi & Butler, 2004; Champagne, Klopfer, & Anderson, 1980; Gunstone & White, 1981). Similarly, adults are no more likely than children to anticipate forward parabola when objects fall from moving carriers, or even when they roll over cliffs (McCloskey, 1983; Whitaker, 1983). Moreover, it is obvious that adults do talk to children about the physical world, and therefore there will be ample opportunities for their misconceptions to be made explicit during adult–child interaction.

One set of opportunities is undoubtedly the why-questions that abound during the preschool years, for instance "Why is the sea blue/the ice slippy/the metal cold/the stars twinkly?" It is significant therefore that, as Candice Mills and Asheley Landrum show in their contribution to this volume (chapter 4), children can be undiscriminating over whom they choose to question and how they interpret whatever answers are given. In addition though, conceptions about physical relations can be presupposed in talk rather than attested explicitly. Here too, it is easy to imagine instances that might lead children into error, for example "Close the door to keep the cold out," "You'll go down the slide faster than anyone because you're so light," "The sky's getting very dark and heavy," and "The sun's just about disappeared behind those clouds." In their chapter (chapter 2), Paul Harris and Kathleen Corriveau indicate that what is presupposed during testimony may be even more compelling than what is stated directly. More subtly, talk can frame and consolidate misleading physical perspectives, as with films where "10, 9, 8 . . . 1, GO" can herald a flurry of bombs or paratroopers falling *backwards* out of aircraft: backward motion is the illusion created when object fall is viewed from inside a carrier. Predicting backward motion was, as noted above, the modal error in Howe et al.'s (2012) research, and consistent with an origin in talk and media images it actually increased with age: it accounted for nearly 60% of the errors made by 10-year-olds but less than 20% of the errors made by 6-year-olds.

In sum then, the research reported in this volume can help to explain why: (a) children who possess representations that allow them to discriminate between natural and non-natural events do not necessarily use these representations when reasoning; (b) the representations deployed during reasoning typically contain substantial misconceptions. On the other hand, the research probably cannot provide a full explanation for erroneous reasoning, for misconceptions have also been reported with topics that are almost certainly represented adequately in adult talk. Flat Earthers are, for instance, rare in contemporary society, and therefore talk about the earth's shape will typically endorse the received perspective. It will also refer to people and animals living in all parts of the world. Cultural artefacts like globes and photographs from outer space will underline these messages. Yet research in many cultures has shown that up to about 6 years of age, children typically believe that the Earth is flat with the sky up above, and even when they start to appreciate the spherical shape they often imagine that people live at the top to avoid falling off (see Brewer, 2008, for a comprehensive review of research in this field).

Most likely then, talk in general and testimony in particular are the source of only a proportion of the conceptions that children call upon when reasoning. Conceptual systems are networks, with linkages made and weighted through a combination of automatic associative mechanisms and more active processes of categorizing and analogizing. They are only partially driven through external factors like talk. Furthermore, the line that I have been developing in this section does not deny a role for direct physical experiences. On the contrary, I stressed earlier that reflection upon the representations used in recognition is probably that starting place for everyday reasoning about the physical world. However, I also suggested that through being reflected upon, the representations used in recognition become fractionated and simplified, and of course the consequences of these processes need not be identical across each relevant occasion. Thus, there is a degree of imprecision about physical experiences once they become the objects of reflection and inference, and the proposal is in effect that talk can help to provide anchors. The specific point is that with physical relations, the anchors are not always beneficial as regards knowledge and understanding: they can lead children to error. The general point is that the proposed dynamics fit well with key themes within this volume.

Everyday reasoning and school science

Reasoning about the physical world becomes part of children's everyday lives from early in the preschool years. Therefore, no matter how the research discussed in the previous section is to be interpreted, it can be assumed that by the time children start school, their reasoning will involve rich but often flawed conceptual frameworks. Studies with 5-year-olds reported in Duit's (2007) bibliography provide concrete evidence. While at school, children typically study science, where reasoning with adequate conceptual frameworks is invariably a curriculum target. The implication is that, to reach the target, science teachers need to construe their role as supporting conceptual *change*, and while the implication has been accepted for some considerable period of time, implementation has not proved straightforward. Misconceptions held by adults have been highlighted already, and indeed many of the studies covered in Duit (2007) used adult samples. Frequently, the samples comprise university undergraduates, whose overall performance at school must have been good.

From the perspective taken in this volume, this resistance to conceptual change might seem surprising. It is teachers who convey the received message, and the perceived trustworthiness of teachers would appear second to none. They will score highly on what Melissa Koenig and Elizabeth Stephens' chapter (chapter 1) indicates is the all-important dimension of perceived competence, and in many cases they will also fare well on the complementary dimension of perceived benevolence/warmth. They are unlikely to be regarded as deceptive or treated with skepticism, even when from research covered in the chapters from Gail Heyman (chapter 6) and from Olivier Mascaro and Olivier Morin (chapter 5), children are capable of taking these factors into account. However, teacher testimony is not necessarily the key vehicle for effecting conceptual change in school science: traditionally the received message has been relayed less directly through physical evidence (Scott, Asoko, & Leach, 2007). In particular, great store is placed upon "critical experiments," that is controlled investigations, which if conducted correctly will produce results that are simultaneously incompatible with existing conceptions and supportive of curriculum targets. In fact, the approach survives despite an extremely patchy record of success (Duit, Treagust, & Widodo, 2008). Indeed, the brain areas associated with learning may not even be activated when evidence is incompatible with prior conceptions (Fugelsang & Dunbar, 2005).

My own earliest research relating to physical understanding provides specific examples of preconceptions surviving in the face of counter-evidence (Howe, Rodgers, & Tolmie, 1990). The research comprises two studies where 8- to 12-year-old children worked in groups of four on tasks that highlighted the factors relevant to whether objects float or sink. One study focused on the properties of the objects themselves and the other focused on the properties of the fluids in which objects are immersed. In both studies, the tasks involved series of items where the consequences of immersion had to be predicted, observed, and interpreted, with the groups encouraged to discuss and reach agreement. Items were selected so that object density or fluid density (depending on the study) was the only factor that could account for all results. Yet the children who participated in 50% of the groups made no progress whatsoever over conceptual understanding: when these children were individually post-tested a few weeks after the group tasks, their performance was identical to their performance on individual pre-tests which took place prior to the group tasks. The empirical evidence had no effect.

Progress was however detected amongst the children who participated in the remaining groups, but what differentiated these children from their non-progressing counterparts were not the test results they witnessed. These were identical for all groups. Rather it was the groups' conceptual make-up. Half of the groups were formulated to contain children who displayed similar preconceptions at pre-test, for instance all members had repeatedly claimed that light things float and heavy things sink. These were the groups that produced no pre- to post-test change. The other groups were formulated to contain children who displayed differing preconceptions, for example to include one child who emphasized mass, another who highlighted shape, a third who stressed the material objects are made of, and a fourth who focused on whether or not objects are hollow. These were the groups that stimulated progress.

Over the years, my colleagues and I have conducted twelve further studies that demonstrate benefits from participating in groups with differing preconceptions. Participation in groups with similar preconceptions has been found repeatedly to have little or no benefit, despite access to equivalent physical evidence (see Howe, 2010a, for a summary). Our studies have been conducted with all age groups from 8-year-olds up to undergraduates, and with pairs and triads as well as foursomes. In addition to further work with floating and sinking, the topics have included heating and cooling, evaporation and condensation, light and shadows, and other aspects of object motion. Moreover, these subsequent studies did not merely analyze progress as a function of group composition; they also looked at the relation between group dialogue and pre- to post-test progress. Without exception, they showed that discussion of differing opinions was the key predictor of positive conceptual change. So in addition to suggesting that physical evidence is insufficient, my research also highlights a key role for talk. As noted, this role is not necessarily emphasized in science classrooms.

Apart from their educational relevance, my results might also appear to provide further evidence for the line developed in the previous section and hence for equivalent links with research presented in this volume. In reality, the situation is more complex. For one thing, there was seldom any direct relation between dialogue within the differing groups and the ideas that the children expressed at post-test. This means that group "testimony" cannot have been the source of subsequent conceptions. In fact, post-test ideas were usually superior to anything expressed during the group tasks, despite being strongly predicted by group interaction. My colleagues and I now believe that the expression of difference during the tasks typically left children in a state of "stimulated uncertainty," which primed them to be alert to (and make good use of) relevant events that they experienced subsequently (Howe, 2009; Howe, McWilliam, & Cross, 2005). Our evidence comes from studies where we exposed children (without comment) to potentially relevant demonstrations, for instance large objects floating when small objects of equivalent mass sank. Some children had completed group tasks a few weeks earlier, while others had not done this. The former children made much better use of the demonstrations than the latter, so long as their group discussion had involved opinion exchange.

The post-group events that we focused on were physical ones. In principle these events could also have included expert testimony from teachers, parents or even, remembering work described in the chapter from Elizabeth Robinson and colleagues, printed texts (chapter 3). However, given that our events were physical, the stark message with which this section began can now be qualified: children can, after all, make use of physical evidence, but only when talk renders this a meaningful thing to do. At the same time though, the qualification implies a second departure from the line followed in the previous section. There I proposed that talk anchors nebulous messages from the physical world. Here anchoring through talk is presupposed, and I am proposing that physical evidence can be used to clarify uncertainties arising through talk. Usage is probably challenging for children, for otherwise the differing groups would have employed results obtained during the group task itself. They would not have had to depend upon post-group experiences. Nevertheless, the physical world is referred to and indeed, as the following sequence illustrates, accorded priority. The sequence occurred when, after lengthy discussion, three 10-year-olds jointly predicted that a toy vehicle would reach the middle of three squares drawn on the floor when it rolled off a slope (Howe, Tolmie, & Rodgers, 1992). A fourth child, Amran, had dissented, predicting the square nearest the slope without hitherto giving reasons:

Nebeela: Why do you think it stopped in the nearer square?
Amran: Because I knew it was going to stop in the nearer square.
Jeffrey: How did you know Amran?
Amran: I knew that.
Jeffrey: You didn't, you're not psychic are you?
Amran: Because when your friend came in we had a chance to work out which one it would go to, so he put his car where you put your car and we saw where it went.
Jeffrey: That's not part of what you think. If you've seen it before, then you know.

Conclusion

In general then, my research suggests two relations between the verbal and the physical, one where talk helps to define how physical experiences should be interpreted, and one where physical experiences are used to resolve differences of opinion that emerge through talk. The first relation has to be presumed from early in the preschool years, for that must be when children start to build everyday conceptions that depart from what they use in recognition and what they will be expected to use in science. Since everyday conceptions (in particular, variability amongst children over what these conceptions involve) underlie the differences of opinion that the previous section considered, the second relation is to some extent dependent on the first. At the same time, the first relation may also sow the seeds for its own destruction: by providing children with the tools for differences of opinion, it is creating contexts where they will look beyond talk for resolution, with physical experiences obvious candidates for attention. In other words, the initially blurred relation between the verbal and the physical both supports and is undermined by their eventual separation.

I have already argued that the first relation is grounded in children's acceptance of what trusted others say, focusing on adult–child interaction. I illustrated the second relation with reference to interaction within groups of children, and Piaget (1932) stimulated a long tradition of research that regards peer interaction as *essential* for the "decentration" required to operate this relation. I do not entirely agree. For one thing, Gabrielle Principe's chapter in this volume (chapter 9) shows very clearly that on occasion children take their peers' (erroneous) claims completely on trust. For another (as detailed in Howe, 2010b), it is inconceivable that any cognitive processes could have evolved in a fashion that restricts them to peers. Nevertheless, I accept that the relatively equal relationship children have with peers makes it easier than it would be with adults to regard expressed views as contestable. Peers probably do not "require" higher levels of autonomy as Olivier Mascaro and Olivier Morin suggest (chapter 5), but they most likely support this. In any event, like Mascaro and Morin, I regard children's developing perspective on testimony as dependent upon factors that lie within, rather than beyond, the discursive relationship.

No matter whether the focus is upon my first and second relations or on Mascaro and Morin's analysis of lies, one aspect of children's developing perspective is the growth of *mistrust* in testimony, that is willingness to challenge. In addition though, I have, with reference to my own research, indicated that mistrust is relevant for learning: trust is important for the acquisition of everyday concepts, but (at least in contexts of group work amongst children) mistrust supports the transformation of everyday conceptions into something closer to the target science. Thus, for me, relations grounded in trust and relations grounded in mistrust are both part and parcel of the learning process,and, reviewing the other chapters, this may be where I am saying something different. Whether I am correct or not is for others to judge, but there is one further point to stress in conclusion: I reached my position after looking at learning across a broad domain of knowledge. I understand why at this early stage, researchers in the sub-field that this volume represents focus upon specific information. I enjoyed reading about their work and applaud what they have done. It made me think, and clarified some issues in my own research. Nevertheless, I feel that, to take the field further and perhaps to make a theoretical contribution as well as a descriptive one, a more ambitious perspective may be required.

References

Asch, S. E. (1956). Studies of independence and conformity. A minority of one against a unanimous majority. *Psychological Monographs, 70* (9, Whole No. 416).

Brewer, W. F. (2008). Naive theories of observational astronomy: Review, analysis, and theoretical implications. In S. Vosniadou (Ed.), *International handbook of research on conceptual change* (pp. 155–204). New York, NY: Routledge.

Cahyadi, M. V., & Butler, P. H. (2004). Undergraduate students' understanding of falling bodies in idealized and real-world situations. *Journal of Research in Science Teaching, 41*, 569–583.

Carey, S. (2009). *The origin of concepts.* Oxford, UK: Oxford University Press.

Champagne, A. B., Klopfer, L. E., & Anderson, J. H. (1980). Factors influencing the learning of classical mechanics. *American Journal of Physics, 48*, 1074–1079.

Duit, R. (2007). Bibliography STCSE (Students' and teachers' conceptions and science education). http://www.ipn.uni-kiel.de/aktuell/stcse/stcse.html

Duit, R., Treagust, D. F., & Widodo, A. (2008). Teaching science for conceptual change: Theory and practice. In S. Vosniadou (Ed.), *International handbook of research on conceptual change* (pp. 629–646). New York, NY: Routledge.

Fodor, J. A. (1980). On the impossibility of acquiring "more powerful" structures: Fixation of belief and concept acquisition. In M. Piatelli (Ed.), *Language and learning* (pp. 142–162). Cambridge, MA: Harvard University Press.

Fugelsang, J. A., & Dunbar, K. N. (2005). Brain-based mechanisms underlying complex causal thinking. *Neuropsychologia, 43,* 1204–1213.

Gunstone, R. F., & White, R. T. (1981). Understanding gravity. *Science Education, 65,* 291–299.

Hast, M. (2010). Explicit versus tacit knowledge in early science education: The case of primary school children's understanding of object speed and acceleration. Unpublished doctoral dissertation, University of Cambridge.

Hogarth, R. M. (2001). *Educating intuition.* Chicago, IL: University of Chicago Press.

Howe, C. (2009). Collaborative group work in middle childhood: Joint construction, unresolved contradiction, and the growth of knowledge. *Human Development, 52,* 215–239.

Howe, C. (2010a). Peer dialogue and cognitive development: A two-way relationship? In K. Littleton & C. Howe (Eds.), *Educational dialogues: Understanding and promoting productive interaction* (pp. 32–47). London, UK: Routledge.

Howe, C. (2010b). *Peer groups and children's development.* Chichester, UK: Wiley-Blackwell.

Howe, C., McWilliam, D., & Cross, G. (2005). Chance favours only the prepared mind: Incubation and the delayed effects of peer collaboration. *British Journal of Psychology, 96,* 67–93.

Howe, C., Rodgers, C., & Tolmie, A. (1990). Physics in the primary school: Peer interaction and the understanding of floating and sinking. *European Journal of Psychology of Education, V,* 459–475.

Howe, C., Taylor Tavares, J., & Devine, A. (2012). Everyday conceptions of object fall: Explicit and tacit understanding in middle childhood. *Journal of Experimental Child Psychology, 111,* 351–366.

Howe, C., Taylor Tavares, J., & Devine, A. (2013). Children's conceptions of physical events: Explicit and tacit understanding of horizontal motion. *British Journal of Developmental Psychology.* Advance online publication. doi: 10.1111/bjdp.12026.

Howe, C., Tolmie, A., & Rodgers, C. (1992). The acquisition of conceptual knowledge in science by primary school children: Group interaction and the understanding of motion down an incline. *British Journal of Developmental Psychology, 10,* 113–130.

Kim, I. K., & Spelke, E. S. (1992). Infants' sensitivity to effects of gravity on visible object motion. *Journal of Experimental Psychology: Human Perception and Performance, 18,* 385–393.

Kim, I. K., & Spelke, E. S. (1999). Perception and understanding of effects of gravity and inertia on object motion. *Developmental Science, 2,* 339–362.

Koenig, M. A., & Sabbagh, M. A. (2013). Selective social learning: New perspectives on learning from others. *Developmental Psychology, 49,* 399–403.

Kotovsky, L., & Baillargeon, R. (1998). The development of calibration-based reasoning about collision events in young infants. *Cognition, 67,* 311–351.

McCloskey, M. (1983). Naïve theories of motion. In D. Gentner & A. L. Stevens (Eds.), *Mental models* (pp. 299–324). Hillsdale, NJ: Lawrence Erlbaum Associates.

Needham, A., & Baillargeon, R. (1993). Intuitions about support in 4.5 month-old-infants. *Cognition, 47,* 121–148.

Piaget, J. (1932). *The moral judgment of the child.* London, UK: Routledge & Kegan Paul.

Plessner, H., & Czenna, S. (2008). The benefits of intuition. In H. Plessner, C. Betsch, & T. Betsch (Eds.), *Intuition in judgement and decision making* (pp. 251–265). New York, NY: Lawrence Erlbaum Associates.

Scott, P., Asoko, H., & Leach, J. (2007). Student conceptions and conceptual learning in science. In S. K. Abell & N. G. Ledermann (Eds.), *Handbook of research on science education* (pp. 31–56). Mahwah, NJ: Lawrence Erlbaum Associates.

Whitaker, R. J. (1983). Aristotle is not dead: Student understanding of trajectory motion. *American Journal of Physics, 51,* 352–358.

Index